The
EVERYTHING®
Great Sex Book

Dear Reader:

We love what we do. We love that we were blessed to find a calling in life that thrilled us, gave us a voice by which to make a difference, and provided us with the feedback necessary for our own continued growth. Over the years both of us have delved deeply into the subjects that this book brings forth. The results have often been exquisite, but sometimes the feelings don't sort themselves out until later, when we could truly say we were the wiser for the lesson.

It has been said that "Life is the only game you ever play where you're not told the rules first" (Ashley Montegue). That's what we love about relationships and sexuality. If you treat life as a game, one you want to play but don't need to "win" over an opponent, then the exploration of new, wonderful sexual techniques and relationship tips will actually create the game—the game of love.

That's what turns us on—learning and creating our realities. This book will guide you with what you need to thrive in your sexual relationships. We are thrilled to be able to provide you with some lessons in the game of love!

Siegie Heumann

Susan Campbell

The EVERYTHING® Series

Editorial

Publishing Director	Gary M. Krebs
Managing Editor	Kate McBride
Copy Chief	Laura MacLaughlin
Acquisitions Editor	Gary M. Krebs
Development Editor	Julie Gutin
Production Editor	Jamie Wieglus

Production

Production Director	Susan Beale
Production Manager	Michelle Roy Kelly
Series Designers	Daria Perreault
	Colleen Cunningham
Cover Design	Paul Beatrice
	Frank Rivera
Layout and Graphics	Colleen Cunningham
	Rachael Eiben
	Michelle Roy Kelly
	Daria Perreault
	Erin Ring
Series Cover Design	Barry Littmann
Cover Illustrations	Susan Kaye
Interior Illustrator	Susan Kaye

Visit the entire Everything® Series at everything.com

THE
EVERYTHING®
GREAT SEX
BOOK

From sensuous to sizzling,
the hottest tips, tricks, and techniques
for spicing up your sex life

Suzie Heumann & Susan Campbell, Ph.D.

Adams Media
Avon, Massachusetts

To the future explorers of great sex—pleasure is your birthright!

An Everything® Series Book.
Everything® and everything.com® are registered trademarks of F+W Publications, Inc.

Published by Adams Media, an F+W Publications Company
57 Littlefield Street, Avon, MA 02322 U.S.A.
www.adamsmedia.com

ISBN: 1-58062-739-0
Printed in the United States of America.

J I H G F E D C B A

Library of Congress Cataloging-in-Publication Data
Heumann, Suzie.
The everything great sex book / Suzie Heumann & Susan Campbell.
p.   cm.   (An everything series book)
ISBN 1-58062-739-0
1. Sex instruction. 2. Sex. I. Campbell, Susan M. II. Title.
III. Series: Everything series.
HQ31.H4748 2003
613.9'6–dc22

2003014833

This book is available at quantity discounts for bulk purchases.
For information, call 1-800-872-5627.

Contents

Acknowledgments

We would like to thank the intrepid sexuality and relationship researchers, writers, and teachers who have come before us. To our lovers, family, and friends—without their love this book could not exist.

Top Ten Benefits of Great Sex

1. Physical health. Statistics show that you will live longer and stay in better shape if you are having great sex. Learning proper breathing techniques and doing your Kegel exercises will add quality of life as well.

2. Mental health. Great sex contributes to a better sense of personal growth, strengthens the connection with your partner, and has a calming effect in your life.

3. Emotional health. Happiness and satisfaction with life come with having a great sexual connection.

4. Knowing that you are a great lover will make you glow.

5. Your lover will greatly appreciate the bliss in your relationship.

6. Very cost-effective marriage therapy. Practicing the communication techniques included in this book will greatly enhance your relationship skills.

7. Long, luxurious, sexy, creative, affordable dates. You and your partner will learn to cherish your time together and make every moment count.

8. Ongoing development of your creativity muscles. The more you engage in great sex, the more you think up new, interesting positions, techniques, and places in which to have it.

9. Knowledge, advice, and conversation to share with your friends. You can pass on tips to your friends to help them improve their relationships as well.

10. You'll have a lot of fun!

Introduction

▶ SEX, OR THE *IDEA* OF IT, is everywhere, all around us, and yet most of us know very little about it. Sex sells everything from new cars to aged whiskey, but when it comes down to having it, we often feel confused. Whether we're young or older, many of us feel that society sends mixed messages about sexuality.

Exploring and learning about our sexual nature comes easily to some people and seems challenging to many others. We aren't taught much about sex unless we were lucky enough to have parents who weren't afraid to talk about it. Young people learn about sex from their peers or from experimentation. The older a person gets before he or she has experienced some kind of sexual encounter, the more ill-equipped that person will feel when actually entering a sexual relationship.

When we feel well informed, practiced, and excited about sex, it becomes an awesome experience. We are born with all the right equipment for sex. What we need is a sort of "owner's manual"—a guide to help us learn, give us ideas with which to experiment, and supply the guidelines to let us know that we are on the right track.

Every couple and every sexual encounter that that couple has is unique. It may not feel that way to you right now, but, as you begin to learn more about your sexual nature, you will begin to observe the differences each time you make love. By doing this you will have a basis from which to expand even further. Becoming conscious—but not self-conscious—while having sex is the key to having each separate experience feel new, exciting, and creative.

Each one of us is responsible for our own sexual happiness. It isn't our lover's responsibility, though it is wonderful if we feel partnered with someone who wants to have sexual happiness, too. *The Everything®* *Great Sex Book* is designed with the goal of giving you every tool necessary to have a complete, satisfying, expansive sexual and sensual experience.

The topics included in this book make it a complete resource for relationships, sexuality, and exciting new ideas for intimacy. It will help you put a lifetime of fun into your intimate life. From male and female anatomy lessons and erotic sexual positions to effective communication techniques and ideas from the Kama sutra, it will enlighten and inform you. This book has been designed to be useful again and again, delving deep into the information you need for a lifetime of great sex.

One of the differences you will encounter with this book is that the authors have infused the content with the concept that personal growth is a component of great sex. The belief that being in a relationship and having a great sex life can actually make your life more empowered, healthier, and happier is a relatively new concept but one that many psychologists now subscribe to. The experience of great sex is a result of passion, information, trust, vulnerability, practice, creativity, fun, and much more.

You won't find a more complete book than this on any bookstore shelf. It is a guide that will inform you for many years to come and provide the insight and knowledge needed for a future of great sex. A long life, a healthy life, a happy life, and a great sex life all go together! A new journey awaits you.

Whatever you can do,
Or dream you can
Begin it.
Boldness has genius, power
And magic in it.
Begin it now.
—Johann Wolfgang von Goethe

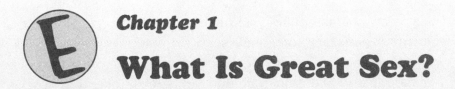

Chapter 1

What Is Great Sex?

For some people, just being able to have any sex at all is considered "great." For others, great sex must transport the partners to a state of blissful oneness of body, mind, and spirit. For most people, great sex is any sex that brings a deep sense of satisfaction and fulfillment to both partners. What does great sex mean to you?

Why Can't Sex Be Simple?

Why all the fussing and fretting about sex? Why can't sex be simple? Well, it could be, if the human mind didn't have the tendency to want to be in control of the human body. Most people have been taught to trust their minds and to ignore the messages from their bodies. All the major institutions of socialization—churches, schools, businesses, and even the family—teach you to control your impulses so you don't get into trouble or embarrass yourself or someone else.

As you get older, the mind begins to exert yet another type of control. You learn that it's not safe to do things that might offend or upset people. So you learn how to behave to get other peoples' approval. By the time you have your first adult sexual experience, the whole area of sexual relationships has gotten pretty complicated. You have learned numerous strategies for controlling yourself and for manipulating the opinions and feelings of others. This situation does not bode well for enjoying a lifetime of great sex.

ALERT!

Worry is one of the "common killers" of great sex. Humans worry about everything. Most of the time it is a futile exercise that keeps us from diving deeply into intimacy.

In spite of this early conditioning, the life force remains strong. It just needs to be encouraged, and it will bounce back. This book can help you get back into harmony with your own essential nature and reclaim your own life force. With a little patience and practice, your sex life can be transformed from something mundane or problematic to something wonderful and fun.

Not Just Maintenance Sex

Great sex is not just any sex at all; it is certainly not what may be called "maintenance sex." Maintenance sex is what most people do most of the time when having sex—where partners perform sex more as a routine than as a conscious, intentional celebration of their love.

Maintenance sex is entirely acceptable, but it is not to be confused with sex that is *really great*. Maintenance sex generally involves some degree of compromise—a step or two down from one's ideal. Perhaps only one partner is in the mood, and the other complies. One of the partners may be trying to appease the other. Or maybe, at times, one or both partners simply want to do the minimum to maintain their sense of being sexually connected.

By contrast, great sex is usually transformative and healing for the partners. Partners feel loved and cherished, and all seems right with the world. Great sex can help us transcend our separateness from each other. We both become part of something larger—a spiritual connection that puts us in touch with the oneness of all creation. Great sex may not happen automatically. But it can be learned. To have great sex requires knowledge, skill, patience, time—and practice!

Great sex will usually take more time than maintenance sex—the time spent staying in shape for it, the time spent preparing for it, and the time spent doing it—but all the extra effort is surely worth the results!

And Much, Much More

After having great sex, people often report that petty ego concerns and personality conflicts seem unimportant. Competitive ideas about feminine and masculine roles or responsibilities tend to fade. The stresses of "looking good," being in control, feeling separate, or being "on guard" disappear. Great sex involves honesty, trust, letting go, merging, and just "being."

Great sex is not so much about technique as it is about presence. The most technically skilled lover is nothing without an open, trusting presence and attention to her or his partner. Learning new positions, techniques, and tricks is only a vehicle for experiencing each other's presence in new ways.

Great sex is a type of intimate communication. It is one of the most important ways in which you, as a human being, share who you are with your partner. Really great sex is like melting or dissolving into the Divine, that universal state of oneness—with the lover and the universe—that gets you in touch with the sacredness of life.

ALERT!

Think of great sex as a bonding experience. Sharing your vulnerability with your partner creates a special connection that can help you deal with the not-so-fun parts of the relationship.

What It Really Takes

There are only a handful of key elements to having great sex: curiosity, openness of heart and mind, the willingness to try new things and learn, and a willing partner or partners. Within that handful, though, there is a vast array of possibilities for self-expression. The skills and techniques in this book are meant to enhance your own unique self-expression—this isn't a one-size-fits-all cookbook.

Sex As a Metaphor for Life

One could say that how you "do" sex is a metaphor for how you "do" life. Your sexual relationships reflect the same habitual patterns and survival strategies, learned as a child, that you exhibit in other areas of your life—except these patterns are often even more pronounced in the sexual arena. If you want to change one or more of the habitual ways you react to things, sex is a good place to start.

If you have trouble asking for what you want, for example, sex is a good learning laboratory. It's an area of life that is concrete. The feedback you get from your actions is clear: You either ask or you don't—and you either get what you asked for or you don't. With such clear and unequivocal feedback, learning is more likely to occur. And when you learn a basic life skill such as self-expression, this learning will easily transfer to the other areas of your life. It is the premise of this book that a life of consistently great sex is possible and that it can be fun to "train" yourself to get there.

Beyond Your Wildest Dreams

Learning new sexual and sensual techniques can bring you more than simple physical pleasure. You may also find yourself feeling a sense of ongoing unity with your lover. Healing can occur not only with respect to your sexuality, but also in your faith and trust in life, your emotions, and your health. Your overall self-confidence will grow as you learn to communicate and understand each other better.

Sexual healing has vast ramifications. Whenever you experience healing of past blocks or inhibitions, you tend to become happier, more generous, and more self-trusting. And you tend to pass this happiness on to those around you. When you feel loved, understood, sexually fulfilled, and connected, you become much more powerful as a human being. This is especially important for those women and men who were taught to suppress or deny their natural sexuality.

◀ Open, honest intimacy is a key to great sex.

Relating, Not Controlling

You cannot manipulate yourself into wanting great sex. And you certainly cannot manipulate someone else into wanting it with you! If you are willing to be open about what you do want, without attempting to control the outcome, then you may just get it. If you want to have great sex, don't have sex out of obligation, and don't ever force it upon your partner.

There is a basic principle governing intimate relationships that most people are just beginning to discover: When you try to make something happen the way your mind thinks it should happen, things rarely work out exactly as planned. The issues of "getting it up" or "getting it wet" are two good examples. The more you think and plan and strategize, the less you are "in your body." You are in your head, or your mind. And when you are in your head, you're not very sexy.

Another way to say this is that in any given moment, you can *relate* to the person you are with or you can try to *control* that person. You can be a part of what is actually going on—feeling what you feel and sharing this energy with your partner. That's *relating*. Or you can try to make yourself or your partner feel something that you don't or maybe hide what you are feeling in the interest of creating a particular impression or achieving a particular outcome. That's *controlling*.

FACT

In a recent Tantra.com online survey, 2,400 people responded to this statement: Making love to my partner is more than sexual release; it's an experience of union with what I think of as spirit or our souls meeting. Of those surveyed, 40 percent responded "frequently," 45 percent—"occasionally," and 15 percent—"never."

In sex, as in other forms of human communion, relating works. Controlling usually backfires. As you read this book, you will encounter numerous examples of how this principle works. The goal here is to help you enjoy great sex by learning to let down your guard, trust yourself, and, ultimately, trust life. Then, the need to control things that are not in your control anyway will fall away.

Basic Assumptions of This Book

Every book or author has a point of view, a set of basic assumptions that underlie the principles and practices that the author writes about. We all bring our personal history, education, and experiences to the table when we speak or write. The first and foremost assumption in this book is that life is a precious gift that each person is entrusted with at birth. You are given a body, a mind, and a set of circumstances (resources and limitations) to work with. It is up to you to use what you have to make the most of what you have been given. The purpose of life is self-realization—to realize your true nature and potential.

How Is That Related to Sex?

Sex is a vital aspect of life that can result in both new life and in a profound experience of oneness between partners. As such, it holds the potential for allowing you to partake in the divine nature of creativity, which includes both procreation (birthing a child) and co-creation (birthing new ideas, products, services, or works of art). Sex can also be a great source of pleasure, joy, and fun!

The experiences of a lifetime are the curriculum that allows you to learn about your true nature and develop your innate gifts and talents. If life is a school, Sex and Intimate Relationships is the advanced course. If you welcome these lessons as opportunities to learn about yourself and to expand your capacity to deal creatively with life, then you will feel happy most of the time.

Life operates on the principle of mutual benefit. A relationship, as a living system, is a good place to experience this principle. The more high-quality attention you put into your relationship, the more high-quality benefits you will derive.

Honesty Is a Prerequisite for Intimacy

If you want to have an intimate relationship, not a superficial one, complete honesty is necessary. If you keep secrets from your partner, you are affirming that you cannot trust that this person has your best interests at heart. If you do not trust a person in this way, ask yourself, "Why would I want to have sex with this person?" If mistrust is present, it's a good idea to be honest about this. Often, honest communication reveals your own projections, baggage, or recurrent fears held over from childhood. Expressing them honestly can allow you to get over them.

Your feelings of mistrust may reveal more about you than about your partner. This is one reason it's good to share what you feel and think—so you can discover the hidden layers of truth about yourself that may underlie your feelings about your partner. Sometimes fears about telling the truth are based on false beliefs learned in childhood. Now that you are an adult, it's time to update your beliefs about what is really safe and what is really dangerous.

Risk-Taking Leads to Confidence

If you fear doing something that you really want to do, it is usually a good idea to go ahead and take the risk. You may want to pause and honestly assess the risk before doing so, but more often than not, the risk will turn out to be more about damage to your ego than to your essential being. Most interpersonal risks are not life threatening. Remember that fear is not a sign to turn back but rather a sign that you are moving into unknown territory. If you take the risk and survive, which you probably will even if it doesn't turn out as you'd hoped, your confidence will grow.

You Are Responsible

You are responsible for your own experience. Whatever you feel or think about another person is a mirror of where you are. If someone does something that upsets you, you are responsible for your feelings of being upset. Likewise, when you feel satisfied with something your partner did, you are responsible for that, too. The other person does not "make" you happy. Likewise, he or she does not "make" you upset.

Your lover or partner is not responsible for your pleasure. You are. Learning about your own body—what you like, how you respond, and how to ask for what you want—are essential skills for great sex. Blaming your lover for not giving you orgasms or not doing it "right" will get you nowhere. Empower yourself to learn the skills to ask for what you want in a straightforward, loving, and truthful way.

Saying that you are responsible in no way implies that you are to blame or that it is your fault. Concepts like "blame" and "fault" are fabrications of the mind. They represent the mind's attempt to be in control by "understanding" what happened. They are not real.

Presence Is the Prize

The only time a relationship really works is when both people are in the here and now. This principle shows up most dramatically in sex and lovemaking. If your mind is on something else, you cannot make authentic contact. Presence is a prerequisite for great sex. And great sex is a pathway to greater presence. Practicing the exercises and suggestions in this book will give you the tools you need to be more present during lovemaking and in each and every moment of your life.

Pleasure Is Your Birthright

Our bodies are pleasure instruments that need to be played to stay in tune. Why would nature have given you erogenous zones if you weren't meant to do something with them? By learning to play that instrument, with all the skill you can develop, you train your body to receive great amounts of pleasure. When you know how to receive, your view of the world changes. You begin to see the world as benevolent and trustworthy. Then you give that energy back to the people in your life.

The Adventure Before You

This book has been designed to be both a resource guide and an inspiration to you. It covers a vast array of information on anatomy, intimacy, relationships, latest discoveries, and fun sexual and sensual techniques. Good relationships and great sex go together, so you'll find both topics covered here.

You'll see how old attitudes from your past can block pleasure and honest self-expression. You'll have the opportunity for self-assessment so you can get an up-to-date view of yourself instead of operating from an outdated self-image. You will be guided to understand where you are now and to develop a plan for where you want to go. You'll have better tools to decide what you want out of life.

ALERT!

Transforming some of your sexual experiences into sacred rituals will help your bodies to remember the event. This will cause you to look forward to more sexual and sensual experiences, which will then begin a feedback loop that becomes self-reinforcing. Life will look fresh and alive.

Sex is one of life's most wonderful gifts—whether, at any given moment, it is wonderful for you or not. It can be a great teacher. Although it can be fraught with anxiety and stress, it can be easy, fun, and relaxing. If you want to discover your highest potential for great sex, trust yourself and don't be afraid to try something new. If you do, one thing is for sure—your capacity for aliveness and pleasure will grow. At the very least, this book could lead to some of the cheapest and best dates you've ever had in your life. Use it well and enjoy.

Chapter 2

History and Mythology

Knowing where you've come from can help you see where you are going. It can be instructional to look at sex and love from a historical perspective. Our biological nature, the role of religion, family structures, and the constraints of culture—all have affected the history of sex and love.

A Brief History of Sex and Love

Sex has been on our minds and in our loins forever—all throughout human existence. Though most of us relate to sex from our own relatively limited perspective, many varying attitudes have been present throughout history. Even today there is a wide range of acceptability when it comes to human sexuality.

At the Dawn of Civilization

Early humans didn't know that it took a man's sperm to fertilize the woman's egg to create a baby. Whether they thought the gods, spirits, or the woman herself created the baby, they didn't connect the act of sex with procreation. Family units as we know them today didn't exist, and few human societies had monogamous relationships we now know as marriage.

It is believed that many ancient societies were actually matrilineal or matriarchal. But by the time the world's cultures had developed writing, women's status had diminished tremendously. Men prevailed in most aspects of the culture, with a few rare exceptions.

FACT

Eros, the ancient Greek god of love, is equivalent to Kama, the Hindu god of love. Psyche, or Soul, is the Greek counterpart to Shakti, the supreme Hindu goddess.

India and most of the Far East, while in essence being patriarchal, held the status of women higher than other cultures of the times. They held sexuality and the woman's role in it very high regard. The woman was the initiatress and the energy behind the sexual life force. In Eastern culture, sexuality achieved the status of an art form.

As a result, ancient treatises on love like the Kama sutra, the Ananga-Ranga, and the Ishimpo, traditionally passed down as oral histories, were recorded in written form for future generations.

But even in India and other countries of the Far East, sexuality eventually lost its sacredness and society became more sexually conservative.

In the Middle Ages

Following the fall of the Roman Empire and the spread of Christianity, sexuality became limited to procreation. The romantic, courtly love of the Middle Ages is well known for its purity and piousness. The troubadours sang, recited verse, and spoke of their true love but didn't do much more about it. Sex and morality were, for the first time in history, converging.

However, the Christian church put many dampers on the family, sex, and even having children. Strict theologians went so far as to recommend abstinence on Thursdays, in memory of Christ's arrest; on Fridays, in memory of his death; on Saturdays, in memory of the Virgin Mary; and on Sundays, in honor of the Resurrection. Mondays, Tuesdays, and Wednesdays were often religious holidays and fasts, so intercourse was banned on those days as well. Throw in Lent (which lasts forty days and ends on Easter), Pentecost, and Christmas, and you have a whole year of virtually no sex.

It wasn't until the mid-1600s that Europe began to transform. Within a few short years, sanitation, science, life expectancy, and the nuclear family all began to flourish.

Organized religion played a great role in the formation of one partner and one family. Great constraints were placed upon couples and society to conform to the moral imperative of the times. Our modern ideas of sex as sinful arose afresh during this time.

The Victorian Age and Beyond

The age of modesty, imposed leisure, and protection from the dangers of the world put middle-class women into a long period of forced retirement during the Victorian Age. Menstruation was considered a disability and sexual desire was not appropriate for a virtuous woman. Men were the superior gender. And yet, during this time of restraint, prostitution flourished, both in Europe and America, because men would go to prostitutes so as not to bother their delicate wives. This was a time of misguided virtuous behavior.

The advent of World War I brought women into the modern world with work opportunities and a bit more independence. By 1920 women in Britain, Australia, New Zealand, and America could vote. They were beginning to join the work force and they were gaining new freedom.

Sexual Liberation

This was the start of the feminist movement and the beginning of a new sexual liberation for women. Through the struggles of the last century we have come to a fresh, modern perspective. Men and women are finding their ways through the maze of new relationship and gender problems and opportunities that are the hallmark of modern society.

QUESTION?

How have your attitudes about sexuality changed over the years? Have they stayed the same, expanded, or perhaps gotten narrower?
Take a good look at your sexual history and evaluate where you have been and where you'd like to go.

Sex and Intimacy Today

In many ways, the world seems to have turned a corner in recent years. With the advent of satellite communications, cellular phones, computers, and the Internet, you can contact anyone at the snap of your virtual fingers. It's one kind of intimacy but not the kind we all desire more of.

Openness about sex and sexuality is blossoming. The print media has played a big part in contributing to the comfort of talking about sex. Major magazines, both men's and women's, compete at the newsstand with headlines that boast the latest techniques and secrets. Talk shows dealing with relationships and sex are among the hottest on TV.

Yet, the stress of our modern lifestyle moves us to feel a desire for more. Personal growth, deeper intimacy, and closeness are our heart's desire. The quality of our lives is now often equated to the deepness of our intimacy—intimacy with ourselves, our partners, our friends, and our families.

Lifestyle Options

Today, more than ever, there are many diverse ways of being in a relationship:

- Marriage
- Celibacy (no sex)
- Celibate marriage
- Marriage without living together
- Living together without marriage
- Monogamous relationship without marriage
- Serial monogamy (being married or in a committed relationship multiple times)
- Being single but sexually active
- Homosexual relationship
- Polygamous (group) marriage

FACT

The divorce rate has grown steadily to 50 percent in the last several decades. There are more second, third, and fourth marriages, and they have less of a stigma attached to them than in the past.

Westerners in particular are becoming more tolerant of diverse partnership models as the population grows and we see daily news about different groups that struggle with freedom of choice. Though some religions struggle with questions of acceptance of nontraditional relationships, even in that arena changes are occurring.

Symbols of Sex and Regeneration

Ancient men had many symbols for sex, regeneration, family, and love. Artwork from as long as 35,000 years ago and all the way through to modern times depicts the importance of sex, procreation, and love in our lives. Sex has been recognized as *the* force that controls the universe and programs our lives, both biologically and emotionally.

The downward pointing triangle, with a small vertical slit at the bottom point, has been used as a symbol of the vulva and the female genitals since the beginning of human time. Its triangular symbol has been seen in cave drawings and carvings throughout the world. It was the first written word symbol for "female" used by the Sumerians around 3,500 B.C.

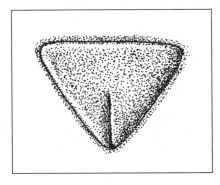

◀ Ancient symbol of the feminine

The phallus has been worshiped for thousands of years as the symbol of all that is male. From ancient stone megaliths, cave drawings, and objects fashioned as sex aids, the phallus symbol remains alive and well today. One need only look at our modern skyscrapers, missiles, and monuments to see how pervasive the phallus is.

Eyes—Windows to the Soul

It may be said that the eyes are a sexual symbol as well. Indeed, they are love's powerful allies. Ancient philosophies see the open eye as a metaphor for an open life and an open heart. It is said that the eyes are the "seat of the soul" and the gateway to the heart. Intimacy, or the act of showing one's self to another, has a direct path through the eyes.

What the Eyes Tell Us

Eyes tell us truths that the tongue won't. Eighty percent of the personal energy we put out to others comes through our eyes. Humans avert their eyes when they aren't quite telling the truth or they feel uncomfortable. When people are embarrassed they tend to look away.

You become coy with your eyes, inviting another in by looking and then looking away and then looking back. You can inflict pain and suffering with your eyes. You can hold another's gaze in a kind of game to see who will look away first. If you need alone time, you might avert your eyes, giving yourself a sense of privacy.

Pay Attention to Your Eyes

To gain a more conscious awareness of how you use your eyes, pay attention for the next few days to how you use them. Notice if you aren't willing to meet someone else's glances. Notice when you do and how it makes you feel. Try giving a person you are having a conversation with your full attention with very open, attentive eyes. See if they become more comfortable and relaxed with you.

Keep the Lights on, Baby

To enhance your intimacy and connection with your partner, keep the lights on while you make love. The lights should be soft but bright enough for the two of you to see each other well. Lie facing each other and simply let your eyes gaze at each other for five minutes. Or you can try this exercise while sitting up.

This may be difficult for you, but stay with it and practice it often. Take it into your lovemaking. See the beauty in the person you are with. Very soon you will be wondering how you ever made love without having your eyes open.

The Italian anatomist Falloppio invented condoms in the 1500s as a way to prevent contracting syphilis; it was only later that condoms came to be used for the prevention of pregnancy.

Let Your Eyes Speak the Emotion

Play some eye-flirting games with your partner or with someone with whom you feel safe. You can consciously set up a game by challenging each other to display certain emotions. Ask your partner to use her or his eyes to express the different qualities of the emotions associated with rapture, longing, neediness, coyness, and devotion. Then try it yourself. Use some of these expressions in your lovemaking.

Drink in the Feelings Expressed

Receiving information with the eyes is just as important as is giving information with the eyes. Keep your eyes soft and receptive. There's no need to react, raise your eyebrows, or frown. Just be. Let your partner in. Take a deep breath and relax. Develop the capacity to soften to an even deeper level.

The Myth of Eros and Psyche

The Greek myth of Eros and Psyche demonstrates the deep connection between love, sexuality, and the soul. It can inform us, even today, of the journey of the soul that deep intimacy demands. It is a tale of love, trust, growing up, and the lessons learned in the process. This tale is so universal that no one can truly love without going through its lessons today.

According to Greek mythology, Eros was the son of Aphrodite, the goddess of sensual love. Psyche was the youngest of three daughters and her beauty was said to rival Aphrodite's. Because of this, Aphrodite becomes jealous and asks Eros to have Psyche married to a monster that will then devour her. But one of Eros's own arrows pricks him and he falls in love with Psyche.

◀ Young Eros is also known as Cupid, the mischievous lad whose arrows were believed to make people fall in love.

Eros then puts her in a beautiful garden and castle and comes to her only at night. He tells Psyche that she is forbidden to look upon him or he will leave her forever. Eventually, Psyche disobeys and looks at Eros, so he leaves her. But by this time, Psyche is pregnant. Eventually, Psyche goes to Eros's mother, Aphrodite, the woman who hates her beauty and thinks she is dead. (How often does a mother think that the woman her son has chosen isn't good enough for him?)

Aphrodite gives Psyche four tasks that she must accomplish. The tasks are so hard that each time Psyche has no choice but to give up. But nature always comes to her aid in some way, helping her to complete the tasks.

On the fourth and last task, Psyche falls to the ground as if dead, and Eros finally "wakes up" from his stupor and saves her by going to Zeus. Zeus helps in a way that does not interfere with his daughter, Aphrodite—he makes Psyche (the Soul) immortal, and both she and Eros take their places among the gods. They have experienced loss, broken trust, separation from parents, and have grown up. They have found deep, trusting, and compassionate true love, yet they have gone through a "trial by fire" to get there.

Stand by Your Man (or Woman!)

The challenge today is to get through the trial by fire. In this "me first" culture, the will to go through the fire and come out the other side to true love has many roadblocks. There is always another woman, another man, or another relationship to move on to if this one just doesn't seem to be "working."

ALERT!

If you are in a loving relationship and you love sex, it's because you feel that you are getting what you want from it—deep, conscious intimacy. If you are addicted to sex, just for the physical part, you are probably afraid of intimacy.

Yet, most commonly, one relationship after another will only lead the person to yet another partner just like all the others. The same struggles, drama, complaints, and problems will come up eventually. If you pick wisely and you are in a nonabusive partnership, why not try to stick it out and grow together? This book is dedicated to helping you have more knowledge and fun on that path.

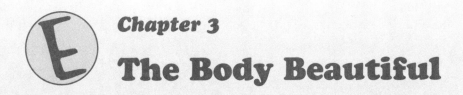

Chapter 3

The Body Beautiful

Ancient cultures, which held a positive view of sexuality, believed that your body is a temple. You receive your body to care for in this life. If you don't take good care of it, who will? You are at your best when you are healthy, happy, and balanced. And, of course, having a healthy body leads to great sex! In fact, aerobic fitness has been found to be one of the factors that contribute positively to both a man's and a woman's sexual experience.

Body Image in Our Culture

Today, even supermodels may complain about how imperfect their bodies are. If they can't accept their bodies, how can the rest of us accept ours? Men and women are bombarded with images of the perfect body. Women are told to suck in their stomachs, wear high heels to appear taller and slimmer, and wear tight clothing. One of the reasons Western cultures have illnesses like anorexia is because we teach our young women that thin is the only way to be.

Self-consciousness and self-doubts get in the way of surrender to full sexual expression. They can occupy your mind and keep you from focusing your attention on the physical sensations that bring you pleasure. Yet many lose themselves, agonizing over whether they're "good enough" or "pretty enough." Don't fall into this trap!

For some of you it will be a long process to unlearn the negative attitudes you inherited about bodily pleasure as children. You probably weren't encouraged to learn about your body and what brings you pleasure. When you "touched yourself," some bigger person would move your hand away from "down there."

Others received more painful negative reinforcement. You may carry guilt and shame regarding your sexual feelings, desires, and actions. Your body may carry the physical memories of those hurts just as your mind and emotions do. It's important to understand that the hurts and injustices you may have experienced in your early years can hold you back from being a fully expressed sexual and sensual being.

Learn to Love Your Body

When men and women love their bodies, they naturally eat right, exercise, and stay healthy without worrying about the details. But getting to that place of acceptance and love so that you can nurture your body temple may be a challenge for you. Your family history, the stresses of modern life, and perfectionist ideals you hold may stop you from full acceptance. Once you become aware of your unfriendly attitudes toward your body and understand how you learned them, you can begin the journey to greater self-love.

You can start to change your negative attitudes by learning to love your body right now. If you do, you won't have to look back forty years from now and say, "Why didn't I just love myself the way I was?" Start now.

ALERT!

Don't ever let anyone be critical of your body. It's okay to ask for advice and comments, but it's not appropriate for anyone to be critical of any part that is you. It is emotionally dangerous to have someone else dictate what is right and what is wrong with your own body.

Begin by noticing how often you worry about what your lover might be thinking of your physical features, whether it's breasts, hips, or tummy (if you're a woman), or penis, muscles, or hair (if you're a man). Notice how you talk trash to yourself. And start talking back. Tell yourself what you appreciate about your body. When you appreciate the gifts you have been given, the journey toward learning to love and honor your temple— just as it is—can begin.

Body Image Exercise

When you recognize that it is only you who hold yourself back, you can take back your power and discover your freedom. If you decide that as an adult you do not agree with some of the things you were taught as a child, you can make the decision to reclaim your vitality and your capacity for bodily pleasure. Here is a simple exercise that will be useful in all areas of your life:

1. Create an image in your mind of a situation or time in your life when you have felt really good about yourself. You feel empowered, smart, and capable.

2. Close your eyes and breathe deeply into your belly for a few minutes while you hold on to that feeling. Really feel it and breathe it in.

3. Now, imagine that you are feeling that way about your body: It is strong; it is healthy; and it is beautiful. Drink in that feeling and bathe yourself in it for a few minutes.

You'll find training for increasing the pleasure you feel in your many erogenous zones in an upcoming chapter, but for now, know that this little exercise, if you practice it, will vastly improve your sex life. Practice loving yourself!

Take Care of Yourself

When you view your body as a temple, you honor and hold it sacred. When you feel sacred and honored, you feel good about yourself. And when you feel good, you're more able to experience your fullest sexual pleasure.

Today we live in ever-increasing "busy-ness." The thing we all want more of is time. Women will often put themselves last on a list of the things that must be done in a day. There are the children and the dinner and the office and the laundry and so much more—the list goes on and on. But who's taking care of the caretaker? She must take care of herself, or she won't be able to care for anyone else. As the caretaker, you are relied upon, so you must take care of yourself.

And men don't have it easy either. Men today have very different lives than those of even one generation ago. You're commuting longer distances to work. If you have children, you are probably spending more time at school events and your children's sports interests than your father did. A higher percentage of wives are working today, so you probably help with some of the driving, shopping, and other household tasks. It's a very active life. Taking time for yourself is often last on the list.

Here's a hint about time: It all comes down to priorities. There is time for the things you really value when you schedule them in. You put meetings, project dates, social events, work, and your favorite TV show on your calendar, so why not schedule time for a long, sensual bath? Value yourself as you value these other things. Plan time for yourself, and put it on your schedule. Soon, it will get to be a habit.

Take a long bath. Put on music. Take a glass of sparkling apple cider in with you. Put a few drops of an essential oil in the tub. Pour in some bubble bath. Sprinkle in a few fresh rose petals from the garden. Any one of these things is so simple and yet will relax you and make you feel special.

Give yourself a pedicure. Do some stretching or yoga. Give your feet a little attention. After all, they are your foundation. Find something for yourself that is a "treat" and make time for it. Everyone in your life will be happier that you did.

Try Another Body Image Exercise

Find an hour to yourself, a time when you'll have quiet and peace. Take a shower or a bath. Wash yourself lovingly and really feel your skin on your thighs, your chest, your buttocks, and your face. Let your fingertips move slowly and lightly over your skin. Your fingers should be enjoying the touch of your own body. Towel-dry and put on a soft robe.

Go into the room that has the largest mirror in your home and do the following:

1. Gaze softly into the reflection of your eyes for a few moments. (This may seem difficult, especially for men, but don't be afraid to try it.)
2. Smile softly at yourself. Breathe deeply.
3. Separate the front of your robe and look at your body, slowly, with focus and attention. Notice all of the parts that you like. Why do you like each part? Has a lover said that he or she likes that part?
4. Take an inventory of the places and parts that you like and the reasons for liking them. Now, what parts are you not happy with? Why? What is it about those parts and places that you don't like? Can you identify whether these parts really don't satisfy you, or whether

your judgment has been affected by cultural stereotypes of how you're "supposed" to look?

5. If you have any complaints about your body, say them out loud. Say them again, for as many times as it takes for you to understand that that is all they are—complaints. We start sounding a little ridiculous to ourselves when we repeat a complaint again and again. Do this now and do it up big time: complain, complain, and complain!

When you've finished, ask yourself how you feel. Often simply expressing a feeling can help it dissolve or change. Can you gaze upon your body with a little more acceptance and love? Spend just a final moment gazing in the mirror again. Relax, smile, and thank yourself for the new level of understanding you have.

The Capacity for Pleasure

The truth is that you have the same working parts that everyone else has, and that is all it takes for great sex. One culture will love big bottoms, another will love small breasts, and yet another will prefer hairless men. It doesn't matter what happens to be in vogue in your present time and place. You've got what you've got and your friend has what she has.

When you realize this, you'll be free to be in your body and experience what it is capable of. When you consider that it has been said that your brain is your biggest erogenous zone, you start to think about how little you might actually be feeling, and then you can begin using your body to its fullest pleasure capacity. When you get past focusing on your shortcomings, then you can begin to have access to your full pleasure.

Erotic Presence

Erotic presence, the way you radiate your erotic nature, is a key component that is missing for some people. This is not to say that you must become alluring, coy, and seductive but rather that you become aware of your capacity for a natural eroticism. Grace, energy, and confidence allude to an erotic nature. Take the opportunity to notice what your style is and how you might develop it.

If you go dancing, try upping the ante a little. Don't worry about technique; consciously throw yourself more fully into the steps and the swing. Be the dance. Let the energy flow through you.

◀ You can find inspiration for erotic dancing in the art of *raqs sharqi*, or belly-dancing.

If you feel self-conscious about erotic presence, try dancing at home just for yourself. Choose a time and place where you have privacy. For both men and women, you might want to dress in a sarong or something a bit sexy. Find a scarf or a hat or a feathery boa you can wave around. Put on music with a good rhythm and start to move. (Men will usually want something with a good, strong beat.) You can dance in front of a mirror if you'd like.

Do a Body Wave

Stop censoring your movement—just let yourself go. Try a new move. Wave your arms around. Keep it light. Loosen your pelvis up with some body waves. To do these, stand with your feet a little apart and bend your knees. Relax. As you begin the movement, stick your bottom out and then gently swing your hips forward. When you feel comfortable with this, begin to let your upper body move to the wave. Your spine will become looser and the wave will move up to your neck and head. Do this slowly and as you repeat it, begin to smooth out the movements. Let your head go and include the natural action of your arms. Go with the flow.

This is an excellent way to warm up for lovemaking. You may even get to the place of being able to dance for your lover. Pretend you are a temple dancer. What better erotic foreplay could you imagine?

Add a little lingerie to your lovemaking. Women can try wearing a demibra or a push-up bra, especially when they are on top. Men can keep their silk boxers or a muscle shirt on while making love.

With a little practice it will become easier for you to let yourself go. You'll begin to notice other areas in your life where you can apply this same idea. The big shift will be apparent in your lovemaking; but, beyond that, a sense of erotic presence will energize your whole life. Find opportunities to be graceful and confident. Notice how you might add a bit of spice to that moment—especially if your partner is around to reap the benefits.

Erogenous Zones

Your whole body is one big erogenous zone. Touch applied to your hair follicles and nerves on the skin travels to the brain and is translated to erotic, sensual feelings of pleasure. But some areas are more sensitive than others, so your body's erogenous zone can generally be divided into three different types:

1. **Primary (first-degree) erogenous zone:** Mucous membrane tissues that comprise the lips, genitals, and nipples. These areas include the anus, penis, vaginal lips, and inside the outer third of the vagina. They are rich in nerves and the nerve endings are very close to the surface of the skin. These areas are very responsive to touch.

2. **Secondary (second-degree) erogenous zone:** Parts that have a sparse amount of hair and are often found in the regions next to the third-degree areas. These parts are not as sensitive as the primary erogenous zone, but are more sensitive than the areas covered by hair.

3. **Tertiary (third-degree) erogenous zone:** The areas of the skin that are covered with hair—your arms, legs, parts of the chest, and so forth. These areas have fewer and more dispersed nerve endings, so they are the least erogenous. Nevertheless, the hair follicles' ends, down under the skin, help stimulate the nerve endings that are buried near them.

QUESTION?

What are the "erogenous zones" and where does this term come from?
The word *erogenous* comes from Eros, the name of the Greek god of erotic love, and *genous* is a suffix that means "producing" or "generating." So erogenous zones are areas that generate erotic love.

Humans need touch from the time they are born to become healthy individuals. Our skin and nerves grow in their ability to feel more fully as we develop. This process can be expanded your whole life long. You will always have the ability to increase your capacity to feel the pleasure of touch.

A Key to Great Touch

A key ingredient to great touch is this rule: The hand that is giving the touch should feel just as good (or better) than the body part receiving the touch. In other words, the Giver should be in pleasure along with the Receiver. Think about this—it's quite a concept. The next time you give pleasurable touch to a person, think about your fingertips. Are they enjoying themselves? How could they be enjoying this experience even more?

When you start paying attention, you will find that you can really enjoy being the Giver. You'll find new ways to touch that will open up the experience for both of you. This simple practice will transform sensual touch for you *and* your partner. It even works when the Giver and the Receiver is the same person. Try it in a fun way; be light and playful.

The Pleasure of Touch

Here is a fun exercise for increasing erotic, physical pleasure through touch. You can do this alone or with a partner as an experiential evening of erotic play. If you do it with a partner, it will involve direct sexual activity. If you are practicing solo, you can self-pleasure your genitals with one hand and stimulate other erogenous zones with the other hand.

The training idea behind this practice is to make new or deeper neural connections between the excitement you feel in your genital area and other areas of your body. For instance, let's take a basic example. Women, let's connect the pleasure you feel in your clitoris with your nipples. You or your partner would stimulate your clitoris to the point of arousal and then begin to simultaneously stimulate your nipples in whatever way you like. This could be orally or with either of you using your fingers and hands.

ALERT!

If you're doing this exercise with a partner, make sure you are lovingly communicating what works and what isn't working for you. You may want to refer to the communication exercise in Chapter 17 so that you get the most from this activity.

Men, you would be stimulating your penis and your nipples. If you are doing it with your lover, have your partner stimulate your penis and you can arouse your nipples or any area of your choice. Remember to breathe fully into your belly. Keep the stimulation up. Take it to the arousal point and then some. Breathe in the pleasurable energy.

Next, continue the genital stimulation but switch to another erogenous zone. Connect each new area with the direct genital excitement you are feeling. Some areas will work better than others, but remember that every inch of your skin is covered in nerve endings that can learn to experience more pleasure. Even the areas between your fingers and toes are exquisitely tender and sensitive when touched lightly and playfully.

More Erogenous Areas

Here are a few other erogenous areas you may concentrate on as you perform this exercise:

- Breasts and underarms
- Toes and feet
- Buttocks and anus
- Inner and outer thighs
- Neck area, ears, and face
- Love handles and sides of the torso
- Back of the knees and inside the elbows
- Fingers and wrists

Let your imagination run wild, but be respectful of your partner and his or her likes or dislikes. Remember to ask permission to touch an area you think might be risky or extrasensitive.

By working on your secondary (second-degree) and tertiary (third-degree) erogenous zones, you are training your body to feel much more. After some practice, it is even conceivable to reach orgasm just by having your nipples sucked. As some of you might imagine, the possibilities are endless.

When the breath is connected to this practice, it too can be used as the vehicle to orgasm. Eventually, it may even be possible for you to breathe the way you did during this exercise and reach orgasm without physical contact. This is not far-fetched and is, in fact, a common practice in tantra. Can you imagine how beneficial this will be in helping you to achieve an orgasm *with* genital stimulation?

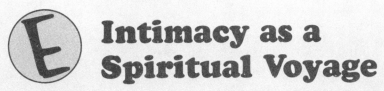

Chapter 4

Intimacy as a Spiritual Voyage

The word "intimacy" comes from the Latin *intimatus,* meaning "to make something known to someone else." When you make yourself—your feelings, your desires, your fantasies, even your upsets—known to someone else, you are contributing to deeper intimacy. An intimate sexual relationship is indeed both a journey to know your partner as well as a journey to know yourself.

Dealing with Fears of Intimacy

Everyone has one or two "favorite fears." For some people it's rejection. For others, it's abandonment or betrayal. Then there's the fear of being misunderstood or not being heard, and, of course, the old standby, being smothered or controlled. These fears originate in childhood, but even when we become adults, fears have a way of finding their way into the bedroom.

FACT

An intimate sexual relationship can provide a safe place to uncover and own up to your fears. While this might not sound like much fun, it is a very valuable thing to do. When you can admit and speak about your fears to your partner, this is a big first step toward healing whatever early wounding led to the fear in the first place.

Recognize Your Fear

Here is an example: When Lila was a little girl, her mother ignored her when she cried loudly for what she wanted. As a result, Lila came to the unfortunate conclusion that "it's not safe to ask for what I want." Now, in bed with Steve, she is hoping he'll stroke her head as part of their foreplay. But she can't force herself to ask, because she is afraid he will just ignore her. Instead, she attempts to override her desire and just enjoy the feeling of Steve's hands on other parts of her body.

The only trouble is, Lila isn't really able to push her real desire out of her thoughts and cannot be fully present to enjoy Steve's touch. She's "in her head," worrying about what to do, rather than "in her body," enjoying this present moment with her lover. When you have a feeling that you try to push away, it usually won't go. This is especially true if the feeling is related to a childhood-based fear that needs to be addressed and healed.

Conquer Your Fear

If you find yourself in a situation similar to Lila's, first gently remind yourself that the beliefs about what is and isn't safe that you learned in childhood are not true. That was then, and this is now. When you were little and dependent, it was indeed scary if you asked for something and got ignored. As a little person you were totally dependent on the big people for your survival. Now, you are a self-supporting adult.

If Lila asks Steve to stroke her head and he ignores her, or if he does it but not the way she really likes, she will survive. So the idea that it's not safe to ask for what you want is an old, outdated belief that she now has the opportunity to heal or outgrow. If she asks and doesn't get what she wants, at least her asking gets her back into the present time with herself and her lover.

The healing comes, not so much from asking and getting, but from asking and finding out that just the act of asking is an act of affirming yourself. Becoming self-validating or self-affirming is what adults do. Waiting for someone else to make you happy is what children do.

If you decide to take the risk and ask for what you want, it's often a good idea to mention also that you are feeling some fear associated with asking—that you are feeling tentative and vulnerable due to old fears in your mind. Letting your partner know that your fears are about you and not him or her can help your partner not to take your feelings personally.

Voice Your Concerns

Here is how an intimate request like this might go: "Darling, I'm feeling very close to you, and I'm also feeling that I want to ask you to touch me in a particular way . . . but I'm afraid to ask. I know this fear is something very old, something I've always had, long before you and I met. So what I want is for you to stroke my head as you were doing last night while we were watching TV. That always feels so special when you do that for me."

Mentioning your fear out loud also helps you accept yourself just as you are. And it helps you take your fear less seriously and get over it. After expressing a feeling, the feeling usually changes. Funny how that works!

Sexual Vulnerability

If you want to have great sex and experience intimacy, the willingness to be sexually vulnerable is a must. Most people protect themselves when they are around other people. This is true even in sex. We tend to be wary of others hurting us, so, just in case, we keep a layer of protection around our hearts. Then, if they do something that we associate with rejection, criticism, or any of our other favorite fears, we say, "I knew it! I knew this would happen! It's a good thing I didn't let myself get completely vulnerable—because then, I'd be even more hurt."

◀ Allowing yourself to be vulnerable is the only way to achieve real intimacy.

Opening up to your partner is an act of great trust. It is the most important thing you can do for yourself if you want to heal your old wounds and realize that you're big now—that you can trust yourself to deal with whatever happens to you.

Being openly vulnerable can also help you see that the pain that another person's behavior triggers in you is useful information about what you still need to heal in yourself. Pain can reveal to you the areas in your unconscious belief structure that need to be updated. So pain is not a bad thing. It shows you where you need to focus in your journey toward wholeness.

What are your areas of potential vulnerability with respect to sex and lovemaking? For many, the area of "asking for what I want" is the big one. We considered one way of dealing with this fear in the example of Lila and Steve. Another way is to simply ask for what you want while feeling your fear, but not explicitly speaking about it. Experiment with both approaches. Sometimes one way will be more real for you, and at other times the other way will feel better.

ALERT!

Intimacy isn't about doing things and going places together as much as it's about "being" together. Close experiences, relying on each other, talking, sharing hurts and frustrations—that's intimacy.

Let Go of Your Fears and Inhibition

There are other ways of being sexually vulnerable. Just allowing the other to see exactly what you are thinking and feeling is a wonderful gift—to yourself and to your partner. Some people are afraid of "not looking good" when they are in the heat of passion. If you have this fear, please talk to your partner about it. It is very likely you will be reassured to know that most people feel honored to be trusted with that level of vulnerability from someone they love.

Other ways to practice being open and vulnerable are:

- Look into each other's eyes while in the heat of passion.
- Tell your partner exactly how something that he or she is doing feels.
- Let your partner know when you are feeling unsatisfied or when you are in a state of longing for more closeness (without blaming your partner for your feeling).
- Ask your partner for feedback about what you are doing to pleasure him or her (with an attitude of sincerely wanting to please).

Practice Enhancing Intimacy

You can create intimacy between you and your partner through effort and practice. There are several exercises that will help you enhance intimacy in your relationship as well as build on your self-knowledge.

An intimate sexual relationship can make who *you* are more known to yourself. That's the other side of the intimacy coin: As you get closer to your partner, you will discover feelings, desires, fantasies, and, yes, even upsets—that you didn't know you had.

Creating Safe, Sacred Space

Whenever you and your partner have something important to discuss, it's a good idea to have a special place in your home that you set aside as a safe space or sacred space. This is where you go to talk about matters of importance. To sanctify this space, you might light a candle, burn some incense, or "smudge" by burning herbs. Whenever you enter this space, even if there is disharmony in the air, you enter it with an attitude of openness to *what is*—willing to speak about and hear whatever is ready to be revealed.

Word Fasting

If you and your lover are planning to spend the day together, try agreeing to be totally silent the whole time. Some people like to do their word fasting while taking a long hike in a beautiful natural setting. Looking at each other, touching, pointing, laughing, and any form of nonverbal contact is permitted, but no talking or writing notes in the sand is allowed. This kind of contact can be a wonderful thing to experience with someone you care about. After the day is over, you can have a conversation about how it felt.

Free Association

This practice is modeled after the free-association technique used by Sigmund Freud and other psychoanalysts. The two of you lie on a bed or on the floor in a comfortable nest of pillows and blankets that you have created for the occasion. Just lie there; you may be looking at each other or somewhere else.

When something to say bubbles up from your subconscious mind, speak it aloud. It could be something related to the present situation, or it could be a memory, a feeling, a thought, a wish, a dream fragment, or a theory. You share anything and everything that enters your consciousness, uncensored.

ALERT!

When you try free association, allow plenty of space between the shares. And do not try to have a regular conversation, although if conversation happens, that's okay, too.

Meditation

Meditation is usually practiced alone, but you can also do it with your partner, side by side or facing each other. There are many traditions of meditation, such as Zen, Vipassana, and transcendental (TM). There are also a number of acceptable postures, including sitting and standing. Basically, the practice involves being in each other's presence and at the same time being totally present to yourself. Paying attention to your breathing, to your physical sensations, or to a mantra that you repeat silently to yourself can help you stay present.

Overcoming Differences

The intimate journey of two people toward wholeness will inevitably involve differences and conflict about these differences. Communicating openly about these differences can feel scary, and that's normal. But open communication can also lead to an actual expansion of each individual's sense of the self, resulting in a deeper sense of unity, not only with each other, but with all of life as well. To illustrate how this happens, here is a true story of a couple conflicted about the issue of whether to continue their monogamous relationship or to switch to a more open lifestyle.

Paula is fifty. Paul is forty-six. They have been married for ten years; this is the second marriage for both. When they first got together, they agreed to be monogamous, but now things have changed. Paul believes he has "only a few good years left" in terms of his sexual vitality. He has only had four sexual partners in his life, and he's feeling a need to experiment with other lovers.

He also has the idea that being monogamous is killing his passion and his sense of vitality as a man. He sincerely believes that it is dishonest for him to pretend to be satisfied with just one sex partner. He loves Paula and enjoys what he and she have together, but he keeps noticing his sexual attention being drawn toward other women.

Paula is beside herself with grief and anger. She wants to stay monogamous. She believes that sex is a sacred act, and she has not had any desire to be with other sex partners.

If you can stay in the impasse for enough time, allowing the difference to exist rather than rushing prematurely to a resolution, you will be changed by the experience. This change is not predictable. It doesn't take the form of giving in or compromising but rather of expanding yourself.

As a result, the couple is at an impasse. Paul feels strongly that he cannot be true to himself and stay monogamous. He also feels genuine empathy for Paula. It hurts him to see her in pain. Paula imagines that if Paul has sex with other women, she will not be able to be as open and vulnerable with him. She trusts what Paul says about himself—that he feels dishonest pretending to want to be monogamous. She wants Paul to have what he wants, and, at the same time, she thinks she'd be untrue to herself staying in a nonmonogamous relationship.

What Would You Do?

If you were Paul or Paula, can you imagine how you might experience such a predicament? Can you imagine feeling two contradictory things at once: the wish to have what you want alongside the wish for your partner to have what he or she wants? This is often what it feels like to hold differences. It's like being in an unresolved predicament without knowing if there will be a resolution.

FACT

Some people can't stand the tension, so they jump to a premature conclusion—like "I'm out of here" or "I know I'm not being fair to you, so I'll just leave." Yet sometimes when you do stay with your experience, you get to a deeper level of what the conflict is really about. It can be intensely painful, but if a couple can stay with their pain, with awareness, a breakthrough will occur.

A Good Resolution

In Paul and Paula's case, after they had stayed with their pain and uncertainty for about six months, they both stated that they felt a sense of ego transcendence. Paul discovered that his need for other lovers was actually connected to some unresolved anger at both Paula and at his mother. After he was able to express his anger to both and to get over it, here's what Paul had to say about the experience: "What I thought I needed for my survival doesn't seem so crucial now." Paula also got a deeper look at herself after staying with her pain. She remembered a time early in the marriage when Paul broke one of his agreements with her—an agreement that had to do with money, not sex. After she cleared this up with Paul, by expressing her resentment, she then saw that "breaking agreements" had been a trigger for her all her life. She did some crying and grieving for some of the disappointments she had felt as a child. Afterward, she was finally free enough of old baggage to say truthfully, "I feel a lot safer, like my security doesn't depend on other people, like I'll be okay if the relationship ends, even though I still very much want to be with Paul."

Outcomes like this often feel magical or unbelievable to the people involved—when they consider where they were before they got unstuck. For so many just staying in the impasse, holding their differences for a period of time, produces an inner expansion or transformation that enables them to experience a deeper level of what's real for each of them.

Practice Holding Your Differences

To help you experience holding differences, pick an unresolved conflict between you and your partner. Sit facing each other. Let's say that the woman opens the dialogue by sharing something she resents about the other partner. She begins by using the sentence structure, "I resent you for . . . " and then sharing bodily sensations, self-talk, or anything else related to the resentment. The man actively listens, mirroring back what he has just heard.

What is active listening?
It's a communication practice that helps you stay present to what your partner is saying without getting defensive. It also lets your partner know that you are attempting to hear her accurately.

Then, when the woman says she is satisfied with how her partner listened to her, he shares what he is experiencing right in the moment. He does not debate the content of her message. His experience can be whatever he feels, thinks, or says to himself after hearing what his partner said. The woman actively listens and then shares her present experience. They keep going back and forth like this for five to ten minutes.

A Sample Conversation

Here's an example of how you could conduct your conversation:

DAN: I resent you for not initiating sex with me more often. You've only approached me three times in the past six months. I feel a tightness in my jaw and in my throat. And my self-talk is,

"I'm not a priority in your life."

DORA: You resent me for not initiating sex. Your jaw and throat are tight. And your self-talk is that you're not a priority in my life. Is that what you said? (Dan nods.) Okay. I resent you for saying I never initiate sex. I feel that in my face and in my arms and hands. They're tense.

DAN: You resent me for saying you never initiate sex. Your face and arms and hands feel tense. Did I hear you correctly? (Dora nods.) And I resent you for saying the word "never." I didn't say you never initiate. I said you have done it three times in the last six months.

DORA: You're saying you resent me for saying "never," and that what you really said was I only initiated three times in the last six months. Did I get it? (Dan nods). And I'm feeling sad. I'm saying to myself that I'm not so good at initiating even though I'd like to. I'm unsure of myself in the arena that you're so good in.

DAN: You're feeling sad and you're thinking that you don't have confidence in your ability to initiate sex. Is that right? (She nods.) And right now I'm feeling softer toward you. I can feel a relaxation in my belly and around my heart.

DORA: You say you're feeling softer toward me. Yes? (He nods.) I feel the tension going out of my face, and I'm feeling a little bit softer and more relaxed now, too.

In this example, Dan and Dora started out resenting each other and ended up feeling softer toward each other. Things don't always happen this way, but often they do. This sort of change is most likely to happen when the two people stay present to what the other has just said and share their here-and-now response. Paying careful attention to your own experience and to each other allows for feelings to be experienced more fully so that they can be released. It also teaches you both the art of holding differences.

Overcoming Long-Term Conflict

If you and your partner have a long history of conflict, it would be a good idea to try this exercise with another person or pair observing. Having a witness or witnesses helps you stay with the exercise, which can be very difficult. Couples are accustomed to bypassing their present experience and going immediately into their interpretations, generalizations, stereotypes, knee-jerk reactions, and self-protective judgments about each other. It's highly unusual for people to simply share their present experience.

Dan and Dora's conversation took place between a real person and a real person instead of between one's interpretation and the other's interpretation. The latter would look more like this: "You don't care about my needs. I've told you a hundred times what I want." (This is an interpretation followed by a generalization. He can't really know what she does or does not care about.) "Well, you don't care about my needs either! You never treat me with respect." (Another interpretation and another generalization.) Does this sound familiar?

ALERT!

If the pain or tension of holding differences becomes too great, it's okay to agree to set the subject aside for several days or even weeks and come back to discussing it at an agreed-upon time in the future.

Well, if you've ever been married for any length of time, it probably does! Mates who have been together for a while tend to camouflage the really painful unfinished situations by making interpretations, generalizations, comparisons, and assessments. They apparently hope that this sort of more distant, less intimate, language will keep them a safe distance from the pain.

Holding differences trains you to tolerate more intensity of feeling, whether it is painful or pleasurable. As a practice, it helps you stay with the discomfort and fully experience the moment, until clarity is reached. It also helps partners discover what is real for each other, instead of getting caught up defending their interpretations and stereotypes. Using active listening with the intent of staying in your experience is a very effective tool for helping you to stick to *what is*, rather than escaping into explanations or defensiveness.

A Connection with Your Partner

As you embark on your voyage toward greater intimacy and mutual awareness, you can practice positions of nurture that will help you to restore and harmonize your energies after a fight or disagreement. And if you still don't feel comfortable doing these with your partner, practice on your own, in front of a mirror.

Eye Gazing

Choose a quiet place. Sit in a comfortable position, with you and your partner facing each other. Preferably, you are on cushions on the floor, sitting cross-legged and face-to-face, as close to each other as possible. You may sit on chairs with a straight back so you sit up straight. Relax and breathe into your belly.

With your eyes open, look at your partner. Your eyes should be soft and inviting. You don't have to smile or look fascinated—just relax, breathe, and allow yourself to open up to the moment. Stay together in this way for about five minutes.

One of the benefits of eye gazing at close range and breathing together is the exchange of pheromones, the sexual scents that induce arousal. They are passed through bodily secretions and the breath. When you are engaged in activities that promote pheromone release, you will develop stronger bonds.

Next, each of you should place your right hand on your partner's heart and your left hand over your partner's arm, on your own heart. The palms of your hands should be flat so that they are touching your partner and yourself completely. Breathe and eye gaze. Relax into the feeling of complete surrender. Stay present with your partner and focus your awareness on only the two of you.

Examine Your Experience

After you have tried eye gazing, think about how this exercise affected you. Here are a few questions you may want to ask yourself:

- Did I have any trouble looking into my partner's eyes? Did I only look at one and not the other?
- How did it make me feel?
- Was I comfortable or uncomfortable?
- Would I be able to sustain this exercise for five to ten minutes?

Also talk to your partner about this exercise. Share your feelings and ask how he or she felt about it.

Eye gazing during the sexual act is a very powerful experience. We are open and vulnerable at that time. Once you are more comfortable with doing it, see if you can look into your lover's eyes while you orgasm. This may be more difficult—you're probably conditioned to "go inside," thinking you'll feel the experience more. In truth, you may actually be able to expand the orgasmic feelings more when you are fully connected to your partner through your eyes.

Heart Hold While Spooning

This is an excellent exercise to clear negative "energy" that can arise from everyday fights and disagreements. Lie on your side with your partner, with one of you in front of the other, like spoons in a drawer. If you are in back, place your top arm over your partner and hold your hand to his or her heart. If you are in front, have your partner place his or her hand on your heart. Relax and breathe together. Do this for at least five minutes.

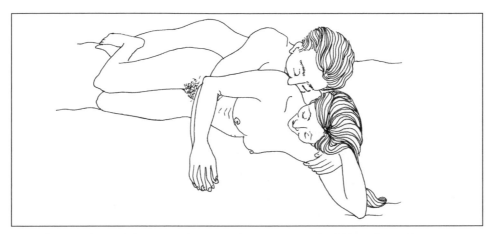

▲ In this version of the spooning position, partners hold hands as they lie side by side.

After a few minutes, you can also try some slow, gentle undulating together. One of you starts and begins to rock from the hips. Cradle your partner in your arms and hold firmly. This is a good tool for "getting in sync," or harmonizing. Ⓔ

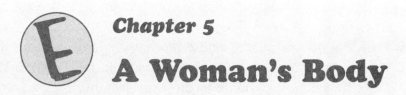

Chapter 5

A Woman's Body

In various cultures, the female sexual anatomy has been likened to a flower. Her parts are delicate, sturdy, exotic, soft, intriguing, and colorful—all at the same time. A woman's sex organs must be strong and resilient enough to bear children. Yet they are also exquisitely sensitive during the act of lovemaking.

Woman—a Unique Being

Female sexuality is a complicated thing. The woman is the only animal who is able to conceive during a portion of every month, all year round. When the issue of sexual intercourse comes up, most heterosexual women under the age of fifty must also consider the issue of possible pregnancy. Sex is not simply an act of sharing intimacy or pleasure, since it also carries the possibility of pregnancy.

A woman's primary sexual response mechanism is her genitals, but she has many secondary and tertiary sexual parts. In fact, every inch of her body can be very responsive to touch—especially her breasts, nipples, buttocks, hips, neck, and face.

During heightened arousal, a woman's chest, vulva, and face will often change color. The sexual flush is due to increased blood flow in these areas. It's easiest to see the flushing in these spots because the skin is particularly sensitive and somewhat thinner. When pink skin turns to deep red, this can be seen as a sign of sexual readiness.

Female Anatomy

Unlike men, women's sexual parts are diminutive and somewhat hidden, especially before sexual stimulation. They're not easily found and investigated. Women are generally taught not to touch or explore themselves; often, they aren't familiar with even the most basic information about their own body. Statistically, the more a woman knows her own parts and explores her sexual response, the more orgasmic she will be.

Outer Genital Area

Known as the vulva, the exterior genitals are made up of the pubis, mons veneris, the labia, and vestibule.

The pubis is the triangle of hair that covers the genitals. The skin of the pubis is quite sensitive and the multiple hair follicles are receptive to sensual touch. Gentle stroking, rubbing, and even light pulling have a very erotic feel when combined with sexual stimulation of the vulva and clitoris.

Some women and their partners like to shave the pubis area, finding this "virgin look" to be erotic. Keep in mind, though, that if you decide to try shaving, you may be missing the experience of the erotic feel that the hair follicles add to the sexual experience. The ancient Chinese considered thick, abundant pubic hair to be a sign of sensuality and passion.

FACT

The vulva ("exterior parts") is the area of the female genitals that is exposed, or on the outside of her body. The vagina ("inner parts") is the area inside her body. A woman's reproductive parts are buried even farther inside the body, beyond the vagina.

Underneath the pubis is the pubic bone, which covers the interior genitals and protects them from exterior injury. It helps support the front area of the vagina and offers the pivot point for the man to rub against during sexual intercourse. Covering the bone is the fatty tissue known as the mons veneris, or the mound of Venus. The tissue provides a cushion for the pubic bone.

The Labia

The labia majora and labia minora are the tissues that form the lips of the vulva. The labia majora are the larger lips that have hair on the outer side and are smooth and hairless on the inner side. These lips protect the delicate tissue of the inner lips and the rest of the vulva.

As the genitals become sexually stimulated, the labia majora will become engorged with blood and will begin to separate and open to expose the inner sanctuary of the vulva. The tissue will change color as sexual excitement mounts. The typically pink skin will turn to deeper shades of pink as it becomes filled with blood.

The labia minora are the more delicate inner lips of the vulva. Here begins the mucous membrane, smooth tissue that is hairless and pink. This tissue is soft and porous and has many more nerves than the outer tissue of the labia majora. This skin forms the inner lips that meet at the top of the vulva and form the hood over the tip of the clitoris.

Women's vulvas vary tremendously, as men's genitals do. If you are a woman who has not had an opportunity to see female genitals, you may want to consult the Internet or rent a few adult videos. It is quite instructive and valuable information.

The inner lips contain sweat glands and scent glands that secrete moisturizers to lubricate the vulva and pheromones to signal sexual readiness. As the genitals fill with blood, the lubrication is literally squeezed out by the pressure buildup in the tissue. The pressure can build to such a degree that the lubrication can actually flow out of the vagina, making it easier to insert the penis during lovemaking.

The Clitoris

The clitoris is actually much larger than it appears—most of it is buried on the inside of the woman's body, so the hood and the clitoral tip are all we see. The inner part is reminiscent of a smaller penis; it is a shaft that splits into two forks, or *crura* (legs), as it goes deeper into the body. The urethral sponge, or G-spot, sits between the two crura.

The clitoris, its shaft, and the crura are composed of the same spongy material that makes up the penis. During arousal, it expands with blood and causes an erection of the clitoral tissue. The clitoris has the highest concentration of nerves of any part of the body, male or female.

Clitoral Hood and Tip

The clitoral hood is a movable fold of skin that is formed by the tissue of the labia minora where it meets at the top of the vulva. It covers the clitoral tip and the portion of the clitoris, or clitoral shaft, that is buried under the skin.

The clitoral tip is the exposed part of the clitoris. It is rich in nerve endings and is made up of spongy tissue that holds blood during sexual excitement. It can increase greatly in size during sexual stimulation and will also change color as it becomes engorged with blood. The clitoral tip is perhaps the most sensitive part of the female body.

Vestibule

The doorway to the vagina, the vestibule, is the area that is surrounded by the labia minora. It contains the opening to the urethra, the entrance to the vagina, and the glands that secret lubrication and scent.

FACT

The Bartholin's, or vestibular, glands secrete lubrication and produce a scent that is thought to carry the pheromones of sexual excitement. These glands are the source of the musky or earthy scent of the vagina.

Perineum

The perineum is the area located between the anus and the opening of the vagina. It is rich in nerves and sensitive to the touch. The perineum is a place on both men and women that can be pressed or stroked for added sexual excitement.

Inner Genital Area

The vagina is the interior portion of the woman's genitals. The vagina is deeply folded and is the area the penis enters during intercourse. The tissue is highly elastic in nature and can accommodate a wide variety of penis sizes. During sexual excitement the vagina narrows at the first third and can expand and lengthen toward the back.

The vagina is typically between 3 to 4 inches deep. If a woman who has a smaller-than-average vagina is matched with a man with a larger-than-average penis (over 7 inches), the couple will have to get creative with positions and stimulation techniques to relax the woman, allowing her to open more fully.

Most women and men are not very familiar with the inside of the vagina. It helps to know about these parts—both for sexual enhancement and health reasons. Here are some of the main parts of the vagina.

The Hymen

The hymen is a flap of tissue that covers the entrance to the vagina, and it is present in most (but not all) virginal women. This thin membrane is broken at the time of first intercourse—or during a strenuous physical activity—and is then dissolved.

It is a myth that the hymen is an irrefutable sign of virginity. According to this common belief, the small amount of blood that is often produced upon penetration is a sign of virtue. Many cultures value this blood as a sign of virginity.

Urethra, Urethral Sponge, and G-Spot

The urethra is the canal, or tube, that carries urine from the bladder out of the body. It is short and ends just above the vestibule, or entrance to the vagina, below the clitoris. The urethra runs through the urethral sponge, or G-spot. It is also believed to be the delivery source for female ejaculate.

Many medical professionals still speculate on the existence of the G-spot, or G-area. Most doctors and sex educators now acknowledge that the G-spot exists. It is made up of several glands, including the female prostatic gland, blood vessels, spongy material that holds fluids, and ducts that deliver the fluids out of the body.

This area is located just inside the vaginal opening, on the top part of the vagina, directly beyond the area of rough, bumpy skin that pads the pubic bone. It is behind the pubic bone, tucked against the back side of it.

Cervix and Os

The cervix is the protective tip of the uterus. The os, or entrance to the uterus, is at its center. The cervix can be felt inside the vagina and is sometimes bumped during rough sex, causing pain.

The os typically remains very small, but changes wondrously to stretch and open up to over 10 centimeters during childbirth. During the conception of a baby, the sperm from the father must travel through the os to get to the uterus and then on to the fallopian tubes. Menstrual blood passes out through the os and then the cervix during a woman's monthly cycle.

Reproductive Organs

A woman's reproductive parts are hidden and well protected. In addition to their reproductive role, these organs also play a vital part in hormonal distribution and regulation, thus affecting female libido and monthly cycles of fertility and responsiveness.

FACT

Though once thought odd and embarrassing, in a recent online survey at ✍ *www.tantra.com*, 47 percent of 1,048 women reported that they ejaculate a fluid when they orgasm. It is much more common than once thought.

Uterus

The uterus is where the fertilized egg lives and develops for approximately nine months before birth. The tissue that forms the uterus is made up of powerful muscles that expand or contract according to need, with soft tissue on the inside to protect and nourish the growing fetus. The uterus is small when the woman is not pregnant—about the size of a pear—but it can stretch to considerable size when holding one or more babies.

Every month during a woman's menstrual cycle the uterus fills with blood and tissue in order to prepare for possible fertilization. If the egg is not fertilized, the blood leaves the body in the form of the woman's menstrual period. The cycle then begins over again.

Fallopian Tubes

The fallopian tubes are each connected, on one end, to an ovary and, at the other, to the top of the uterus. They deliver the egg that travels from the ovaries through the fallopian tubes and into the uterus. Sometimes, though rarely, an egg can get embedded in one of the fallopian tubes, become fertilized, and develop there. This is called an ectopic pregnancy and must be terminated, as the fetus cannot grow in the tube.

Ovaries

The two ovaries are the vessels where the eggs, the female's contribution to new life, are stored. A woman has all the eggs she will ever have in her two ovaries by the time she is born. Every month, as the hormones dictate, one of the ovaries will release an egg into the fallopian tube. That egg will descend to the uterus where it will either become fertilized, leading to pregnancy, or pass through the os of the uterus with the monthly menstrual blood.

Pelvic Floor Muscles

The pubococcygeus (PC) muscles make up the web of muscles that support the pelvic floor in women as well as in men. Some run front to back and others run side to side, crisscrossing to form the support system. It is these muscles that stop and start the flow of urine and bowel movements, keep the bladder from leaking, contract during orgasm, open for birthing babies, and hold the internal organs in place. Keeping these muscles toned is very important to sexual and genital health. These are the muscles that are strengthened by doing Kegel exercises.

A Personal Sexology Exam

Every woman should know her body well, especially if she is interested in being powerfully erotic and sexual. A personal examination is an important first step to great sex. A personal sexology exam is usually done alone. Set aside some quality time to investigate your "Jade Garden," as the ancient Chinese called a woman's vulva area.

Let's Begin Your Exploration

Start by taking a shower or bath and relaxing. If you have never done this before, view it as a way to know and love yourself better. As you relax, allow any negative imprinting, from societal or family influences or from past partners, to dissolve away. Remember that many cultures have worshiped the feminine genitalia. For this moment, pretend you are a member of one of those societies and rejoice in the wondrous gifts you have been given just by being a woman!

Did you know? Ancient societies that practiced loving as an art form often had special names for sexual parts. Some of the names used for the female genitalia were Lotus Flower, Perfumed Garden, Jeweled Vessel, and Precious Gateway.

Stand near a full-length mirror and observe your body. You're not looking at yourself critically. Rather, your attitude is one of openness, interest, reverence, and perhaps awe. Notice your hips. They have soft curves that draw the attention of potential partners. Your waistline may be smaller than your hips. This "hourglass" shape is very attractive to the opposite sex. Notice the softness of your skin.

Look at your breasts. No other mammal has breasts that stay full when they aren't nursing a baby. And yet, many cultures aren't as fixated on breasts as our culture is. Explore your breasts—to see how they feel to your own touch and to discover how you like to be touched. You might want to use a little massage oil for this exploration.

Exploring Your Vulva

Now, find yourself a small hand mirror and sit comfortably on a mat or towel. Slowly and softly rub your hand over the pubic mound of hair between your legs. Feel how soft it is. Notice the sensations that translate through to your skin from the hair follicles. Give a slight tug to the hair with your whole hand and see how it feels when those nerve endings are stimulated more forcefully.

With both hands, gently separate the hair and open up the outer lips of your vulva. Look at the outer and inner lips in the mirror. Notice the colors, and see where the hair starts and stops. See the entrance to the vagina and look for the tiny opening, just above it, that is the end of the urethra. Notice the glistening, wet skin.

Exploring Your Clitoris

Apply a small amount of lubricant to your vulva. With your thumb and forefinger, feel along both sides of your clitoris. Also explore the clitoral shaft buried just under the skin below the clitoris. You will have to squeeze your fingers together slightly to feel along the shaft. This is easier done when you are turned on, as the shaft and head of the clitoris fill with blood and are more prominent. This is also a great stroke to use when pleasuring yourself.

Now look at and feel the hood over the clitoris. Pull it back gently to expose the head, or tip, of the clitoris. Run your finger gently over the head and feel its sensitivity. This is the most concentrated bundle of nerve endings on your whole body.

Exploring Your Vagina

With a little more lubricant, explore the inside of your vagina. At this point you may want to get up and sit on your knees. This position will give you better access to your vagina and G-spot. Feel the lining of the vaginal walls and the folds that make up the interior area.

The Kama sutra divides men into three categories by penis size: the Hare, the Bull, and the Horse. It also divides women into three categories of vagina size: the Deer, the Mare, and the Elephant. The perfect union is said to be between equals: the Hare man with the Deer woman, and so on.

As you put your finger inside your vagina, check the strength of your PC muscles by tightening on your finger. The walls should feel thick and strong. If they don't, start doing those Kegel exercises today. You'll feel improvement within a few weeks.

Where's the G-Spot?

It's difficult for women to reach their own G-spot, so you'll have to twist a little to get access to it. Your hand will probably be facing palm up, although don't hesitate to spend a little time exploring the area down toward your anus. The membrane between the anus and the vagina is thin. Because of this, the G-spot can be stimulated through the anus, too.

Just beyond the entrance to the vagina, on the top, you'll feel a mound of skin that is ridged and plump. Slip just beyond that and you've hit the G-spot area. It is neatly tucked behind the pubic bone and needs a surprisingly firm touch to be felt. It is much more responsive when you are turned on, so you may want to arouse yourself and then explore more.

When touching your G-spot, you will probably feel an area of heightened sensitivity. Touching it might even feel uncomfortable at first. You may feel slight pain, tickling, erotic sensations, or the urge to urinate. Or you may not feel much this first time. For now, just see if you can identify any spot that feels a bit more sensitive than the surrounding tissue, and just press on it or massage it for a minute or two.

Reaching the Cervix

In this position, on your knees, you may be able to feel your cervix. In some women the uterus is tipped forward, and that brings the cervix into reach. It is toward the back and is relatively large. It will feel soft and puffy. You may be able to feel the edges and the os. It may be somewhat sensitive, depending on where you are in your monthly cycle.

Some women report that they have a very sensitive turn-on area right above the cervix on the top part of the interior of the vagina. Other than this area and the G-spot, most sexologists agree that the vagina is not a particularly sensitive area. So if you ever wondered if there should be more happening in there or believed that maybe you were different, don't give it another thought.

Nevertheless, the sensitive spots you do have in your vagina are exquisite and deserve all the attention you can give them. The more you stimulate them, the more they will give you back. This is why the angle of penetration during intercourse is so important to women.

Completing the Exercise

When you feel your exploration is complete, remove your finger and simply hold your hand softly over your vulva and mound and take a few deep breaths. Relax and appreciate yourself for this time. Honor yourself and all women. Be grateful for being given these parts that function so miraculously.

As you wrap up this time with yourself, reflect on what you thought about your private parts before you began this exercise. In particular, try to answer the following questions:

- Has your view changed?
- What did you discover?
- Do you feel more relaxed and accepting about your parts or not?
- Is there someone else you can talk to about your discoveries and feelings? (If so, spend some time with this person talking about your experience.)

This is a fun and interesting exploration to do with your partner, too. Be vulnerable and ask him to do this with you. Then, you can switch roles so that you can watch your partner explore himself, too.

QUESTION?

How do I figure out where my PC muscles are and how to control them?
If you aren't familiar with your pelvic floor muscles, pay attention next time you pee. As you urinate, see if you can stop the flow. It's your PC muscles that are allowing you to do this.

Classic Kegel Exercises

The pubococcygeus (PC) muscle exercises known as Kegel exercises have many advantages. They are best known for their help in strengthening and toning the whole pelvic floor to prevent incontinence later in life. But they are also the secret to stronger orgasms and *pompoir,* the art of "milking" the penis during intercourse (see the end of this chapter for tips on practicing *pompoir*).

Doing Kegel exercises will definitely improve your and your partner's sexual experience during intercourse. In fact, once your PC muscles get regular exercise, you will find that pumping them actually turns you on. Furthermore, training these muscles will help you better identify and distinguish your G-spot and anal muscles.

As you perfect these exercises and strengthen the muscles, you'll begin to notice that you can isolate distinctly separate groups of muscles in your pelvic floor. This enables you to isolate your clitoris, for instance, and stimulate yourself at any time. It's an excellent trick for getting "juiced up" for a hot date or romantic evening.

Kegel exercises also increase blood flow to the pelvic region, which aids in the increased flow of hormones and helps engorge the vaginal area. With increased blood supply and stronger muscles, you will prep yourself for better, stronger, and more amazing orgasms.

Are You Ready to Begin?

Sit comfortably in a chair or on the floor. You should be sitting up straight, but with a relaxed attitude. Or you can use a large rolled-up towel—sit on your knees and put the towel between your legs, so that you're sitting on it. You should be able to feel slight pressure on your pelvic floor.

Take a few slow, deep breaths to begin. Really relax. Breathe fully into your belly. On an in-breath, tighten your PC muscles. Hold for a moment. Now, on the out-breath, relax them. Focus on the relaxing. This is very important. Let your muscles go to a completely relaxed state. Make sure you do this after every Kegel. As you increase or decrease your speed, your breath will follow automatically. Tighten and relax, tighten and relax.

Try to start with about fifty of these every day for a few days. Your muscles may hurt a little, as in any new exercise, but that's how we know we're doing the work. Eventually, you can work up to 200 repetitions a day. You may do several sets a day, if you wish.

ALERT!

A set of 200 Kegels takes about five to ten minutes. They can be done while sitting anywhere. You can even do them standing, but you'll find the exercise is harder that way.

What Do You Notice?

Generally you will notice the difference within a few weeks. After about a month, you can usually begin to isolate the different muscle groups that comprise the pelvic floor. As you continue working on your PC muscles, take notice of how they feel. Are you getting turned on just by doing the exercises? Has your partner noticed any change during intercourse?

Don't be discouraged if you don't notice much of a change right away. This will take a little time, as any muscle conditioning does, but the benefits are well worth the time and effort. You should notice that you have a better "grip" when you insert two fingers into the opening of the vagina.

Advanced Kegel Exercises

When you have mastered 200 repetitions a day and feel like your muscles have caught up to the new exercise demands you have placed on them, you can add a set of sustained Kegels to your repertoire. When you first try these, you should probably be sitting in a chair with your feet on the ground.

Begin by slowly tightening your PC muscles to the count of ten (or to whatever number you can get to when you're beginning). Hold and take one long, slow, deep belly breath and let that breath out without letting your muscles go. On the next in-breath, tighten one more time.

Remember—only do what feels comfortable at any one moment. You can always come back to the exercise. Don't continue if you feel like you're hyperventilating. It will often take a little while to get into the flow of these exercises. Be gentle with yourself and enjoy them.

Begin to slowly let that breath out and let your muscles relax in a gradual letting go. Do this in steps of ten if you can—it may be very hard at first. Eventually, you can work up to twenty repetitions. You can put these into the middle or at the end of your 200 regular Kegels.

Pompoir, or Milking

The art of *pompoir,* or milking the penis, is a marvelous technique to use with many different lovemaking positions. Most of the ancient love manuals mention some version of it. It's an art that the best courtesans were adept at, but many wives mastered it just as well. Try it while practicing some of your favorite positions to see which ones it works best with. To perform this technique, you contract your PC muscles while the penis is inside you, simulating a "milking" action. *Pompoir* does take a while to perfect, but it is well worth it.

Once you've mastered the basic Kegel exercises, begin to add a sustained set in which each contraction lasts five to ten seconds. Build each contraction in steps, like you are going up the stairs. This is the same technique you will use in *pompoir.* You'll notice that at first you may not be able to distinguish between that many levels in your muscle group. Eventually, though, you will notice increasing strength and awareness of these multiple layers. On the out-breath, let your PC muscles completely relax, but again, let go in layers.

Do a minimum of twenty repetitions of this longer hold at the end of your regular Kegel exercises. You can also practice your Kegels while you are having intercourse. When you both need to slow down a bit, try doing your twenty long holds while your lover is still inside you. Have your lover do a set, too. Then try doing them in unison.

ALERT!

Even if you do not make time to do the full twenty longer reps of Kegels every day, don't give up the practice entirely. Do as many as you can whenever you think of it—in the car, while on the phone, or even in line at the supermarket.

You'll have the strength in no time at all! As your muscles grow in strength, try longer periods of holding and letting go to create the action of "milking." Try different positions to see what works best. Subtle shifts in the depth of the thrusting can enhance the effect. You may be able to grip better if the head of the penis is caught just behind the pubic bone where the G-spot is. This will also provide subtle yet stimulating pressure for the G-spot and the head of the penis. Ⓔ

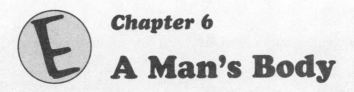

Chapter 6

A Man's Body

Like women, men are rarely encouraged to know their bodies intimately and to explore their full sexual potential. They may feel more permission than women to be open about their desire for sex, but this does not mean that they have really explored their full capacity for passion or their deeper, subtler sensitivities.

Male Sexuality

It's a cultural stereotype that sexuality comes naturally to men. In fact, many men feel stymied by cultural and family beliefs that stigmatize male sexuality. In many cases, a young man's sexual experiences begin with quick, furtive exploration. He may learn to reach climax quickly during masturbation and then, when it comes to sexual excitement with a potential lover, his body may react too quickly. This pattern can be very difficult to change, leading to insecurity and fear of underperforming.

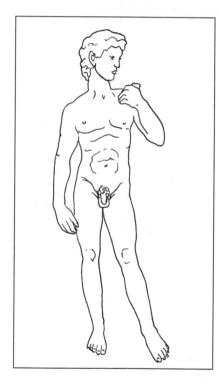

◀ David, an ancient symbol of masculine beauty

The male ego is very much tied to sexuality—issues of acceptance, performance, attractiveness, and youthfulness really do matter for men just as much as for women. When you add to this the stress levels of modern life, things can get tough. Lack of good communication skills between couples and the changing roles of men and women compound the problem. Often the last thing on the list is to take the time to develop skills as a great lover.

We live in exciting times for new understandings and break-throughs in sexual research. The willingness to learn, to talk openly, and to bring greater understanding to our sexual issues will open doors to deeper intimacy.

The Male Body

The male body is very different from the female body in terms of its reproductive organs, but new advances in medical understanding of both the male and female anatomies is revealing more similarities than differences. Modern researchers are discovering that men and women have internal and external sexual parts that are of the same origin. As the embryo develops, these parts take different developmental tracks, as directed by male and female hormones, which exist in different ratios in the male and female bodies.

Pubic Mound and Pubic Bone

Men and women both have a soft, fat-padded pubic mound, which protects the pubic bone. It is covered with hair and has scent glands that distribute pheromones, sweat, and sexual stimulus scents. The hair and hair follicles add extra erotic input by stimulating the nerve endings under the skin. Gently tugging, pulling, and scratching this area can be a turn on.

The pubic bone protects the male's internal sexual parts from outside damage. In the right positions during sex, it can be effective in rubbing against the woman's clitoris for stimulation.

Scrotum

The scrotum is the sac that hangs down under the penis and contains the testes and the ductwork that allows the sperm to enter the penis and be ejaculated. The skin of the scrotum is soft, pliable, and covered sparsely with hair. Some men enjoy stimulation of the scrotum during sex.

Makeup of the Penis

The penis is comprised of several parts. On the exterior, the penile skin has an amazing capacity to expand and shrink within minutes or even seconds. As the tissue underneath fills with blood, the penis goes from flaccid to erect. Blood vessels can be seen just under the skin. These become much more prominent as the erection becomes harder.

ESSENTIAL

Many ancient cultures understood the sexual arts both as a science and as a spiritual path. The phallus was worshiped as a powerful creative force. These cultures bestowed names on the penis like Thunder Bolt, Wand, Jade Flute, and Arrow of Love.

At the tip of the penis is the foreskin. Just like the clitoral hood protects the clitoris, the foreskin covers and protects the delicate tip of the penis. If it has been removed via circumcision, the head of the penis is always exposed. The foreskin has many nerve endings and scent glands buried in it.

The penile shaft has several nerves, veins, and arteries running through it and includes the urethra, which runs through the middle. The shaft is made up of the same spongy material as the clitoral shaft—the corpus cavernosum. When this spongy material fills with blood, the penis becomes erect.

Up to one-third of the penile shaft is buried under the skin. At the other end, at the tip of the penis, is what's known as the Lowndes crown. It is buried under the tip, or head, of the penis and may be likened to the tip of the clitoris. It is highly likely that the nerve endings here are chiefly responsible for the exquisite sensitivity of the frenulum, the membrane that connects the foreskin to the shaft and glans, close to the tip of the penis.

The glans of the penis is the very sensitive tip area. It contains a large number of nerve endings and plays a key role in male arousal. The urethra, which connects the bladder to the penis, ends here and is used for the elimination of urine; it is also used during ejaculation. Two spermatic ducts feed semen into the urethra during the ejaculation process.

At the base of the penile shaft are the two Cowper's, or bulbourethral, glands. They excrete small amounts of an alkaline fluid that neutralizes any acidity in the urine and urethral tube. This enables the sperm in the semen to travel in a favorable environment.

Prostatic Glands, or the Prostate

The prostate is actually a group of glands clustered together at the base of the penis. The duct that delivers the sperm and the two ducts that deliver the seminal fluid all convene here, so the prostate is instrumental in male ejaculation. During ejaculation, the prostate contracts and "pumps" the fluid out through the urethra.

FACT

The prostate is thought to be the equivalent of the G-spot in the woman. When directly stimulated, it is reported to add additional heightened sensuality to a man's orgasmic experience. See Chapter 15 for more on this subject.

The Testes and Sperm

The testes are two egg-shaped glands that produce sperm. They are connected to the prostate gland, where the sperm are combined with the seminal fluids to form semen, which is then ejaculated through the vas deferens, or spermatic duct. The sperm contain the genetic material that the male contributes to fertilization. Although there are many sperm in each ejaculation, it takes just one to fertilize the egg during conception.

Prior to ejaculation, the sperm is held in seminal vesicles, sacs that hold and nourish it. The sperm bathe in a solution of simple sugar and fluids that thickens the blend until it is needed in the ejaculation process.

Perineum

The perineum is a soft spot on the exterior of the body, between the anus and the base of the penis (or, in the case of women, the vagina). Although it's not always apparent that this is a sexual part, the many nerve endings that surround the anus make it very sensitive. You can experience great pleasure when the perineum is pressed firmly, perhaps because it stimulates the prostate gland in men.

Kegel Exercises for Men

If you've read the chapter on the female body, you already have an introduction to Kegel exercises. Women aren't the only ones who benefit from using their PC (pubococcygeus) muscles. In fact, PC muscles are just as useful for men. They hold up the pelvic floor, hold the internal organs in the body, and generally help counteract the downward gravitational pull. Having strong PC muscles aids in stronger erections that last longer and increases libido. Kegel exercises also help massage the prostate gland.

PC muscles must be relaxed in order to urinate. They can be tightened to prevent ejaculation from occurring (although that's not necessarily the best method), and they can and should be strengthened. Men can test their PC muscles by trying to use them to lift the erect penis. The higher you're able to lift your erection, the stronger your PC muscles actually are. Men, you will notice that you can "lift" your erection a little higher when you squeeze.

The angle of the penis at the time of erection varies from man to man. Younger men tend to have angles that point upward. As men age, they tend to lose the upward swoop. This angle directly affects the stimulation of the G-spot in the woman during intercourse. Kegel exercises can strengthen the muscles that control this arc.

Men can use the same Kegel exercises described in Chapter 5. Once you feel your muscles are strengthened, you can further exercise them by using a wet washcloth or a sock draped over your erection. Lift it up and down as you are tightening and relaxing.

Does Size Really Matter?

Penis size is the subject of magazine articles, talk shows, kitchen table gossip, locker-room whispers, and you name it. As a result, many men feel self-conscious about their penis, afraid that they're just not measuring up. But the truth is, size doesn't matter—what matters is the man's self-confidence and skill. Much more important than what you've got is what you can do with it.

Becoming a wonderful, attentive, and caring lover is far more important than the size of your penis. Having a very large penis can actually be a problem. Though the vagina can expand and shrink according to fit, some vaginas are smaller than others. Difficulties can arise when two people are mismatched in this arena. A man with a larger-than-average penis may have trouble getting full satisfaction for himself because he can't penetrate deep enough to stimulate his whole shaft. Furthermore, some women complain that they experience pain from their partner's thrusting techniques, and the pain may be due to the size of the penis.

The Lock and the Key

One reason the size of a man's penis isn't very important is that the G-spot is only 1½ to 2 inches inside the vagina, and during intercourse the goal is to stimulate the G-spot to an orgasm. The head of the penis does most of the stimulating of the G-spot. As the head passes the G-spot area, on both the in- and the outstroke, it catches slightly; that's what causes stimulation. Particularly on the outstroke, the head of the penis rubs up against the pubic bone and causes friction in the G-spot area.

Women often mention that the girth of the penis is more important to them than the length. But even the girth isn't that important, as long as she does her Kegel exercises. With stronger PC muscles, a woman will be very satisfied with a penis of any size—and she will also have much more sexual vitality and orgasmic potential.

The Soft-On

Men—don't be upset if occasionally you can't get it up. There are plenty of great sexual possibilities that aren't centered around a hard-on.

Take the focus off intercourse and try a side dish for a change.

When you have a soft-on, your partner may want to give you attention orally. If she usually has difficulty taking you into her mouth, now would be the perfect time. Try some new techniques and let go of performance worries. You'll enjoy yourself a lot more if you relax and go with the moment.

ALERT!

The incidence of prostate cancer is growing. Having a lot of satisfying sex can help keep the prostate healthy. Vitamins, minerals, and nutrients, especially zinc, along with a healthy lifestyle, are invaluable aids in staying sexually happy and healthy.

A Personal Sexology Exam

Because a man's sex organs are more external than a woman's, men are more likely to have explored them. He knows more about their capabilities and limitations than a woman does about her parts. Yet, that knowledge is sometimes limited to the basics. The following exploration is suggested for you to become more intimate and connected with your body and your sexual parts.

Beginning Your Exploration

Make sure you have privacy, though you may choose to do this exercise with a partner. (If you choose to do this with a partner, make sure you take the lead. Your partner may ask questions, but the focus should be on you.) Start by taking a bath or shower and relaxing. Close your eyes and breathe for a few minutes.

Stand in front of a full-length mirror and observe your body. Look at your chest and arms. Notice how they are shaped. No judging yourself now—you are simply looking for the universal symbols of your maleness. Notice your hips, legs, muscles, and torso. Do you have a lot of body hair? How does it feel?

Begin by cupping your penis and scrotum in your hand and gently holding yourself. Notice the heft and feel of the weight. Where is your mind? Do your thoughts turn sexual immediately? Just breathe and relax.

Lightly pull the skin that covers your scrotum. Use both hands for this and experience the stretch and elasticity it has. Notice if your testes, or balls, are the same size. Just as women's breasts are often different in size, men's testicles may be, too. Rub your hand very gently over the hair on your pubic mound. How does that feel? If a partner has touched you in that way in the past, did you like it?

Exploring Your Penis

Now, cup just your penis in one hand. If it is getting hard, relax and come back to this exercise in a minute. If you are uncircumcised, pull the foreskin forward and consider how it covers the tip and then some. Wet your fingers and gently run them around the frenulum. That's the area on the shaft of the penis just immediately below the head.

Notice the veins that are apparent on the outside of your penis, along the shaft. Now, if possible, guide yourself to an erection and look at those veins now. Notice the work they are doing to supply the blood that causes your erection. By just thinking about that blood, you may be able to pump more blood into your penis with some focus.

QUESTION?

Are you a "shower" or a "grower"?
You may have heard this expression before. Some men look fairly big when flaccid but don't add much length when they get turned on. Other men appear to be on the smaller size when flaccid but when erect grow more proportionally. You cannot judge a book by its cover.

Arouse yourself with some of the hand techniques covered in Chapter 15, using a good-quality lubricant. Remember to focus on breathing into your belly. Then, observe yourself. What do you notice? Is your scrotum loose and relaxed or tight and up toward your body? Has its texture or color changed in any way? How does it feel to pull down gently on your scrotum as you pleasure yourself? Do you ask your lover to do this during lovemaking?

Add a bit more lubricant to your genitals and feel your scrotum again. Feel the testes in the sac. You may even be able to feel the vas deferens, the tube that delivers the sperm to the seminal vesicles. Be gentle. These are delicate parts.

Buried Treasure

Lie down. Place your hand behind and under your scrotum and feel for the base of your penis, which is buried under the skin. You should be able to grab it and even stroke it with enough lubrication. How does this feel? Can you tell if you are more sensitive on the upper area of the base or the under part?

Now, with the same hand, feel the area of your groin that is directly next to the base of your penis. This is the space that connects your legs with your torso. The next time you have sex and your lover is stimulating you, have her massage you in this area while you are aroused. If she strokes with her fingers close to the base of your shaft, it should add to the sensual feelings.

If you feel tight in this area, massage it without sexual arousal and practice relaxation and breathing techniques. You'll gain benefit from easing those muscles later, when you are engaged in lovemaking. This is very appropriate for women, too. Try it on your lover next time, as part of the foreplay.

Men—if you'd like your partner's vagina to be tighter, don't just complain about it. Instead, tell her that you would like to practice lasting longer and suggest that she practice some of the arts of loving, too.

Moving on to the Perineum

Put some light pressure in the area between the base of your penis and the anus. Press more firmly. Do you notice any sensations? It's an indirect way of stimulating the prostate gland and can feel very good when combined with heightened arousal. If you want to, lightly feel your anus around the outside. It has many nerve endings and can be highly erotic during sex. See Chapter 15 for more detailed instruction on internal prostate massage. This is a sexual secret few men or women know about.

Chapter 7

Sexual Response in Men and Women

When you're hot, you're hot, and when you're not, you're not, and many factors determine how turned on you are at any given time: The quality of communication between partners, self-esteem, stress, feelings of warmth or closeness, family problems, stimulation or lack of stimulation, fatigue, aerobic fitness, and religious beliefs all affect your libido.

Ready or Not

You can't expect to always be ready for sex. Yet many people would rather fake interest than communicate openly about their feelings. The problem with this is that it further increases the emotional distance between partners and makes great sex even less likely in the future. When you don't feel like talking much, you can simply say, "I'm not ready for lovemaking just now, but I sure would love to snuggle or spoon with you," or "I sure would love to give or receive a massage." (Chapters 4 and 17 have in-depth discussions on honest communication.)

> To help yourselves get the most out of sex, it's good to understand some things about how men and women work. Let's look at the general sexual response patterns of men and women and then expand on the possibilities.

A massage can help both men and women get into a loving mood. Some men feel they should be the macho, sexy guy who is just supposed to "get it up" anytime. The fact is, especially as men get older, they too need to be warmed up to enjoy sex to the fullest.

Sexual Response Curve

Sexual response in men and women can vary greatly, despite the common belief that men are always ready for sex. In reality, men need touch, desire, and attention to feel turned on, just as much as women do.

Take a look at the chart that depicts the typical sexual response cycle for both men and women. As you can see, the basic steps are the same—excitement, plateau, orgasm, and resolution.

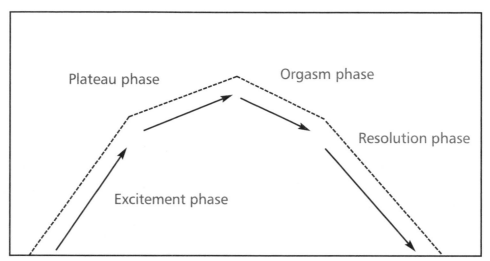

▲ Sexual response cycle in men and women

Sexual Response in Men

Preconceived notions of male sexuality can actually hinder a man's full sexual response. Fortunately, ancient techniques have been rediscovered that can help him to achieve the fullest expression of his sexuality.

Men tend to be visual responders. They are stimulated by the sight of breasts, hourglass waistlines, and buttocks. When a man sees a woman walking down the street, his testosterone kicks in, and as his penis expands, his self-control shrinks. The typical male sexual response pattern unfolds like this:

1. **Excitement phase:** This phase begins with imagination, touching, innuendo, kissing, fondling, looking at the partner, flirting, dancing, or any other activity the man finds exciting. As excitement builds, his erection hardens. On an arousal scale of one to ten, this phase takes him to about five or six.
2. **Plateau phase:** An increase in excitation occurs. The heart begins to beat faster, the erection gets firmer, the sense of separateness fades to the background, and body movements become more involuntary.

The testicles and scrotum tighten and pull closer to the body. Breathing patterns can be shallow and fast. His turn on reaches a level of six to eight. Premature ejaculation sometimes occurs during this phase.

3. **Orgasm phase:** For men, the point of no return occurs as he begins to move toward orgasm and ejaculation. The penis thickens with blood and the head often swells as he gets closer to orgasm. The typical arousal level at the point of no return is at eight to nine. With ejaculation mastery, that point might be at nine and three-quarters. During orgasm without ejaculation, that point would be the full ten, but ejaculation would not occur.

4. **Resolution or refractory phase:** Within minutes of ejaculation, the body relaxes, the breath deepens, and the blood begins to flow back out of the primary erogenous zones. The body comes back to its static state, before it was turned on, though much more relaxed and satisfied.

An ancient Taoist love text says that a woman's sexual energy begins in her heart and then moves to her genitals. For the man, the energy starts in the genitals and then moves to the heart. This difference, when worked with consciously, can bring about the healing of misunderstandings between men and women.

Depending on the age of the man, the last phase may last for ten minutes or many hours. Without ejaculation, the orgasm energizes the man and he goes back to about a level of eight, unless he rests a little longer, in which case he will relax into a level four or five. He may start again after a few minutes at the four or five level.

Sexual Response in Women

It may be a myth that women take longer to warm up to the idea of sex than men do. For women who are very familiar with their bodies, not much time is needed for them be lubricated and ready. Many women reach orgasm quickly through self-stimulation but take longer to arouse and orgasm when having sex with a partner.

Regardless of individual arousal time, a woman's sexual response usually begins with feelings of emotional intimacy. She may not need such intimacy every time she makes love, but things generally go better if she feels she is getting the intimacy she needs. Tender words, touching, loving gestures, and sexual foreplay are ways to begin to warm up a woman.

As a woman becomes sexually stimulated, her chest may flush, her vulva will begin to swell, and she'll start exuding lubrication in her vagina. Her nipples may become erect and her breasts firmer. Her heart rate and breath will speed up.

FACT

In the 1960s, sexologists Robert Masters and Virginia Johnson were the first modern doctors to research and describe in detail what we now call the female sexual response pattern.

The typical female sexual response pattern looks like this:

1. **Excitement phase:** The energy builds during this first stage of sexual excitement. Vaginal tissue swells, and lubrication of the membranes occurs. The supporting muscles of the pelvic floor tighten and pull upward. This expands the back of the vagina so it can accommodate the penis. On a scale of one to ten in terms of excitement, this phase may be rated at one through seven.
2. **Plateau phase:** The excitement response builds to a certain plateau and tends to level off. The turn on becomes sustained and consistent at between seven and nine. Breathing patterns can be shallow and fast, and the erogenous zones change color to brighter pinks and reds. It is during this period that tantric breathing can play an important part in increasing and sustaining the sexual feelings being generated.
3. **Orgasm phase:** The recognition that orgasm will occur has a distinct beginning. Many women feel this moment coming only to experience it fading and then returning. That pattern may occur several times before the orgasm phase moves into its final release. Many women experience frustration at this juncture and find that the actual orgasm may be elusory. If the orgasm does come, a very pleasurable

explosive release of pulsating energy occurs. There may be multiple phases of pulsating explosion and release.

4. **Resolution or refractory phase:** The body relaxes, the breath deepens, and the blood begins to flow back out of the primary erogenous zones. The body comes back to its static state, before it was turned on, though much more relaxed and satisfied. For some women this phase will last for just a few moments; others will feel complete and won't want to be aroused again for some period of time.

ALERT!

When it comes to research of human sexual problems, men get most of the attention. In the United States, 95 percent of all funded sexual dysfunction research goes to find cures for male sexual problems.

Experiencing Multiple Orgasms

Many men experience having multiple orgasms when they are in their twenties, and these almost always include ejaculation. As men enter their thirties, though, changes begin to occur. The refractory phase lasts longer in older men because it takes longer for the penis to refill with blood after a first orgasm with ejaculation. Men can learn to shorten this refractory phase (as described later in this chapter), or they can try to achieve orgasm without ejaculation.

In women, multiple orgasms can be defined several ways. The orgasms can be back-to-back responses that have distinct beginnings and ends, or they can be so close that it doesn't feel like any refractory period has occurred.

During extended multiple orgasms experienced by a woman, constant waves of involuntary muscle contractions occur. As the vaginal walls contract, the vaginal fit usually gets tighter. Rather than diminishing the woman's sexual energy, multiple orgasms often get successively more intense.

Take a look at the extended sexual response cycle chart, which shows multiple orgasms or back-to-back orgasms. It consists of peaks that get higher and higher on the chart. They are not followed by the typical refractory or resolution period.

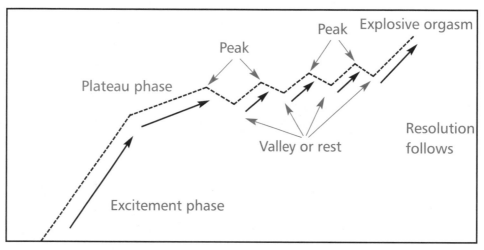

▲ Extended sexual response cycle in men and women

A Variety of Ways

Back-to-back orgasms can occur through clitoral, G-spot, or vaginal stimulation. With these women, there is virtually no refractory or rest stage. They move almost immediately into repeated plateau stages and then orgasm.

Typically, if a woman were able to have several clitoral orgasms in a row, they would occur with a distinct beginning and end with a fairly short refractory phase. She would be ready to go again very quickly and could take clitoral stimulation again, though she may have to start very softly the second time around.

In the case of G-spot or vaginal orgasms, they can occur like clitoral ones where the response cycle is repeated in its entirety, or the orgasms could be indistinguishable from one another. There would be no refractory period and the orgasmic state would simply continue—often being experienced as successively more intense rather than diminishing.

Take Yourself into a State of Bliss

Some women report sustaining a state of orgasmic bliss without dips for several hours. While this may be surprising, these are women who have learned to do this through practicing the exercises that are presented in this book. A woman can train herself to experience great amounts of pleasure. This is something any woman can do—with sufficient motivation and focused attention.

To facilitate becoming multiorgasmic, practice the deep-breathing exercises suggested in this book. Also, learn to "drive," or enable, your orgasms by consciously increasing the pace of your breathing. A great pattern is to pant into your belly eight to ten times and then take a deep breath in and let it out very slowly through slightly pursed lips. Focus on feeling erotic pleasure in and around your genitals when doing this breathing practice. Repeat as often as you want.

Mastery over Ejaculation

Tantrics and Taoists practice ejaculation control techniques that are said to allow the *chi,* or life force energy, to build in a man as he ages. The teachers of these practices today say that a man may have orgasms but should retain his semen, to increase his energy and sexual drive. These techniques take some practice, but in most cases, if you or you and your partner are willing to learn them, you are almost guaranteed results.

It often takes just a few weeks to become very proficient. You'll last a lot longer and your lover will feel the benefits, too. Within a month you should be able to actually feel the orgasmic sensations without ejaculation and the loss of fluid. You'll feel much more energized and sexually alive instead of depleted after sex. (Specific techniques for holding your sexual charge longer are covered in Chapter 14.)

Now that you are aware of the basic structure of the orgasmic response cycle and you've seen the chart that illustrates the extended cycle, you can visualize what is possible. Keep this chart in mind when you need a little help in self-control. Very soon your body will know the difference and your leap of faith will be rewarded.

As you advance in these practices, you'll begin to notice that you are actually getting so close to the edge that you are experiencing orgasmic sensations over and over. Waves of orgasms and energy can flood your body. As you begin to have multiple orgasms, you'll notice that your penis will be anywhere from very hard to firmly soft. You can go on and on without the refractory period.

FACT

In 2000, Tantra.com surveyed 1,377 men about their control over ejaculation. The survey revealed that 20 percent ejaculate earlier than they would like to, 35 percent have control over when they ejaculate, and another 45 percent only have control some of the time.

Enhancing the Female Orgasm

There are several ways in which women can enhance their orgasms, whether they're clitoral, vaginal, or G-spot orgasms. Arguably, the easiest type of orgasm to achieve is the clitoral orgasm. As a woman becomes more stimulated and turned on, the shaft and crura of the clitoris become engorged with blood. As this happens, the shaft straightens out and becomes erect, much like a penis. In the process, the head of the clitoris actually becomes more buried under the clitoral hood. This can become a problem if the woman maintains a body pose that tightens and curls inward as she becomes more turned on. The clitoris tends to get further buried. Learn to relax your body and even arch your back, slightly, if you feel this might be the case.

Some women have learned to facilitate access to the clitoral tip by pulling back the clitoral hood. Usually this will happen after a woman is somewhat turned on already. As she needs more stimulation, she will help expose her clitoral tip, either during oral sex or with finger stimulation. The clock exercise is a very important exercise that is rarely taught. Try it by yourself or with a partner.

The Clock Exercise

Lie on your bed with your partner at your side. On your back, spread your legs open wide and relax. Take in a few deeply relaxing breaths. Now, as your partner watches, take your index finger, with a lot of lubrication on it, and feel your clitoris gently on all four sides. Now, notice if one area or side feels more excitable than another.

You'll be interested to know that on most women, if you use the analogy of a clock, the 10:00 or 2:00 positions on their clitoris are by far the most sensitive. Most women don't know this. It's such a tiny area that most women think that the nerve bundle covers the whole thing. Not true. You will most likely be much more sensitive at one of these points than the other.

When you have found which part of the clitoris is most sensitive for you, have your partner touch you softly so that you can guide your partner to the exact spot. As you move into oral sex, make sure you are in a position that actually focuses on this area. After you have tried the exercise and explored the sensitive areas of your clitoris, take note when you are making love to determine if you are getting the most direct stimulation you can.

FACT

An online survey done in the year 2000 by ✒ *www.tantra.com* found that out of 1,048 women surveyed, 35 percent said they have multiple clitoral orgasms and 24 percent said that they have multiple vaginal orgasms.

G-Spot Clues

Women can also achieve orgasm through stimulation of the G-spot. The more you explore the G-spot and focus on it as part of your sexual experience, the more alive and responsive it will become. At first, some women will experience burning sensations, the urge to urinate, mild pain, or possible numbness. Some women will feel like laughing or crying, or they'll feel waves of emotion. Some will experience sexual pleasure immediately. If you don't experience pleasure right away, take the view that you have at least taken a step on the path to ecstasy. If it feels like a struggle in the beginning, take breaks, but keep exploring. With time and patience, you'll get to the pleasure you're seeking.

Be gentle with yourself the first few times. Don't make it a chore. As you become more aware of your sensitive vaginal parts, you'll begin to notice how much you can feel during intercourse. The more you can feel, the more pleasure you'll have, and the more you will take control of your orgasmic response.

QUESTION?

How often do you think women experience orgasm?
In a recent survey by Tantra.com, 56 percent of 1,087 women said that they always have orgasms when they masturbate. Only 23 percent said they always have orgasms when they have sex with a partner.

Do your Kegel exercises. This can't be stressed enough. They are vitally important because they give you the ability to feel what is going on inside your body. They put you in touch with the interior of your vagina and strengthen your body's response to sexual pleasure.

Female Ejaculation

Until recently, many women have felt ashamed or embarrassed about exuding fluid during sex, but public opinion has changed. Now women tend to feel that the ability to ejaculate gives them a sense of erotic power or a sense of freedom. As more women talk to each other openly about sex, they have empowered themselves to feel good about whatever feels natural and pleasurable.

Ejaculating can be somewhat messy, and it is certainly not necessary for great sex, so it's important to know that it isn't strange or unusual. If you have experienced ejaculation, you might want to be prepared with a towel next to the bed. Some women have been known to ejaculate up to several teaspoons of fluid.

The fluid emitted is exactly like male ejaculate, only without the sperm. It is not urine, though because the ejaculate comes through the urethral tube, it may push out a small amount of urine prior to the release of the ejaculate. Considering that the fluid most often occurs through G-spot or vaginal stimulation, and that the G-spot is the urethral sponge or female prostate gland, this makes perfect sense.

As in the male, the fluid in the female prostatic gland builds up and needs release. Some believe that symptoms of PMS might be greatly alleviated by female ejaculation. Part of the pressure and fluid buildup during the menstrual period may very well be female ejaculate. If you have PMS and know the times of the month when you feel the symptoms the most, have a lot of sex just prior to these times—it may help.

Sexual Dysfunction in Men

Although many sexual problems exist among both sexes, there are several dysfunctions specific to each gender. Common issues confronted by men are guilt about sexual desires and the pressure to perform.

ALERT!

Find a good sexologist or therapist trained in sexuality for problems that persist. If sexuality is important to you, start now. Why waste time? A fulfilled and satisfying sex life is too important to ignore.

Psychological problems with libido, fast ejaculation, not ejaculating, and attaining and maintaining erections often point to the presence of guilt, shame, unfulfilled desire, poor communication, or lack of training. It's amazing what happens when a couple begins to talk honestly about their anxieties, worries, and assumptions around sexual issues. Changes for the better can occur overnight.

Health plays an integral role as well, and factors that lead to problems with libido and erections may be physiological. These can often be treated very effectively with diet changes, herbal formulas, quitting smoking cigarettes, and developing a more healthy diet. Overindulgence in food, smoking, or alcohol cause blood vessels to close down, which leads to lack of adequate blood flow to the penis.

If your efforts do not meet with instant success, don't be discouraged. You are not alone. This is a path that has been traveled by many, over many centuries. With an open mind and a willing heart, anything can be accomplished. For most people the most difficult hurdle to overcome is just getting started. Once you begin, you may be surprised how much reward awaits your efforts.

Sexual Dysfunction in Women

For women, overcoming and transforming problems with orgasmic potential can feel daunting at times. Learning to relax your body can help you learn to relax your mind. This will help take off some of the pressure.

Sit down and have a really good conversation about your beliefs, struggles, inhibitions, and frustrations with your husband, partner, or lover. Be vulnerable and tell your partner your innermost feelings. Lack of communication is the number-one cause of libido problems, so stop beating yourself up and start expressing yourself more. For a little while, have sensual times together that aren't necessarily sexual or don't involve intercourse. You can focus on your partner for part of the time if you wish, but have at least two-thirds of the time together focused on you. Receiving a massage, snuggling together—these kinds of things can help take the worry out of being close.

As you receive the massage, don't expect to end up having sex. Explore your erogenous zones fully. Be touched and learn not to do anything about it except moan. Let your lover know that in learning to receive, you are taking action, and, if he is patient, you will both see great results.

Drop the focus on the big O for a while. Be sensual. Learn to relax and receive. If you are willing, have your partner blindfold you and give you a sensual massage. The blindfold will add a little suspense and newness and will allow you to focus more fully on sensations.

Educate yourself about your own body. Spend as much time as you can to learn what works best for you and what feels great. Experiment. Don't hold back. You have nothing to lose and everything to gain. You are in charge of your pleasure.

If you really feel stuck, visit a doctor of sexology or a psychologist with a sexuality background. You'll learn a lot and discover that you aren't alone. They will have a variety of ideas and, when combined with what you've learned in this chapter, will give you new tools for attaining your maximum pleasure potential. Ⓔ

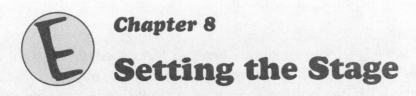

Chapter 8

Setting the Stage

The whole world is a stage, but you and your partner will probably be staging most of your "plays" in the bedroom. Creating an erotic atmosphere that is conducive to your unique style of romance can be a fun activity that you and your partner can do together. The mood you set in your bedroom and your home guides the energy and expands your awareness of lovemaking with your partner.

Rekindling Romance

Setting the stage starts with romance—the little things two people can do anytime of the day or night to communicate, "I love you. . . . I want you. . . . I'm glad I'm with you. . . . I'm looking forward to being intimate with you." The word *romance* means different things to different people. In a sense, it's whatever turns you on.

People feel more romantic when they feel valued. We all want to be appreciated and acknowledged. That's really all that romance is about. There's nothing mystical or difficult to get. Just hold your partner in your thoughts, and the little gestures will follow.

The Little Gestures

Just in case romantic little gestures don't come to you automatically, make yourself a list of some of the simple things you could do to let your lover know you find him or her attractive or to make life a little nicer for that person. Smile when your partner comes into the room. Listen to his or her stories. Make the bed in the morning. Do the things that are out of the ordinary for you. Open the door for your mate. Cook a meal or do the laundry without being asked. Take the dog for a walk, mow the lawn, or clean the garage. It is amazing how much benefit comes from these actions.

Romantic Moments

Create romantic moments as you move through your day together. Americans don't display public affection nearly as much as many other cultures do, but there are things that are certainly appropriate even in our culture. Take hold of the hand next to yours when you are walking. Kiss in public. Play childlike romantic games during the day with each other— play "footsies" under the table or cover your lover's eyes with your hands while sitting down for a meal.

The Great Get-Away

Get away to another world. Go for a miniholiday to a local hideaway. Take all the things you think might be needed for a complete getaway that heals and nourishes your bodies and spirits. This might be going out into nature, or it may be a weekend in the big city. Whatever you choose, it will be remembered for a long time if you take the few things along that will help the memories last.

Ambiance in the Boudoir

The bedroom helps set the mood when you awake in the morning, and it's your last sense of place at night when you go to sleep. To help keep you at your best, create a space that is sensual, spicy, cozy, and private. Your bedroom can be a sanctuary and a hideaway where you start and end your day.

By creating beauty, harmony, and a clean functional space in which to enjoy our sensual and sexual life, we feed our spiritual side as well as our esthetic needs. Living harmoniously with the energy of the surrounding environment is an art form.

FACT

According to Amazing! Feng Shui (✑*www.amazingfengshui.com*) consultant, Gayla Yates, "Good feng shui in the bedroom can dramatically affect your relationships and your relationship to your life!"

Feng Shui in the Bedroom

There is a way of harmonizing two peoples' energies using the ancient art of *feng shui* (pronounced "fung schway"). Feng shui is defined as the Chinese art and science of placement for arranging buildings, objects, and space in an environment in order to achieve the most harmonious balance of energy.

The idea in using feng shui in your bedroom is to blend masculine and feminine energies and create an atmosphere of trust, openness, and oneness between the two. Arranging the energy, or chi, of the room can create harmonization in the bedroom. Your last impressions before falling asleep will filter into your unconscious mind and set the stage for a restful sleep. And what you see upon opening your eyes is your first impression that sets the stage for your relationship to the new day. Does your bedroom welcome you back into consciousness, or are you smacked with overwhelming messages like laundry spilling out of the closet, unread books, unpleasant news in old newspapers, and so on?

In studying the feng shui of the boudoir, we see that the placement of the bed, the availability of light and air, and the flow that is created in the room are important aspects to keep in mind. You may want to consider the colors you have chosen and the comfort level that you desire. Is the room inviting? How does its energy feel to you and your partner?

ALERT!

You can enhance your bedroom with incense and candles, but don't overdo it. When burned, these objects can pollute the air, thus depleting the available chi, so use them in moderation

Make a shift in the position of the bed. If possible, avoid placing the bed directly across from the door or on a wall adjacent to bathroom plumbing. When the bed is placed to the side of the room, but still has a view of the door, a cozy eddy is created. Put desks and exercise equipment into another room; or, if they must stay, use a standing screen or curtain to separate them when they aren't in use.

The Four Elements

The four elements are earth, air, fire, and water, and having a balance of all these elements in your bedroom will help you harmonize its energy. The element earth might be a piece of driftwood you found or a stone that has special meaning to you. Living plants—either freshly cut flowers or potted plants—with rounded, soft leaves, are also a welcome addition to the boudoir.

Air becomes visible when we light incense. Fire is visible when we light a candle. Water might be represented by a small fountain or by a picture with the element water in it—but you should avoid turbulent seascapes and fountains that may become mildewed.

◄ Your bedroom may be enhanced by sensual elements like candles (representing fire) or plants (representing earth).

The Use of Color

Sometimes just small changes can make big differences. Try a change of color to set a different mood. Creamy tones combined with shades of pinks, oranges, reds, and browns help create a warm atmosphere. Pure whites, blues, and greens are cooler colors that don't have the warmth and passion usually associated with sexuality. When you can, use natural fabrics like cotton and wool for the bedding and floors. Natural fibers are friendlier to the skin, since they "breathe" better. They also tend to be more sensual.

Mirror on the Wall

You may also want to add a mirror to an appropriate place on a wall or on the ceiling; if it is on the ceiling, make sure it is not made of glass, for safety reasons. Mylar can be a good substitute for glass, since it is not breakable; and it gives an interesting "impressionistic" aura to the images it reflects. From a feng shui point of view, however, large mirrors are not advised in the bedroom as they affect the free flow of chi.

Background Music

Can you imagine a great movie without the accompaniment of an emotionally evocative soundtrack? Researchers have found that the same pleasure centers of the brain that are positively stimulated by food and sex are also affected by music. Any music that sends chills up your spine has a direct effect upon your mood. When we use music that is particularly stimulating to us in a positive way, we can elevate our mood, feeling more content, relaxed, energized, or turned on.

A Soundtrack to Love

You wouldn't want to leave music out of a great night of lovemaking. Music helps set the mood and can even be used to choreograph an evening of love. You probably have your old favorites, songs and artists that really turn you on and that you and your partner have made love to before. Great! Use them, and also go out and find some music that is new to both of you. You may even want to make a date to go to a music store and listen to a variety of new and different kinds of music.

Listen to new music before you introduce it to the bedroom. Explore unusual possibilities that might include world beats, drums, and exotic cultural music. Introducing new rhythms will open up the two of you to spontaneously trying new positions and practices that wouldn't have occurred to you before.

Make sure that you know the kinds of music that excite your lover. If you like different types of music, take turns creating a mix of both kinds in any lovemaking evening, so you will both feel turned on.

If you have the ability to record, try creating a whole love-track of music to make love to. This could be for a special erotic evening that may be several hours long. It could be a soundtrack you use often for massage dates. Or it could include a hotter, spicier list of tunes that you use when you're feeling especially daring.

The idea of creating your own soundtrack allows you to create the "dance" you want. It can start with soft, melodic pieces that slowly rise in intensity, according to the length and love rhythm that you two have. Maybe you are creating a special birthday ritual and you want to design a new wave of lovemaking that is a gift to your beloved.

At the end of the music mix, include a soft, sensuous ending when you can cuddle, kiss, and take in each other's breath before falling off to dreamland, or before getting up and continuing your day. But whatever you do, be sure to close your lovemaking sessions tenderly and sensitively.

Fragrance and Aromas

Scents and aromas are powerful stimuli; they can affect your mood and trigger memories or particular feelings. Our emotional body stores and recalls events in our lives that often have a smell or particular scent associated with them. We all experience times when we catch a scent of something that reminds us of a childhood experience, a first love, or a favorite holiday.

◄ Essential oils may be used for bathing or sensual massage.

Researchers have found that certain foods with strong odors cause penile blood flow to increase. Dr. Alan R. Hirsch tested thirty scents and forty-six odors with men from ages eighteen to sixty-four. His results found that cinnamon buns caused the greatest arousal and that a combination of pumpkin pie and lavender caused an average increase in penile blood flow by 40 percent. Older men responded more to vanilla and men who had the best sex lives reported a preference for the aroma of strawberries. Every scent and odor that was used in the research caused some degree of increase in penile blood flow.

FACT

Fine Indian restaurants will often have a small bowl filled with herbs of anise, licorice, and flower essences to chew after the meal. Along with cleansing the breath, these delicacies also help stimulate the libido.

Dr. Hirsch also studied the female reactions, which turned out to be markedly different. Among women between the ages of eighteen and forty, licorice was the most sexually stimulating. The combination of licorice and cucumber caused a 13 percent increase in vaginal blood flow. The pumpkin and lavender combination that the men liked so well caused an 11 percent increase. Women had negative responses to barbecue smoke, which caused a 14 percent decrease, and cherry, which caused an 18 percent decrease. In addition, they found that women had a 1 percent decrease in vaginal blood flow when they were exposed to a variety of men's colognes! So men—don't assume that your cologne is a turn-on for your woman.

Experiment with Scents

Humans can detect between 10,000 and 30,000 different scents, so have fun experimenting to find the ones that get you and your partner going. Get a variety of essential oils from a local herb shop or health food store and use them in different ways. Try putting a few drops on the light bulb in the lamp next to your bed. Bring a bowl of fruit to bed with you and try feeding tiny pieces to each other. Before you put the bites in your lover's mouth, inhale their sweet scent and let your lover do the same. You may want to blindfold your partner to really enhance the senses of taste and smell.

Attire in the Love Chamber

Throughout history, costuming and erotic wear has seen many changes. From extremely suggestive, as in bustiers that pushed up the breasts and tightened the waist, to volumes of fabric and veils that revealed very little skin, the designs tended to fit the culture and times. Today, in the privacy of our own homes, we find it a little easier to let our imaginations go wild.

Although eventually you'll end up nude, foreplay can become much more powerful and extended when the element of clothing is added to the scene. Certain clothing elements lend themselves to the erotic.

Buttocks, breasts, legs, and shoulders (in that order) are the body parts that men list as their most arousing. Therefore, plunging necklines, tight skirts, styles that accentuate the legs, stockings, and bare shoulders are evocative ways in which women can create allure. For the bedroom, try looser-fitting garments that allude to the curves of the body underneath the clothing. The fabric should wrap around you to accentuate your own erotic, natural curves.

The Bare Essentials

It only takes a few items to satisfy a hunger for erotic dressing up. You can keep it as simple as this:

- A sarong made from either rayon or silk (to be worn by both men and women)
- A sarong that is either transparent or see-through
- A teddy, matching bra, and underwear or a one-piece body suit
- A robe of velvet, silk, or rayon
- A feather boa

In addition, you could add any number of items that appeal to you and your partner. You can use the following list of items if you're looking for an erotic gift for your partner:

- Additional scarves of all sorts
- Dress-up items from used clothing stores
- Fantasy items that you think might be good additions to your love play
- A wider selection of lacy underwear and teddies
- Feathery fans, masks, and other props that might add appeal
- Jewelry that might lend an exotic feel to your costumes

Choose fabrics like velvet, rayon, and silk—they feel just as good to the person wearing them as to the one touching them. Silk slides under the hand and over the body easily. It shimmers and feels slinky and gives the body a moist, wet look.

Though it's usually women that we think of as dressing in erotic attire, men have a few options available, too. In studies, women say that they appreciate inner strength and caring in a man over physical traits, but when it comes to the physical, they list average build, tight stomachs, and strong arms as their preference. Select silk robes, boxer shorts, and maybe a sarong for your intimate liaisons. For a special evening you may even want to layer a little and put on a pair of men's G-string underwear under your boxers. When selecting items that create a tighter look, with the bulges in all the right places, pick fabrics that will breathe and that aren't too restrictive. It's a well-known fact that a man's sperm count goes down when his scrotum is up close to his body for long periods of time. Select items that leave your whole body available for touching.

Men, do you dare to catch your partner by surprise?
Learning to wrap and wear a sarong is quite convenient for those moments you have to get up for something you've forgotten. It may even come in handy when you decide to create an erotic dance for your partner some evening.

Food as an Aphrodisiac

Sensual foods have a definite place in the bedroom. They are especially welcome if they are juicy, soft, mysterious, and sweet. If the foods are evocative reminders of sexual organs, there's even more reason to include them as part of your lovemaking ritual. You'll find more information on foods as aphrodisiacs in Chapter 13, but here are a few ideas for starters.

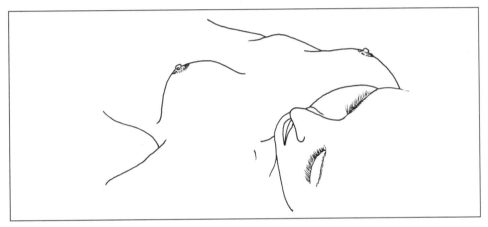

▲ Here's another idea: You can use your body as a serving platter for your lover.

Lots of fun can be created with food in the bedroom. Food can be used for stimulating the senses. Try an evening of lovemaking that involves blindfolding your partner and offering him or her different sorts of fruits, chocolates, and desserts that are suggestive of softness or juiciness, or just plain fun. This is more about sensing than it is about eating. Keep the bites very small and offer the food gently for smelling and brushing across the lips first, before letting your partner take the bite into his or her mouth.

Whipped cream and chocolate syrup are fun in the bedroom, but there are things to know before you get highly sugared foods near a woman's vagina. Sugar can cause yeast infections in women. If you decide that you want to have a sensual feast on your partner, stay aware of where you are placing the edibles. Keep the goodies on the exterior and take a bath together before you have intercourse.

ALERT!

Too much food in one's stomach during lovemaking can detract from the erotic nature of the experience. A nice dinner beforehand may be romantic as foreplay, but it can temporarily reduce your capacity for sexual pleasure. For a hot night, it's best to eat light!

Nothing Like a Hot Bath

There is nothing like a hot bath to invigorate both your mind and your body. A hot bath can inspire you to relax and stop thinking. It can calm you and create an atmosphere of being in a sanctuary. Taking a bath is a ritual that is easy to do for yourself.

The act of bathing together can be as elaborate or as simple as you'd like to make it. It's easy to add bubbles to the bath water and light a few candles around the bathtub. Or you can get as elaborate as using a Japanese dry brush to pamper and stimulate the skin before you get into the water. Sometimes it's appropriate to bring music, drinks, food, and playful fantasy into the bath. Other times you may want to ceremoniously wash your partner's feet and anoint them with creams and oils. You can even have an important conversation while soaking in the bathtub.

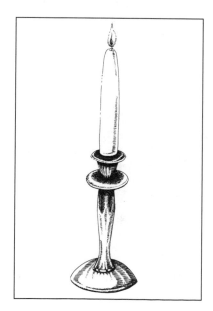

◀ Lighting a candle will help set the mood for romance.

There is no end to the imaginative things you can do in the bath. Get innovative and think up a few wild ideas for yourself. Here are a few suggestions of things to do in the bath:

- Lovingly wash your partner's hair.
- Give your partner a foot or scalp massage.
- Slide your soapy body up and down over your partner's body.
- Put soap on a large soft sponge and soap your partner's body.
- Dry your partner very lovingly.
- Brush each other's hair.

You may also want to add something to the bath water for an enhanced experience. Here are a few ideas:

- Put rose petals in the bath and on the floor of the bathroom.
- Use a few drops of a favorite essential oil in the bath.
- Use herbal and scented soaps.
- Finely grate a little orange or lemon rind into the tub.
- Float a cinnamon stick or a few cloves in the water.
- Use foaming bath bubbles.

Arranging for Worry-Free Time

It's very important to have the peace of mind required for an erotic evening. What keeps men and women distracted are the regular old things that consume our everyday life—work, deadlines, laundry, company coming, kids, and almost anything else that worries us.

Don't feel guilty if you feel that you need a little time away from your kids. It's important to spend time with them, but it's also important that children see their parents in love and connected. The modeling that is provided for children is essential in the creation of their own healthy relationships.

Clear the space as best you can, and then don't worry about what you're not doing. All of that stuff will eventually get done, whether you worry about it or not. The difference will be that you will be much more relaxed and happy. You may even find that when you give yourselves pleasurable evenings to remember, you are more resilient in handling the stresses of your daily lives.

Time Away from Kids

If you have children, try to find friends or relatives to take them for an evening and overnight, if possible. Explore trading this gift with another couple by having each other's children overnight. As time passes and your children get older, you'll get better at carving out time for you and your partner. They'll understand that the two of you want time together and that you need your privacy. In the meantime, set up situations that eliminate the worry and distraction that can occur in a busy household. E

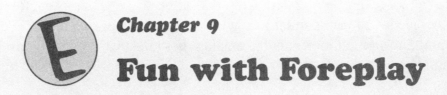

Chapter 9

Fun with Foreplay

Almost anything done at any time might fall into the category of foreplay, as long as it's pleasurable. There are so many ways to give and receive pleasure. Every person and every couple are different. So why not include anything that has ever been associated with pleasure over your whole lifetime in your expanded definition of what foreplay is. A great definition might be everything right up to intercourse!

Foreplay Twenty-Four Hours a Day

It's very erotic to feel loved and cherished. Do you remember the first time you were in love? You probably couldn't stop thinking of your heartthrob. That was nonstop foreplay.

Mature couples usually need a little help to remember that it's important to think of your partner during the day, when you are not in each other's presence. Call your partner to say you are thinking of him or her. Both men and women love even the smallest gestures that show they are in someone's heart.

FACT

In a recent Tantra.com survey in which 2,400 people responded, 30 percent said that they spend less than 10 minutes on foreplay and another 19 percent said that they spend between 10 and 30 minutes. That's probably not enough foreplay.

Inquire about your lover's schedule, and ask often how he or she is doing. Ask if there is anything you can help with. Pack a little note in your lover's briefcase, purse, or lunch pail to be found during the day. Hint at a secret meeting later that evening. Tease a little. Touch each other often.

Of course, the standard things work well, too: flowers, dinner out, a movie, a gift—all are usually welcomed and appreciated. But those things aren't nearly as important as the little remembrances that don't cost much. When you can offer help and assistance, that is foreplay. When you say "I love you" in many different ways—you are having foreplay. And these things are not just for men to do and for women to receive. They are important for both sexes.

Erotic Massage

When we daydream of the perfect sensual experience with a lover, it often includes massage. Nothing can get a couple more relaxed, in the moment, and focused than warm oil and tender hands. Massage is a wonderful way to begin a sexual experience. It gets our bodies and our minds in tune for what comes next.

One of the basic things to keep in mind when giving a massage is to prepare ahead. Where will you give the massage—on the bed, on a massage table, or possibly in front of the fire? When you decide, make sure you have a large-enough towel or an old sheet. You don't want to use oil on or near anything new or valuable.

Warm the massage oil slightly. Get your music selection ready. Warm the room ahead of time. If you are prepared, your participant will feel even more honored to receive this gift.

Begin Massaging Your Lover's Body

When you are ready, have your lover lie down on his stomach. Invite him to relax and receive your love and energy. Ask if there is anything he needs before you begin.

To start, rub your hands together vigorously for a couple of minutes to get them warm and energized. Tenderly place them on your partner's back and let them just lie there for a few minutes as you connect.

Massage is a practice that has been perfected over thousands of years. It is used for stress reduction, relaxation, erotic touch, musculature health, lymphatic health, emotional release, body rebalancing, and much more.

Lightly move your hands in slow, smooth motions over your lover's body. Feel your fingers and palms. Do they feel good? Make whatever adjustments you need to make so that you, the giver, feel comfortable and relaxed, and so that your hands are receiving pleasure as well as giving it. Feel the soft hair on your lover's body. Feel the lines and contour of his calves, thighs, buttocks, waist, back, neck, and arms.

Oil Massage

Apply some warm oil or massage lotion to your hands and begin with the feet. At this point you can use firmer pressure, but remember that sensual massages aren't therapeutic in nature! Remember, you are eroticising the flesh, not pounding it.

Massage the balls of the feet along with the instep, heel, and ankle. Go between the toes and on top of the arch. Send love through your hands to heal and nurture. Move up the leg and spend a little time on the calves, behind the knees, and thighs. It's best to work on one side and then the other.

ALERT!

Try not to make your partner flinch during a massage. Experiment with the depth and pressure of the touch you give. Start with a lighter touch and move into deeper pressure later. Stay sensitive to your partner's response and adjust accordingly.

Move to the torso and gently knead the buns. As you apply new oil, try leaving one hand on your partner and pouring a little oil over the hand that is still on the body. This serves two purposes; it keeps your partner from being shocked by the oil and it keeps you and your lover connected. Your lover won't feel like you've gone away, even for a minute. Try moving your hands in unison over his bottom. Go in circles, first one way and then around the other way. This is relaxing and energizing all at the same time. Ask how he likes it best—whether he wants your touch to be deeper or lighter.

Moving On

As you move up the torso, you can use more oil. Slowly work up the spine but never touch the spine directly. The muscles on either side of the spine support and protect the vertebrae and the rib attachment points. See if you can feel every one of them as you move slowly up the back. You'll find that using your thumbs will work well. As you continue the massage, make sure that your fingers and hands are doing fine and aren't tired or uncomfortable. Remember, this experience should be pleasant for both you and your lover.

Move to the outer area of the back and run your hands up the sides of the body, from the waist to the armpits. Use a long, firm stroke so you don't tickle. Keep your attention focused on the sensations in your hands. There are lots of nerve endings in this region and it can be a major erogenous zone for many people. Spend some time on the shoulders and scapula.

As you work these areas, you can move a little closer and tease your partner with a little verbal foreplay. Tell him how much you're enjoying this moment or anything that comes to mind. Or just plant a simple kiss on the back of his neck.

Finish the sides by massaging each arm and the hands. Our hands serve us well and they get cramped and tired. You can kiss them and knead them lovingly and even speak to them and thank them for all the service they perform. Experiment using both hands to work up and down the arm or hold the hand firmly with one of your hands and massage up the arm with your other hand. This allows for gentle pulling and stretching of the arm.

Face-Up

Gently role your partner over and connect with your eyes for a few moments. Though you can do his feet again, you may want to begin with the front of his legs and thighs. Try moving your hands out from the middle, at the knee, up with one hand to the thigh and down with the other hand toward the toes. You can also stand at his feet and move both of your hands up each leg in unison.

FACT

If the massager is a woman, she can use her breasts in the massage. As she reaches toward her lover's inner thigh, her breasts can grace his feet. The breasts are the representation of the heart and can be used to send her love.

The inner thighs are highly erotic areas that generally respond immediately to soft, conscious touch. Notice your partner's breath as you approach this area. Did he make a satisfied sigh? Did he moan?

You may want to encourage your partner to open his legs a little now. The muscle structure of the inner thighs is sensitive, so use a soft stroke.

Lightly play with his pubic hair and really feel the soft hair on his thighs. Hair is highly erotic, and the more softly you can touch it the better it will feel. Gently brush over his genitals, just teasing a little, and move to the front of the torso.

Add more oil and massage the belly and abdomen with the palms of your hands. Be firm but sensitive, especially if your partner has eaten in the last few hours. Then move on to the chest area.

As you move up the body, start in the center, move up between the breasts, and stroke to the outside and around the breasts. Include the upper chest and come down around the outside of the breasts and back down. Start the move again. This is a particularly good massage move to open the heart area. Do it a few times with your attention focused on love. You may even want to speak loving words to your partner.

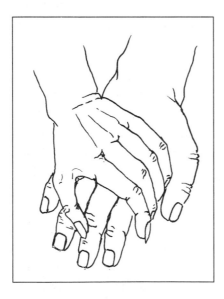

◀ A tender touch is the key to a good massage.

Now, focus some attention on the breasts. Women generally love having their breasts massaged upward and on the outsides, under their arms. Use circle strokes, first one way, six times, and then the other. Massage the areola and nipples gently. Men's breasts can be highly sensitive, too. Focus some attention on them to develop their erotic potential even more.

Finish the main body massage by standing at your partner's head and massaging his shoulders and arms from this position. Knead the muscles in the shoulders and stretch your body over your partner's, using both of your arms to massage down his arms to his hands. Women, as you bend with this move, let your breasts lightly brush your partner's face. Repeat this stroke several times.

A Facial Massage

At the end, you may want to do a facial massage. With a small towel, wipe the excess oil off your hands. Look into your lover's eyes for a moment and acknowledge him. Place your hands as gently as possible on his face, cupping his face in your hands. Stroke his skin as lovingly as you possibly can. Softly pass by his eyelids, lips, forehead, and hair. Caress his cheeks and temples. Do it as if you were worshiping him. (You can also add a sexual massage described in this chapter.)

Electrifying Touch

When it comes to exploring new areas in our lovemaking techniques, we tend to go for the hot, strong, overt qualities instead of moving into the realm of the soft and sensuous. Slowing down and investigating every inch of your partner's skin can, on first investigation, seem too obvious.

But ask yourself, how often have I actually taken the time to discover my partner's erogenous zones? Have I asked her what she likes? When we begin to open up to our partners in these new, subtle ways, we open new doors to a fuller range of intimacy and connecting.

Make a list of all the areas on your body that you either like to be touched or think that you might like to have touched. Then, list the five main places on your body that are your personal favorite erogenous zones. Share your lists with each other.

Erotic touch is an area that has a lot to explore—there are many esoteric ways of touching with hands, feet, and other body parts. For instance, Charles and Caroline Muir, of Source Tantra, teach a technique that refers to the penis as a wand or paintbrush that "paints" and strokes the outside of the vagina. In this form of foreplay, the man uses his penis, which is generally softly erect, to stroke the outer labia. As he gets the go-ahead signal from his partner, he comes closer to the vaginal opening, and strokes from clitoris to anus.

Here are a few more ideas on how to use touch in your foreplay:

- **Touch as light as a feather:** Touch as though you are stroking only the hair on the body. Use the fingertips, your palms, the back of your hand, or your cheek.
- **Light scratching:** If you have fingernails, try scratching your partner around his inner thighs, scrotum, buttocks, back, and head. Move slowly.
- **Light biting:** Nibbling on your partner may be very erotic. Try it around the ears and neck.
- **Pulling:** Gently but firmly pull the hair around your partner's genitals. Do this in a large handful, not little pieces.
- **Blowing:** Use your breath to blow on your partner—behind the ears, over the face, and over the genitals.

◀ A feather touch should feel as light as a feather.

The Art of Kissing

Kissing is an art and can be enhanced with practice and intention. Our lips are extremely sensitive and receptive to stimulation. Many people hold their lips stiffly, not letting them relax and be open to the receiving and giving required for good kissing. Practice using your lips in a soft, open way. Part them slightly and keep them moist. This will heighten their sensitivity.

Practice pouting softly when you are by yourself. This relaxes the lips and exposes more of the fleshy interior. In general, become more aware of your lips. Try eating your meals more slowly than usual and really feel the food passing between your lips. Practice sucking on soft fruit, like a piece of mango, for the effect it has on your mouth and lips.

Kissing Techniques

When you are about to kiss, lick your lips to wet them, open your mouth a little, tip your head very slightly, and go softly forward. At first, leave your tongue out of it. Use your lips to gently explore the interior of your partner's lips. Move very slowly, but with confidence. Go deeper, and open your mouth a bit more as you feel yourself going into the kiss. Create a slight amount of suction as you expand and open your mouth a little bigger.

QUESTION?

How many ways do you kiss?
Have a love contest to see how many different ways you can kiss. Challenge your lover to dueling lips and see how many different techniques you can come up with.

Take your lover's whole mouth into yours. Do this lovingly, as if you were exploring it for the first time. Eat them up—but gently. Now, if you wish to, you can do some "French" kissing—probing with your tongue into your lover's mouth and letting your lover do the same. Let your tongue slowly investigate rather than force its way into your partner's mouth. Tease and let yourself be teased. The subtler you are, the better. Kissing can go on for a long time if it's treated as a playful and erotic activity.

Music to My Ears

The ear is one of your main erogenous zones; it has many nerve endings, and it is situated near the neck, another highly erotic area. Ears are the gateway to hearing, one of the five senses. You can nurture your ears with music, a direct path to the soul.

The ear should be approached slowly, with a little teasing. Try a soft breath to start. Get close to the ear that is about to enjoy being the object of arousal. With slightly open lips, spread your warm breath around the ear and behind it. Move in with very soft and light kisses to the top area and the immediate hairline just above the ear. You might take a small piece of hair in your lips and give it a little pull, just to entice.

Move down the ear slowly to the fleshier areas and the lobe. Kiss and gently blow. Speak to your partner with barely audible words, teasing a little if you want to, or reminding your partner to relax and breathe. As your partner begins to react by moving and making sounds, begin to press your lips a little harder and with more ardor. Take the lobe and lightly press and suck on it with your lips.

ALERT!

Experience lovemaking as a dance, with many moves and sentiments that can be explored on the dance floor of the bedroom. Remember that whatever you are practicing in your lovemaking, the giver should be experiencing as much pleasure as the receiver.

Love Bites

Move briefly to the neck just below the ear and place a few kisses there before moving back to the lobe. Now try a few light bites on the lower, fleshy part of the ear. Be gentle and playful. This is a bite to entice and show your passion; it is not meant to hurt.

After the bites, don't move away without first kissing and sucking a little more. You don't ever want to move away after a tease like a soft bite. Come back and treat the ear to a soft and sensual experience again before going on.

An Exercise in Sexual Communication

This exercise is both sensually fun and a good learning experience. It should be done with a partner, and you should expect to devote one hour for each person. Keep it light, and see what you can discover about your partner and yourself.

This is a practice in sensual touch and will be accompanied by a simple but powerful communication technique. Essentially, you will be asking for different kinds of touch. This will be a practice in learning what you like, how to ask for it, and training your partner in what you want.

This is an activity you can come back to more than once; each time, you can be more detailed and precise. Practicing clear communications in this fun way will help in those times when it's more difficult to communicate.

Feeling worthy of asking for intimacy and having someone honor that request is difficult for many of us. But what you discover is that when you do bring a little more humility and vulnerability into your life, your partner will see more beauty in you than ever before. When you reveal yourself in new ways, you are saying, "I trust you, and I am entrusting my most vulnerable self to you." That kind of thing is irresistible—even if it is a bit new and awkward. Think of awkwardness as a sign of innocence, a signal that you and your lover are entering uncharted territory together. This is the kind of thing that keeps love alive and fresh.

Let's Begin

To begin the exercise, set the scene by lighting a few strategically placed candles. Scent the room; decorate it with flowers; have massage oil and something to drink ready for your use. Make sure the room is warm. When you're ready, proceed as follows:

1. Make a positive statement about the touch you are currently receiving. Keep it simple. "I love the way you look at me when you touch me." Or, "I love the way your fingertips feel on my face."
2. Ask for a change. Keep this simple, too. "Would you please use a little more pressure?" Or, "Would you try that a little faster to see how it feels?"
3. When your partner responds, give thanks: "Mmmm . . . that's great." Anything in a positive tone will do. That doesn't mean you necessarily liked the change. It is okay to say: "Wow. I thought I'd like that, but I was wrong. Thank you for helping me learn that about myself."

Difficulties in Communication

If your partner seems reluctant to communicate, use positive messages to encourage speaking. Ask a multiple-choice question such as, "Would you like me to do this a little harder or softer?" If you're the one who is shier about speaking up, try to find the courage to ask for your partner's encouragement. You might say, for example, "Do you really want to hear what I like? If you do, I'd like you to remind me of that now and then."

Here are some questions to see how you did with this exercise:

- How did this experience make you feel?
- What did you notice about your breathing?
- Were you able to take the focused time that your lover offered and enjoy it?
- Was it hard to receive that much time and energy from your lover?
- Did you get nervous and want to "give back" before your receiving time was over?

Each time you practice this exercise, check back with these questions to see if your responses have changed.

Much, Much More

You'll find great ideas for more sensual and sexual play throughout this book. Some of the more obvious areas to explore are oral sex (Chapter 12), bathing together (Chapter 8), games (Chapter 16), and sexual massage (Chapter 15). Sometimes it's appropriate and exciting to just have fun with foreplay, and skip the main course. Explore and have a good time. Ⓔ

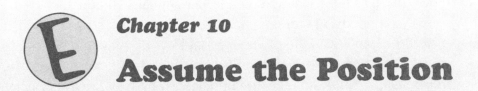

Chapter 10

Assume the Position

New positions are possibly the best way to introduce variety and interest into a sexual relationship. They can be exciting, a little challenging, and often inspiring. There are really only a handful of basic positions, but there are many, many variations on each of the basic ones, and practicing variety will help any couple reach greater pleasure.

Yin and Yang

Many Eastern cultures believe that male and female energies run opposite to each other. The Taoists say that man pulls his sexual and life energy (yang) from his feet, up through his penis and then upward into his heart. Woman, on the other hand, takes her energy (yin) from the top, down through her heart and then to her genitals. Hence, the war of the sexes—she needs a heart connection before she has sex; he needs sex before he can have a heart connection. How do they proceed?

Your choice of positions can have a major influence on your yin/yang relationship. Yin is the receptive principle. Yang is the active principle. The position you choose, and its appropriateness for your particular needs, can make the difference in whether you experience a female/male "energy dance" or a "war of the sexes."

When a woman opens up her sexual repertoire to include trying positions where she is on top and in control, she becomes the "male" principle or the yang in the sex act at that moment. This empowers her, and can give her a growing confidence in taking a more sexually active role. When the male is on the bottom, he can move into his feminine yin side. This takes the heat off, so to speak. He can relax. He doesn't have to be in charge and perform. The simple act of trying a new position can often be transformative for a relationship.

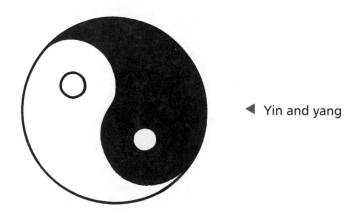

◀ Yin and yang

There's Always Something New

When you investigate a new position, you can count on having new things to talk about and learn together. Exploring new positions should be fun, and you should be prepared to communicate with your partner and laugh at yourself if you don't quite get it right away. You'll probably find that some positions will work well for you, and some just won't at all.

ALERT!

Before you begin learning new positions, you should read the sections of this book devoted to finding the woman's G-spot, enabling the man to last longer, and so forth.

The more positions you try out, the easier it will become to learn new ones, as your awkwardness or reluctance will disappear. You'll find yourself becoming willing to try other new things with your lover. That's what makes exploring different positions so important. This form of trying something new will often lead to a transformed sexual relationship. For couples who want to learn and add to their sexual repertoire, exploring new positions can be one of the best ways to do it.

New positions are not only fun to try out, they are often the key for women to learn how to increase their pleasure and help create the possibility of vaginal or G-spot orgasms. Men will also get much more satisfaction from intercourse by discovering positions that increase their stamina and give them better control.

The Perfect Fit

Experimenting with different positions may also help solve the problem of the imperfect fit. That is, a woman with a large vagina may end up with a man who has a smaller penis. Or, on the contrary, a woman with a tight vagina may have a lover whose penis is too big for her, causing her pain during intercourse.

A couple experiencing these types of problems has to try new positions to get the very best out of their lovemaking. Positions that hurt the woman or don't allow her to move her hips and adjust her body to her partner's are going to contribute to an uncomfortable sexual experience.

Approximately 80 percent of men have penises that are "average" in size, between 5 and 7 inches in length; most common ranges from 6 to 6.5 inches. Girth is commonly between 4.5 and 5.5 inches.

If the woman or man can't communicate problems like this, the couple may begin to shy away from sexual activity. This can be the beginning of a downhill swing to the relationship. The couple may never come out of it, all because neither person could say that they weren't comfortable with the way their sexual experiences were going. Exploring new positions can help.

The vagina will, in most cases, expand or tighten to fit the penis. Foreplay for the woman makes a tremendous amount of difference. It's a rare case that the fit just won't work.

A Great Variety of Positions

There are as many positions as there are possibilities in the creative mind. When trying them out, keep the communication going. Tell your partner what you like and what doesn't work for you.

Very few of us are mind readers, so when in doubt, ask. If your partner is quieter than you are, encourage him or her to speak up. Ask "multiple-choice" questions:

- Do you prefer that I do this faster or slower?
- Do you like this harder or softer?
- Should we move on to another position or would you like me to continue?

Even if the answer is "none of the above," just knowing that you care can give your partner the courage to speak up. Remember, you both really want to know what the other one wants and likes.

There's More Than One Way

There are many subtle variations on each major group of positions. If a new position isn't working for you, don't abandon it right away. See what happens when you move a leg a little to the left or right, or put a pillow under your bottom to lift your pelvis, or shift from one knee to the other.

Have available pillows of varying sizes and shapes like crescent moons, rounds, and squares to use under your head, arms, legs, buttocks, tummies, and feet to subtly change angles and positions. High headboards, love swings, and even the floor may all have their place in your lovemaking repertoire. Get creative and keep it fun!

In recent years, buckwheat-filled pillows of various sizes and shapes have come on the market. There are even a few manufacturers of "love furniture." These are ideal to use during lovemaking, since their shapes can be molded to fit your needs.

The Missionary Position

The missionary position is probably one of the most widely used positions during sex. In this position, the woman lies on her back with her legs bent and her knees pointing up with her feet on the bed. Her partner lies on top of her, generally with his knees on the bed or other surface. The man supports himself with his arms, and the woman's hips support his hips.

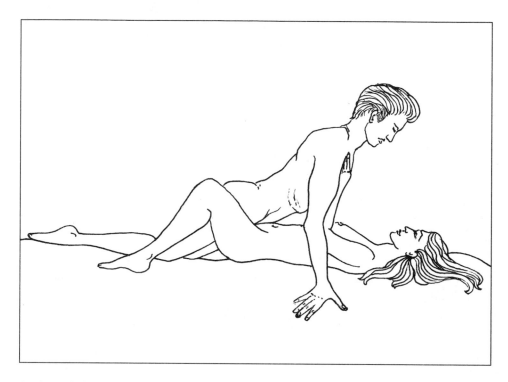

▲ The missionary position

The man does the thrusting and most of the movement in this position. It's a somewhat difficult position for the woman to move freely, especially if the man is larger than she is and leans on her during lovemaking.

Basic variations of the missionary position include having the woman wrap her legs over the ankles, thighs, or buttocks of her partner. She can even move them up to his waist and back. These variations sometimes happen spontaneously as the woman get more excited and turned on. The natural reaction is to move closer to create more contact as the lovemaking progresses.

These positions can stimulate the G-spot and the interior vaginal spots that women identify as pleasure producing. They are also great for eye contact, whispers, loving words, and kissing; and the partners can put their arms around each other. Traditional thrusting, however, doesn't do much for most women because there's no clitoral stimulation.

The Coital Alignment Technique

Also known as CAT, the coital alignment technique is a modified frontal position that improves the woman's stimulation. The CAT is similar to the missionary position, except that the man rises up and moves about four inches forward (up her body). In this position, he can use a combination of small thrusts and rubbing his body up and down to get the woman more excited.

The rubbing action, which both partners can do in rhythm with each other, rubs the man's pubic bone on the woman's pubic bone and clitoral hood. This friction adds enough contact with the clitoris to have her reach orgasm in the act of intercourse. Generally, the CAT position has partners very close, with arms around each other, so that they can create the traction to get the up-and-down rhythm going. It's this back-and-forth friction that excites the woman and may make the man last longer, too.

Yawning Position

Vulnerable and erotic, this position could become one of your favorites. The woman lies on her back and places her legs up and over the shoulders of her partner, who is on top of her. The legs can rest on his shoulders with very little strain to the man. She should not use much of a pillow, if any, under her buttocks, as this will limit her mobility.

With the man on top, you can go from the missionary position to the yawning position very easily. Thrusting should begin gently, as this is a vulnerable position for some women. With her legs on his shoulders, she will have the leverage to lift her pelvis easily and affect the angle of penetration.

FACT

Most women eventually begin to have orgasms at some point in their lives, but not necessarily every time they have intercourse. More women experience clitoral orgasms as opposed to vaginal or G-spot orgasms.

One of the benefits of this position is that the woman can easily rotate her hips for maximum contact to her G-spot. The rotating also stimulates the man and they can both control the movement and the thrusting easily and freely. Furthermore, in this posture the hands are free to stimulate other erogenous zones. The man can use his hands and fingers on the clitoris, breasts, face or any other area on the woman's body where he knows her pleasure will be enhanced. The woman's hands are free to caress her partner's face, back, neck, thighs, legs, and scrotum; gently pull his hair; or wrap her arms around his neck.

She can assist him in having an orgasm but not ejaculating in this position because she can read his energy easily. She is able to move, do her Kegels to grip him firmly, or lie still so he won't orgasm too soon. Lying still, in a heightened state of arousal, with the woman squeezing her PC muscles in this position is pure ecstasy. This is a good way to let the man come back to a more stable state if he is feeling that he might be getting close to ejaculating. Lie still and, if appropriate, pump your PC muscles slowly and keep him just at the edge of excitement.

A variation on this position calls for the woman to straighten her legs and firmly push the backs of her legs away from the man, so that her feet move closer to her head. In doing so she puts a greater angle on her pelvis, and consequently the man's penis accesses the G-spot better. She is more in control of the thrusting in this variation and can control the deep versus shallow thrusts and the speed of the thrusting. This is a little more difficult for some women, but try it before you decide that it's not for you. The more of an angle you are able to put on the vagina and penis, the more pressure will be applied, causing greater pleasure.

Splitting a Bamboo Position

Sir Richard Burton's translation of the Kama sutra includes the following: "When the woman places one of her legs on her lover's shoulder, and stretches the other out, and then places the latter on his shoulder, and stretches the other out, it is called the *splitting of a bamboo*."

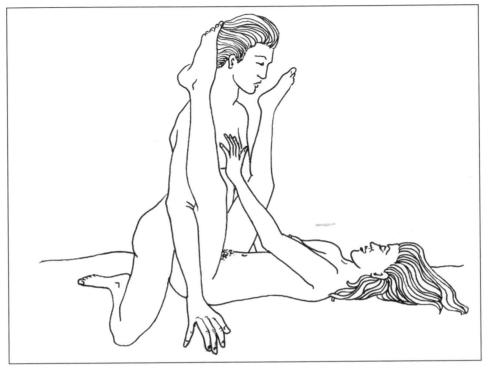

▲ Splitting a bamboo position (with the woman moving her right leg down)

In this position, the woman lies on her back and can be propped up by pillows placed at her back. Her partner squats, kneels, or sits on his feet with a slightly forward tilt. The woman has one leg bent with her foot on the floor or bed. The other leg is on the man's shoulder, with the ankle hooked on it or straight up in the air and held by her partner's hand. At the couple's own pace, the legs are then placed in the opposite position. As in the Kama sutra description, the legs are at one moment split one way and then the other way.

This is a wonderful position for making the subtle shifts that are often required for effective G-spot stimulation. The woman can grind and rotate her hips or undulate and use her PC muscles to create greater pleasure for both herself and her partner. The up-and-down motion of the legs causes an arc to be created that rubs, like the motion of a windshield wiper, back and forth across the G-spot area. This position is more advanced than others, but give it a try. You may surprise yourself.

Woman on Top

Empowering, satisfying, vulnerable, creative, and edgy—all these adjectives and more can be applied to positions where the woman is on top. Often portrayed as either goddess or slut, a woman may have a difficult time assuming both manifestations in one body. Sometimes women want to be "controlled" and sometimes they want to be the one in charge. Assuming the top position can have the effect of bringing out the powerful "animal passion" in any woman. Men will get more of what they want with such a multiflavored lover.

ALERT!

Women, you can help your man last longer during sex. By playing the roll of the sexual initiator and encouraging position changes during lovemaking, you'll slow things down for your man. Pay attention to his breath and movements to know when to initiate a shift in positions.

It's a wonderful lover who will allow the woman her full repertoire of sexual expression. However, women themselves collude with social mores in holding back their sexual energy. It's difficult to overcome the training that the family, community, religion, and culture have put us through. Personal fears often keep women from exploring a fuller range of possibilities when it comes to sexuality. If you haven't tried any of the many top positions, now is the time to try. Be gentle with yourself, and be sure to tell your partner of any vulnerable feelings you are experiencing.

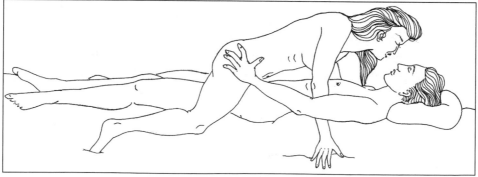

▲ The basic woman on top position

Variations on the Woman on Top Position

The basic configuration for the range of woman on top positions is for the man to be lying on his back and the woman to straddle him, but there are many variations to this basic position—for instance, the woman can be facing forward, sideways, or backward. The majority of these positions call for the woman to be facing forward so that there's eye contact, and the couple may kiss and speak to each other. The forward types are also the best for G-spot stimulation. With the woman on top, the man can have his legs flat along the bed or bent, with knees pointing up. The woman can experiment with any of the following variations:

- **Fluttering and soaring butterfly:** This position, described in the Kama sutra, is performed with the woman's feet on the bed. This allows the woman to raise and lower herself onto the man. The woman is in control of the rhythm, depth of thrusting, speed, and angle of penetration. It takes strong thighs to maintain this position for a length of time. The man can use his hands to help support the woman and guide her timing.

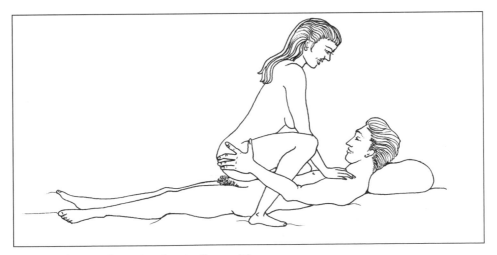

▲ Fluttering and soaring butterfly position

- **Woman upright, with knees on the bed:** This modification of the butterfly position offers a great range of motion because the woman can move up and down as well as forward and backward. She is closer to her partner's face and is often supporting herself with one or both hands. It is possible for her to use one of her hands to caress her lover's face and body.

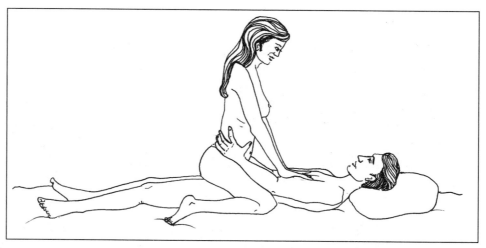

▲ Woman upright, with knees on the bed

- **Both legs straight out in front:** This position is a little more challenging. The woman will have to use her hands to support herself while moving up and down. Try sliding back and forth on your man, but be careful not to hurt him, especially if you are average to large in body size. Try this one facing away from your man, too.
- **Leaning down over the man's chest, with knees on the bed:** This particular position is a good one for clitoral stimulation because the two of you can rub against each other, as in the CAT position. The woman can guide her lover to apply maximum friction where she needs it most.
- **Alternating feet:** In this position, the woman has one leg with the foot on the bed and the other leg with the knee on the bed. This is a good option for women who prefer stimulation of one side of their vagina or G-spot over the other. It's also very powerful for the

woman to put her hand under the man's buttocks on the side with the foot on the bed. She can gently pull him closer and rock him back and forth.

▲ Alternating feet

- **Lying on top:** In this position, the woman lies on top of the man, moving up and down in order to stimulate her clitoris.

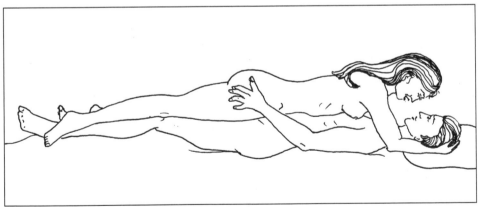

▲ Lying on top, a position that stimulates the clitoris

You can move through each one of these variations, one by one like a dance, as the lovemaking progresses. You can perfect this dance by staying aware, limber, and by sometimes leading and sometimes letting your partner lead. Remember to use your hands liberally to caress your partner. The more loving your touch, the more total the experience.

Rear-Entry Positions

Without a doubt, rear-entry positions are some of the best positions—they enhance G-spot stimulation, they have the advantage of leaving the man's hands free to caress and fondle the breasts, and variety is easy to come by. With rear-entry positions, you can adjust the angle and depth of penetration and the ways you move. This allows the woman to adapt the experience for herself while having a lot of room to increase the pleasure for her partner. It also enables the woman or the man to stimulate her clitoris. For some women, this is an important part of intercourse.

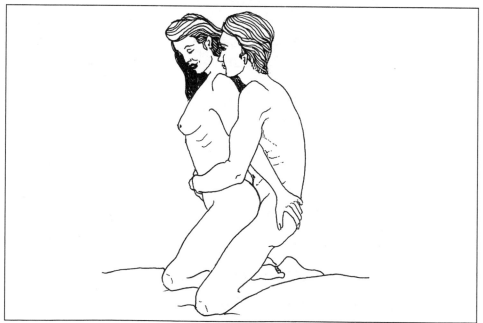

▲ Basic rear-entry position with both partners on their knees

Rear-entry positions aren't always the most appropriate—the moment must be right. Sometimes it's just more appropriate to be facing each other. Eye contact, breath connection, heart connection, and intimacy are all facilitated through facing your partner.

Men may find that they are turned on by the increased control in these positions. You can be in control of the depth, speed, and rhythm. You have a wonderful, archetypal view of your partner, reminiscent of ancient or primitive man. Men can feel powerful and still maintain sensitivity with their partner.

Try this position first with both partners on their knees. It's best for the woman to support herself with both her hands by holding on to the man behind her, so that she can keep her spine moving and undulating. Use the different rhythms and depths of penetration to explore how this basic position feels to both of you. Make a study of how it feels, and communicate your findings for future reference.

Men, try putting one hand on your lover's heart and one on the lower part of her stomach. Undulate like a wave, connected at the core.

Try a Few Variations

As a variation, the man can sit back, his legs folded under him, and have the woman sit back on top of him, still in the rear-entry position (this is known as the "two peas in a pod" position). When you try this, what has changed? Both of you take notice of any subtle changes. The woman can also try holding on to something above and in front of her. This can be the wall or headboard of the bed. Is your G-spot as stimulated in this position? Do you find it easier to rise up and down on your partner? What do you notice?

▲ Two peas in a pod position

Now, try having the woman lean forward and lay her head down. This is a good position for stimulating the man by caressing his scrotum or his inner thighs. You can also help him stay focused on nonejaculatory pleasure by cupping his scrotum in your hands and gently applying pressure with a downward pull.

Be gentle and always ask first if it's something he would like you to try. You may also wish to apply pressure to his perineum (the external area between the anus and the scrotum that covers his prostate gland, or the male G-spot). This will help keep him from going over the top, so to speak.

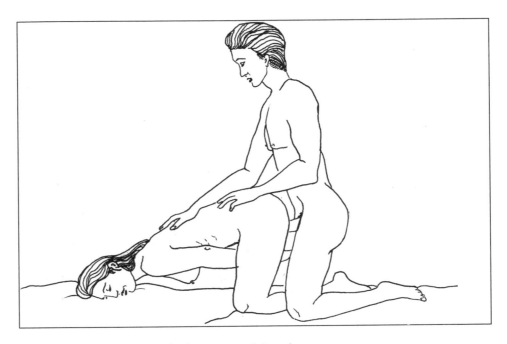

▲ Rear-entry position with the woman lying down

Another position in which the woman is lying down on her stomach is the lion position. This position works best if the woman wants to concentrate on pumping and squeezing her PC muscles (this can be done in other rear-entry positions as well).

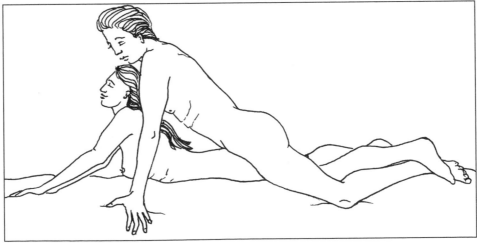

▲ The lion position

Have a small hand mirror available somewhere near your bed. It's invaluable for these positions because you can have the woman hold it so that the two of you can gaze into each other's eyes as you get more and more aroused. Keep these exercises soft, lighthearted, and explorative. Remember—this is lovemaking. Please take your time and enjoy every delicious moment.

Yab-Yum Positions

The basic yab-yum position is a little-known but excellent position to explore. Lovers are face-to-face and heart-to-heart. They are able to keep eye contact, kiss, and caress each other. This position is the best one for extending the sexual experience because it prevents the man from thrusting so much that he ejaculates too quickly. It allows for the deep connection that makes the extended lovemaking experience magical.

▲ Basic yab-yum position

In this position, the man sits cross-legged on the bed or floor and the woman sits astride him. She is facing him and has her legs wrapped around him, with the soles of her feet coming together behind him. Both partners have their arms wrapped around each other, and their faces are very close. The woman can put a firm pillow under her buttocks to help with the pressure on her lover's thighs, if necessary.

If you're not very comfortable in the basic yab-yum position, you may modify it as follows: The man can sit on the edge of the bed or a padded hassock (footstool) with his legs on the floor while the woman sits facing him on his lap. Make sure the man's legs are parallel to the floor from the knees to the hip. This is a good modification for people with lower-back problems.

▲ Modified yab-yum position

The yab-yum is a great position to use when the man starts getting too close to ejaculation. It's a position that is easy for the man to stay aroused in even when there is a minimum of movement. By combining fast, hot movements with slow, steady rocking and even stillness, a dance can be created. This allows you to remain in a high state of ecstatic connection for virtually as long as you want. It's a little more daring and advanced, but well worth it.

Clasping Positions

The clasping positions are postures in which the woman and the man maintain a straight-legged, rather rigid posture in respect to each other. Clasping comes from the idea that the woman must clasp or hold on to the man's penis with her vaginal muscles and thighs. These positions don't allow for much movement. When the legs are stiff, the feet can't be employed to help lift the pelvic region, so it's hard to accomplish any sort of rhythmic swinging motion of the hips.

You can try any of the following clasping positions:

- Woman on her back, with the man on top.
- Man on his back, with the woman on top.
- Woman on her stomach, with the man on top.
- Side by side and facing toward each other or in a spooning position (see following section).

FACT

The Ananga-Ranga, an eastern erotic love text, talks about a clasping position called "the union of balance." It is the position where the couple faces each other while lying on their sides. The front-facing unions give better access to clitoral stimulation for some women. The man's pubic bone will rub against the woman when they move together in an up-and-down direction.

The clasping positions have an advantage in situations where the man has a large penis and the woman has a smallish vagina. It can be very uncomfortable and possibly dangerous for a woman in this situation to completely accept hard, deep thrusting from her partner. Because the closed legs prevent the penis from deep penetration but give ample friction to the man, these positions can facilitate the love act. On the other hand, a woman with a generous vagina partnered with a man with a smaller penis won't get as much out of these positions.

The advantage of any position that allows for shallower rather than deeper penetration is that the woman's G-spot will get more action, as may her clitoris. Remember that the G-spot is nearer the entrance of the vagina, rather than back near the cervix. When there is more frequent thrusting and the man's penetration is shallower, the head of the penis contacts the woman's G-spot a greater percentage of the time, so she'll get excited more quickly.

Spooning Positions

Spooning positions are a wonderful addition to any couple's repertoire of lovemaking. Greatly nurturing, they are especially appropriate for either the very beginning or the very end of a lovemaking session. Partners can use spooning positions to connect deeply before making love or they can use them at the very end, for holding and lying still in those magical moments before drifting off to sleep.

These positions can be used whether the man has an erect penis or not. Just holding each other in these positions has its place in any lovemaking situation. They can also be used when the two of you desire to make love but the woman is low on energy or both of you are more tired than usual and you want to stay very mellow. With the woman in front and the man behind holding her, the couple can gently undulate, whether having intercourse or just bonding.

When trying any new position, take it slowly at first and stay very conscious of your partner and his or her feelings. New positions can trigger long-buried emotions and feelings of vulnerability. Keep the communication open, and be willing to stop and explore the feelings that are coming up for both of you.

Generally, you assume a position similar to spoons lying next to each other. Lie front to front or back to front, with either the man or the woman in front, depending on who needs the most cuddling. Bring the arm and hand that is under you to the front, under the person in front, so that you can hold them near their heart area. The other hand can come over the top to hold their pelvis region close to yours. Pull them to you and snuggle up close.

Never Stop Exploring

There are many other erotic positions to explore. See if you can discover some for yourselves. Just to give you an idea, there's one called "the twinning branches." To get an idea of how this position works, open up both of your hands, make the scissors shape with your first and second fingers on each hand and put them together to "cut" each other. The resulting shape would be the position that the two of you would assume. This position is comfortable and is good for relaxing and resting while making love. Women will find that one side or the other may feel better. See which side suits you.

You'll be able to explore some more exotic ideas and variations in Chapter 14, so have fun and keep in mind that you are taking each other on an erotic journey. Draw your partner in by keeping close contact with soft, intimate eyes. Study each other's facial expressions. Stay very connected. Breathe deeply. Ⓔ

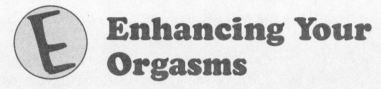

Chapter 11

Enhancing Your Orgasms

The big O—so exquisite, so sought after, so powerful, or so soon, so elusive, so disappointing—and we really know so little about it. We've had to discover the world of sex and orgasm on our own—each of us an intrepid explorer without much of a map. Bound by instinct, hormones, peer pressure, and the deep desire to please and be pleased, we seek to discover the how-tos of the great, soulfulfilling orgasm.

Why Do Humans Experience Orgasms?

The most basic answer to the question of why humans have orgasms is procreation. To ensure that humans will continue to reproduce, nature has given us the orgasm as a sensual reward. Why would we have the drive to have sexual relations if there wasn't something very enjoyable about the act? After all, the clitoris has no biological function other than pleasure, and yet it has the highest concentration of nerve endings in the whole body.

While no two orgasms are ever really alike, nor are we able to describe each man's or woman's individual experience, we know the basic path the orgasm takes each time we are graced with the experience. (Refer to the individual chapters on male and female sexuality to understand more fully what occurs.) The important part is that the orgasm depends on each person's capacity to feel and receive pleasure.

Scientists have discovered that when the female experiences an orgasm, the cervix actually dips down during each contraction and "sips" the semen up into the uterus. It's perfectly clear that throughout evolutionary history both men and women needed orgasmic pleasure to drive the survival of the species.

Pleasure Is Your Birthright

Nature has given us the sex organs, the hormones, and the desire to have sex. We have the capacity to fantasize, to think about sex, and to actualize the act through lovemaking. It is your birthright to have the fullest sexual pleasure you can possibly experience. You may choose to fully partake of your sexual potential, or you may choose to abstain. And, of course, you may choose anything in between.

You, and only you, are responsible for how much pleasure you experience. Your partner is not the responsible one. If you hold ideas about the "shoulds" and "shouldn'ts" of sex that limit your capacity for pleasure, it's time to ferret them out. In a sense, the mind can be the greatest "sex organ" or the worst inhibitor of bodily pleasure.

If you're openly curious about your own sexual response cycle and give yourself permission to have pleasure, you will open up to new worlds. If you shut down your natural openness through false expectations and limiting beliefs, your capacity for pleasure diminishes. Taking charge of your sexual pleasure will empower you and free you in ways that extend beyond the bedroom.

Learn to Enjoy Yourself Again

Men and women are supposed to be good at sex; yet we live in a culture that hides sexuality or confuses it with symbols of power or powerlessness. A society like ours does not educate its young adults in how to honor and love their own bodies. With rare exceptions, every young person must either reinvent the wheel or overcome huge prejudices in order to learn about sexuality and sensuality.

Approximately 26 percent of all women report that they never experience orgasmic release; that number was even higher until the late 1960s. Inability to experience orgasm is a frustrating problem that directly affects our self-esteem and our relationships. Many men ejaculate before their partner is even warmed up! These things can frustrate people so much that they decide it isn't worth it.

Our own problems can look so big and scary sometimes, that we don't realize that almost everyone else has similar struggles. Openings occur when we are willing to talk about our lives with others, when we become vulnerable with our friends and lovers, when we decide to empower ourselves to have more in our lives—more pleasure and more intimacy.

The Keys to Great Pleasure

Don't get stressed out by your quest to achieve the perfect orgasms. Trust that with love, practice, and playful innocence you can begin to have the kinds of sexual experiences that you always dreamed of. The following list summarizes the basic ingredients for expanding the capacity to orgasm (we'll look at each of them in more detail in this chapter):

- Learn to relax. Take hot baths at quiet times. Take time for yourself. Go away for the weekend to a spa all by yourself.
- Become an excellent breather.
- Stay conscious during sex—don't drift away.
- Learn to meditate—it will help you learn to focus your attention.
- Know your body and what you like.
- Make noise. Sound helps your partner know what you like, and it helps you let go into a deeper experience.
- Do your Kegel exercises.

Notice that there isn't anything on this list that even hints at "techniques." While speed, timing, placement, and new techniques are wonderful, they won't help you focus and expand into the pleasure. Personal mastery over the domain of your mind and body will.

Staying Conscious and Aware

Eye gazing with your partner will put you in full awareness and bring you to the "present" with your lover. Leaving the lights on or lighting candles during sex with eyes open is the best way to be bonded with your partner. When we are fully available, open to being seen, our capacity for merging and orgasm goes way up. Once you get used to relating in this way, you won't want to go back to the dark.

Learn to Meditate

What does meditation have to do with great sex? It helps us learn to focus our attention. One of the main things that gets in the way of the orgasmic response in women is worrying. We can't get the kids, bills, phone calls, groceries, business, and so much more off our minds. Meditation for as little as twenty minutes three times a week will give you a wonderful new tool to draw on for relaxation and focus.

Do Your Kegel Exercises

It can't be emphasized enough—both men and women need to strengthen their PC muscles and use them! Once you're good at doing Kegels, you will actually be able to turn yourself on! You can do up to 200 at a time in just five to ten minutes, and it can be done anytime and anywhere—while you're driving, sitting at your desk, in a meeting . . . you get the picture.

Kegel exercises facilitate the flow of blood to your genitals and they keep your pelvic floor muscles healthy. If you do these twice a day, you are going to notice a difference. See Chapter 5 to review how Kegel exercises are done.

FACT

Many studies have reported that up to 46 percent of all women have some kind of sexual dysfunction or unsatisfactory sexual response levels. Doctors are beginning to understand that some of these are organic and physical in nature and some are psychological.

Unlearning Old Habits

There are some women who have learned to orgasm by keeping their bodies straight and stiff. They tend to tense up instead of relaxing into the pleasure. This is how they have taught themselves to orgasm.

These women may have a difficult time learning to relax and open their bodies to new positions and feelings. It can be very difficult for some of them to open their legs into wide positions. The vulnerability of exposing their genitals to be seen, touched, and honored can be a lot to handle. But if you bring a gentle will, a playful and loving heart, and a little patience to the practice, you can reap the benefits of expanding your orgasmic capabilities. Unlearning old habits is always hard but usually worth the work and focus.

Mastery of Your Breath

Breathing is not a conscious activity for most humans. We expect to just know how to do it. Yet the key to greater health and vitality, experiences of expanded consciousness, and the full-body orgasm is mastery of the breath. Yogis place a great emphasis on learning to deepen and lengthen the breath. Becoming conscious of the breath and its patterns is the first step in the process of expanding orgasm.

We're a culture of chest breathers. Chest breathing causes adrenaline secretions that can lead to panic and fear. We're taught to suck our stomachs in and wear tight belts and clothing. This pushes our breath into our chests. We don't know how to belly breathe.

Discovering your G-spot and beginning to develop the capacity to have vaginal orgasms, in addition to clitoral ones, can have the outcome of opening you up. Remember to breathe deeply into your belly, be patient, and love yourself.

You can't relax your genitals when you're holding in your stomach. The body becomes rigid. It's very difficult to tighten and hold your genitals when your stomach is full of breath. Try it. A relaxed body leads to a more relaxed attitude, which will lead to a more relaxed life. The way in which you breathe can make a vast difference in the quality of your orgasms and your life.

Breathing Issues among Women

Women who don't orgasm easily often hold their breath as they get more turned on. As they approach a kind of transition stage on the way to peak arousal, say a seven or eight on a scale of ten, they will often hold their breath, and then nothing happens. The result is that the energy must be built up again, only to have the same thing happen repeatedly. It becomes difficult to transition smoothly to the next level of sensations.

As arousal gets going in women, they will often begin to breathe a little faster. If they become aware of their breath, they can then begin to "drive" the experience by purposely doing faster, focused breathing to increase blood flow and arousal. It helps, exactly as meditation does, to focus the energy and move from a sense of separateness to one of being merged with the energy.

Good Breathing for Men

Once practiced at awareness, men can, when they notice their breath getting faster, consciously breathe slower and more fully. This allows them to move the sexual excitement through their body instead of unconsciously going right past all those exquisite feelings and going "over the top."

A Breathing Exercise

This is a simple but profound practice that should take about fifteen minutes. To get ready, wear loose clothing without a belt and allow at least an hour since your last meal. Lie comfortably on the floor on your back in a quiet place where you won't be disturbed. Rest a few minutes and then begin to notice your breath. How are you breathing? Through your mouth or your nose? Does your chest rise, or is the breath coming from your belly?

FACT

A survey by Carol Rinkleib Ellison in her book *Women's Sexualities* found that 38 percent of 2,600 women studied had not once had an orgasm during intercourse.

After you've briefly observed yourself, put your hands lightly on your abdomen and begin to breathe into your belly, focusing on the spot where your hands are positioned. Take long, slow breaths through your nose and visibly but gently force your belly to rise and fall with the breath. You may really have to focus on this. Don't breathe into your chest. This will be difficult for some people and easier for others.

Practice sustaining this slow, steady breathing as you continue to observe the gentle rising of your abdomen. Take really deep breaths. Make them slow and deliberate. Stay relaxed. If you're having difficulties, don't get frustrated. If this exercise is easy, just keep going. Keep this up for ten minutes.

Take It with You

Try practicing breathing as much as possible to help it become easier and freer. Notice the times during your day that you might be breathing your old way. When we are frightened or upset, we become chest breathers. This creates a feedback loop of increased anxiety. In those moments, attempt to consciously change your breath right then and there. You will calm yourself and be able to function much more effectively.

If you find yourself holding your breath at any time, take a long, slow belly breath and clean out your lungs. Continue with the deep belly breathing. If you notice that you're holding your breath during lovemaking and at the time right before orgasm, relax, let go, and expand your abdomen with your breath. A deep belly breath can open the channels to allow the full-body orgasm. It will help you relax and at the same time build up a charge faster.

Practice with a Partner

You can try deep-breathing exercise with your partner in several variations—as you're in the spoon position or when you're facing each other as you lie down or sit in the yab-yum position.

The spoon position is when the two of you lie front to back, with the person in the back placing a hand over the front person's heart. If you choose to sit face-to-face, sit cross-legged as close as you can get or in the yab-yum position—when one person sits cross-legged and his partner sits astride his lap, with her legs wrapped around him. Face each other, eyes softly focused and open.

Gently begin to breathe together. It is usually best for the slightly faster breather to follow the slower breather. (Often, women are slower breathers than men.) Stay relaxed and avoid making a goal for your breathing. Breathe into your bellies. Continue for about five minutes. You can also try breathing alternately.

Making Noise

Breath and sound go hand in hand. Deep, resonant, low-register notes can transform your orgasmic abilities. They open up the body cavity because the mouth is usually pretty wide open and the energy flow gets much more accentuated. Sound and breath can lead to multiple orgasms.

Making noise during sexual play is a turn-on and helps us know where our partner is in the sexual response cycle. The signs of arousal and stimulation, especially in women, are very hard to interpret even with sound added. When we open up our mouths to let sound out, we literally open up the body cavity and allow the energy and pleasure to be transported through us.

It's almost physically impossible to make deep sounds while in orgasm and hold your pelvic region tight at the same time. Moaning opens up the pelvic region and relaxes the genital area, greatly enhancing the full-body orgasms that follow.

Practice making sounds when you are making love or when you're by yourself, just for the fun of it. Deep breathe into your belly and open your mouth. Let your mouth be loose and relaxed. On the out-breath, feel the sound come from your belly, not your throat. Make low, deep moaning sounds.

If making sounds is new for you, let your partner know that you'd like to try it. It can even feel a little silly at first, but being vulnerable will draw your partner closer, so go for it. Consciously bring sound to your lovemaking so you can really see how it works.

Positions for Increasing Orgasmic Response

Changing and varying positions can be very helpful in finding new ways to stimulate the G-spot in women. They are also valuable in helping men last longer and achieve mastery over their ejaculations. In addition, trying alternative positions keeps the energy new between partners and invites open exploration.

Positions that enhance the connection between the G-spot and the penis in coitus are ones that place the angle of penetration such that the head of the penis is pointing to the top wall of the vagina. Positions in which the woman is on her back and has her legs up or on her partner's shoulders work well to achieve this angle.

When the woman is on top, she can help guide the penis in the right direction and to the right depth for maximum effect. Positions that directly affect the clitoris are the missionary and its close cousin the CAT. It's best to rub back and forth in these positions rather than just thrusting in and out. Thrusting, in general, pulls on the labia minora and the clitoral hood, but the stimulation is, at best, indirect.

Men, Make It Easier on Yourselves

Unfortunately, the positions that create the most friction for women do so for men as well. If you are having problems with ejaculating faster than you'd like to, you may have to train yourself to last longer. Men, if your partner has already had a clitoral orgasm before you have intercourse and you aren't yet able to last as long as you'd like, try positions that don't cause the most friction. Those would be the missionary position, spooning, certain positions that use furniture, sex while standing, and any position where the two of you can eye gaze and stay in deep communication.

Let's Dance

It really helps to make intercourse more of a dance. Speed up; slow down; step this way, then that way. By doing this you can give yourself permission to stop and just breathe together when you are feeling close to ejaculating. If your partner has been doing her Kegel exercises, she can squeeze you while you are in stillness and still keep the sensations going. In other words, introduce a variety of steps to your dance!

Thrusting Patterns

Great lovers have learned that sex isn't just about in and out. Men, when you're doing most of the movement, spend some time teasing by staying shallow and then surprising your partner with three deep thrusts. Create a dance of churning, deep thrusting, and then shallow thrusting, and then reverse the order.

A classic pattern of thrusting, suggested by one of the ancient erotic books, is nine deep thrusts, then one shallow (and slow); eight deep thrusts, then two shallow; seven deep thrusts, then three shallow; and so on. Go slowly, eye gaze, and take deep breaths into your bellies. The breath carries the intense feelings throughout your body. It translates the acceptance of the pleasure to your brain. This thrusting pattern allows the man to get very excited and then transfer that excitement to the woman.

Shallow thrusting stimulates the G-spot area more effectively. Generally, a woman will like deep thrusting and shallow thrusting at different times during arousal. Ask your partner what she likes best. Try making up your own patterns with the help of your partner.

Ejaculation Mastery for Men

This is one of the most common complaints and frustrations men have about sex: "How can I stop from having quick orgasms? Sometimes I ejaculate after fifteen seconds! My partner is not able to climax. Please help me."

What's the rush? The fast ejaculation may be the result of guilty feelings, fear of getting caught while masturbating, being out of touch with one's own body, or honesty and trust issues with one's partners. As a result, very often men have trained themselves to come too quickly.

Over thousands of years, the tantrics and Taoists have developed simple, easy, and fun techniques to help men train themselves to last longer. While whole books are written on this subject, a good grasp of the essence of the practices can be given here. All you need is training, intention, focused attention, and practice. If you put in some effort, the result will be well worth it. Most men see significant results in just two weeks of practice.

Ejaculation mastery is the first step toward multiple orgasms for men. Once you've learned to last, you'll recognize how close you are to having orgasms when you are on the edge of the pleasure plateau. From that point you can begin to fine-tune the experience through breath, awareness, and relaxation.

You are about to embark on a wonderfully fulfilling journey that is remarkably easy for most men. However, there are some men who need to see a specialist—whether it is a psychologist or urologist—for their problems related to premature ejaculation.

Start Your Training

To train yourself to last longer, you can practice by yourself or with your partner. The first step to training yourself is to engage your willpower. You will probably be tempted to just let go, as you always have, in order to achieve brief orgasmic pleasure. But rest assured that if you are willing to trust, and back away from that point of no return a few times, whole new worlds will open to you and your lover. The training will also involve the following:

- Devoting some quality time to these fun training sessions.
- Learning to relax in the excitement of orgasmic bliss.
- Changing your habit of chest breathing to belly breathing.
- Learning simple communication practices with your partner.
- Loving your body and all the wonderful things it's capable of.

If you do this on your own, self-pleasure yourself until you reach an eight or nine (on the scale of one to ten) of your arousal. Stop, relax, and breathe deeply into your belly for a few minutes; then start again. Don't tense your body—relax it. This will require some self-restraint at first. Bring your focus and willpower to bear.

Tension in the body is typically what causes men to ejaculate. By voluntarily relaxing in the high state of arousal and combining that with slow, deep belly breathing, you will create a container for more powerful, long-lasting pleasure.

If you have a partner, it is ideal to practice this together. The techniques are fun and will likely add a new dimension to lovemaking for many couples. It may be a rare experience for a woman to be handed the control button to her man. It may also require both of you to learn a lot of new "hand job" techniques for pleasuring. (You can refer to Chapter 15 for some of those strokes.)

FACT

It's reported that up to 75 percent of all men ejaculate within two to five minutes of beginning intercourse. A survey of 1,370 men conducted by Tantra.com revealed that less than 35 percent felt they had any control over when they ejaculate.

Incorporate What You've Learned

You will very soon understand that as you master the ability to stop before going over the top, you will actually be experiencing orgasmic-like pleasure without ejaculation. After a few weeks of practicing, you're going to want to try it out during intercourse with your partner.

Don't expect to be able to take your new-found control straight to coitus without a few hitches. You will have to start the process over, but it should be much easier this time. You'll have to stop at that eight or nine arousal point and rest. This time, though, your body and mind will be working together and they'll know what to do.

Know What Pleasures You

Changing positions, learning correct breathing, and controlling ejaculation will certainly help you enhance your and your lover's orgasms. But one often-overlooked and yet obvious point that needs to be made is that in order to fully enjoy yourself, you need to know what pleasures you. Take as many opportunities as possible to learn about your hot spots. What gets you juicy or aroused? Do words turn you on?

How about teasing or seduction? Erotic dances from your lover? Small gifts? Tenderness?

Explore your body and how it prefers to be touched. Do you prefer soft caresses or to be squeezed and hugged? Do you prefer to be touched all over, or do you have specific areas that most desire touch? Do you like a single stimulation point, or can you handle two, three, or more? Do you like your nipples squeezed or your whole breast fondled with just a hint of nipple? Do you like your scrotum to be pulled firmly or cupped gently?

A person's preferences usually change from moment to moment. We'll like one thing this time and something else the next. But most of us find that we also have our favorite spots and secret desires when it comes to touch. The problem is, we keep them secret. Let your lover know what you like; but first, discover it for yourself. You won't be able to tell what you don't know.

Our genitals are most sensitive to touch, but there are other erogenous areas you may want to explore:

- Breasts and nipples
- Inner arms and armpits
- Toes and feet
- Buttocks
- Scrotum
- Inner and outer thighs
- Anus
- Neck areas
- Down your sides, from under your arms to your hips
- Love handles
- Back of the knees and inside the elbows
- Fingers and wrists

Try combining one or two of these additional areas with genital stimulation. Vary the touch you give by using your fingertips, tickling, blowing, lightly scratching, or just holding the area. Learning to receive multiple types of touch will create more possibilities for orgasmic pleasure. Ⓔ

Chapter 12

Hot Spots and Sexual Taboos

Sexual taboos vary widely among cultures. Even in our society, some people still see oral sex, anal sex, G-spot stimulation, using sexual toys, and even sexual massage as fringe activities. As a result, these activities may trigger fear, rejection, criticism, or performance anxiety—but these same acts may also excite, titillate, and stimulate desire and curiosity for many people.

The G-Spot, or Goddess Spot

It is widely believed that women have at least two vaginal areas that will respond to sexual arousal. One is located toward the back of the vaginal canal and closer to the cervix (the opening to the uterus). The other is the G-spot, an area located on the upper anterior wall of the vagina, about 1 to 1½ inches in, past the opening of the vagina and just behind the pubic bone. The G-spot lies between the two roots of the clitoris, which are buried under the skin and beneath the pubic bone. It consists of spongy material that is analogous to the prostate gland in men.

FACT

The term "G-spot" comes from the name Grafenberg, the scientist who identified this sensitive area. In recent years, the G-spot has also been lovingly called the Goddess spot. Almost every woman has this spot or area, and most will be able to find it with a little training.

Exploring the Goddess Spot

Let's learn how to access your G-spot and what to expect when you do. By awakening the G-spot, you will have access to a whole new realm of orgasmic potential. Some women will find this exploration easy and some a little more challenging. Old emotional wounding we're not aware of can come up for some of us when the spot is stimulated. Another possibility is uncontrollable laughter. You never know what emotions are there! But whatever you discover, it's all worth it!

The benefits of awakening the G-spot will really show up during sexual intercourse. With a little practice you'll begin to recognize exactly where your G-spot is while in coitus, and that will enable you to subtly position yourself for just the right contact. Your G-spot will be in your consciousness, so to speak. You'll begin to notice it when you do your Kegel exercises and when you're making love. That will help you to empower your own orgasmic potential.

When it comes to exploring your G-spot, it really helps to have a partner. If you don't have a sexual partner, find a friend or buddy who would like to find her G-spot as well. Work together to create a wonderfully intimate learning experience. This will not mean you are a lesbian, if that is something that might worry you. If you're more comfortable doing this by yourself, that's fine, too. Later in this chapter, you'll find tips on positions that will best facilitate solo exploration.

Let's Begin

Be relaxed. Take a bath or shower to help you get into a loving mood. Music, soft lighting, and a massage, if possible, will open the heart and the body to deeper sensing. Spend some time on a little foreplay. Get turned on. The woman may even want to have a clitoral orgasm. This will increase the blood flow to her vulva and vagina and, as a consequence, to the G-spot.

Once you're both ready, the man can use his middle finger to explore the G-spot, which is located less than two inches into the vagina just behind the pubic bone, on the top part of the woman's body. He should lubricate the finger and, looking into the woman's eyes, softly ask for permission to enter the vagina.

It's important to move slowly. As your finger enters the vagina, you'll feel the softness and then an area marked by its ridges. If you move your finger around, you'll notice that there really isn't any other area quite like the ridge area. Come back to that spot and proceed a tiny bit farther, just behind it to an indented space that is directly behind the pubic bone.

ALERT!

If you have been doing your Kegel exercises, you'll probably be able to get in touch with your G-spot more easily. You've been stimulating it during the practice!

Apply very firm pressure. Your finger should be in a "hooked" or "come hither" position. At this point ask your partner what she is feeling. She may already be giving you some indications of sensations. Try slowly moving your finger in the "come hither" motion. Now try slowly sweeping your finger in a windshield washer motion. Is that different? Better? What does your partner like best? You may be amazed how much pressure this area can take. Don't be afraid to try applying more of it.

It is very important at these beginning stages to ask how your lover is doing. Encourage her to use the previous three-question communication technique to be clear with you about what she likes and doesn't like. If this is new territory for her, she is going to appreciate the questions and feel more confident about being able to guide you. She is discovering new things about her body, and if you can both stay open, connected, and in communication, you will both gain not just information, but a whole lot of pleasure.

What to Expect

Many reactions can come up at this point. The woman may feel the urge to pee, she may feel a slight burning, she may feel pleasure, or a combination of any of these sensations. She may feel apprehensive, frightened, or even elated. She may laugh, cry, or cringe in perceived pain. Remember, this is a sensitive area!

When you bring this experience to an end, please make sure to face your partner and thank him or her for the honor of participating in this exploration with you. Communicate the love and gratitude you feel to have this person in your life. You may want to lie together for a moment or possibly try the spooning position.

Most men feel very empowered and successful as lovers when they help their partner discover her G-spot. While you shouldn't let this go to your head, do acknowledge yourself for being willing to help your lover know more about her body and expanding her pleasure potential.

Practice Solo

If this is a solo practice for you, the same information applies. You should find a position that enables you to comfortably put your middle finger into your vagina and have enough latitude to move around some. Good positions for this are on your knees and sitting down a bit on your calves and on all fours with one hand free to explore. These positions bring your uterus down a bit and provide a better angle for your hand to have proper access.

Advanced Practice

The more you practice the finger methods, the more in touch you are going to be with your vagina and your G-spot. You are in the process of awakening a sleeping beauty! As this unfolding happens, see if you notice any changes in your awareness of your G-spot during intercourse. If you're doing your Kegel exercises daily, you should notice even more sensations.

In order to feel your G-spot better during intercourse, have your partner thrust slowly and shallowly at least half of the time. This will cause the head of the penis to rub the G-spot more frequently and produce more friction. Try various thrusting patterns like the following: nine shallow, one deep; eight shallow, two deep; seven shallow, three deep; and so forth.

FACT

Certain positions greatly benefit the stimulation of the G-spot. The "woman on top" and "rear-entry" positions are great for G-spot gratification. Explore some of the ones in Chapter 10.

And, finally, you are encouraged to make sounds. Incredible breakthroughs can occur when we move from the safe comfort zone we normally occupy. Practice making sounds that resonate from deep within your belly. You can do this while you are by yourself and then introduce it to your lovemaking later. Open your mouth and make low-register moans that don't come from your throat but from your abdomen. These kinds of sounds can bring on multiple G-spot orgasms.

Oral Sex

Although times are changing, some men and women have misgivings about both giving and receiving oral sex. Not all couples are comfortable with it and may need some encouragement in this area of lovemaking. Other couples already enjoy oral sex, but they may be able to use new information to improve their knowledge.

Oral sex is often considered an essential part of foreplay. What's less commonly known is that oral sex can also be a very pleasurable stand-alone activity. Many women find that oral sex is the only way they can have an orgasm. While this book aims to help you expand your orgasmic potential, the fact that for many women it's the only way to go (or come!) points to the value of oral sex.

When preparing for this type of intimate contact, cleanliness is important. Bathe together, and pay close attention to the little details. Men, if you aren't circumcised, give special attention to the area under your foreskin. Women, wash with a gentle but effective soap. You'll both be more comfortable and relaxed knowing that you are clean and prepared.

Technique in oral sex is important. Whether it be the fine movements and location when giving cunnilingus or the techniques involved in fellatio, it's important to practice and ask what works for your lover. Try out new techniques and vary things like speed, attention to different areas, and firmness. And always stay playful.

Is It Sex or Isn't It?

It's so very interesting to listen to a variety of opinions on whether or not oral sex is sex. Oral sex is often defined as "not really having sex," as a way of camouflaging one's true actions. Teenagers often hold the position that having or giving oral sex isn't really having sex. This is a form of denial. It is also dangerous in this day and age because of the proliferation of sexually transmitted disease.

No matter what you call it, oral sex is exquisite to receive, an honor to give, and takes practice to master. There are many tricks and tips, but the most important principle to remember is the desire to give and receive it. Forcing yourself or someone else can definitely backfire. If this is a problem in your relationship, open up the topic for conversation. Use one of the several communication tools offered in this book to have a meaningful talk about it.

Practice Enjoying Oral Sex

This exercise may be enjoyed by both men and women. Skin and slice a mango. Pick up a long slice and hold it delicately in your fingers. Now slide it into your mouth slowly and sensually. Really enjoy it slipping past the inside of your lips and the fleshy parts of your mouth and tongue. How does this feel? Try this with a banana or a piece of papaya. Suck it gently. Move it slowly in and out of your lips.

QUESTION?

What are cunnilingus and fellatio?
Cunnilingus is using the tongue to stimulate the clitoris. Fellatio is oral stimulation of the penis.

Buy some fresh peas still in their pods. Split the pea pod open and begin to nibble each pea out slowly with just your lips—no teeth. Feel how sensitive and focused those lips can be. Try taking your tongue and flicking it around one of the peas still in its shell. Play all around the pea. Go from side to side. Try staying right on one small spot at one particular area on the pea. Just use the very end of your tongue. How does this feel?

The mouth is an extremely sensuous part of your body. The mucous membranes and soft tissue that make up the lips and interior regions are full of nerve endings. Evolution has made the mouth sensitive not only so that we can tell what we should put into it, but also so that we can enjoy it.

Stimulating the Clitoris

Clitorises come in many sizes, but they are small in relationship to the rest of a woman's sexual organs. The clitoris is covered by a piece of skin or hood that protects it from being rubbed or irritated during most of the day. The head of the clitoris and the hood are the exterior parts of the clitoris, but there is much more buried under the skin, past the head.

As the woman gets more turned on, the clitoris begins to fill with blood and become engorged. This causes the clitoris to become erect. As this happens, the head of the clitoris "hides" up under the hood more. It's often useful for the woman to help out by holding the hood that covers the clitoris back, out of the way for her lover.

When it comes to oral sex on a woman, you need to be subtle but focused. Pick one area you think is most sensitive and then stick with one speed and one kind of movement for a while. The giver has to develop the stamina required for repetitive movements like these.

It's useful to know that most women have a particular area of their clitoris that is most sensitive. This doesn't mean that it all doesn't feel good, but one area is usually the most sensitive. Most women find that stimulation of the top of their clitoris is the most pleasurable.

You also need to pay some attention to the labia, or lips of the vulva, which are sensitive to touch and licking. Start with the labia and slowly move in to focus on the clitoris after the outer areas have had some attention. You can gently suck, lick, blow softly, and nibble on any of these parts. (**A warning**: Never blow air inside a woman's vagina. This can cause an air embolism that can be fatal.) Try different modalities of touch with your lips, tongue, tip of the tongue, and even teeth if you are very careful. Be very tender in your touch.

FACT

Though very small, the clitoris has approximately 8,000 nerve endings in that one pea-sized bundle. During sexual stimulation, as the nerves are stimulated, the clitoris becomes erect, just like the penis.

Women, when you're receiving oral sex, remember to relax as you get more and more turned on. Breathe deeply and stay aware of your body and what is happening. As you become more turned on, you may notice that you begin to curl up a little. Your stomach, hips, and buttocks tighten up. When you find yourself tensing up, relax again. If you allow your body to curl, the clitoris only becomes more hidden and harder for your partner to stimulate. Open your body up and out and breathe. This will expand your orgasmic potential.

Stimulating the Penis

Receiving oral sex is sometimes the most fantasized part of the sexual experience for men. Usually, men are more open and relaxed about oral sex than women are. Many men have seen pornography that portrays women giving oral sex with wild abandon. They consider it erotic and intimate for their lover to give them fellatio, to ejaculate into their lover's mouth, and to have the lover swallow their ejaculate.

Remember—it's not about taking him over the top too quickly. Train him by getting to know his arousal patterns and then backing off when he's getting close to ejaculating. This training can come in handy when you are having intercourse and you both want him to last longer.

Some believe that oral sex was not common until the 1960s and 1970s, when it became wildly popular with the advent of women's magazines seeking yet another cutting-edge story for the cultural avant-garde. Our parents may not have partaken of these pleasures, but today it has generally lost its taboo status. Though a few states in this country still consider oral sex illegal, its appeal is enormous and lends great creativity and erotic pleasure to any relationship.

It's wonderful to start with a soft penis. This allows the exquisite feeling of having the man respond in your mouth to the touch you are giving. As you begin, touch your partner tenderly with your hands and gently blow on his pubic area. Cup his scrotum in your hands and carefully fondle the hair and skin around his genitals. Begin to kiss and lick his shaft. Start out with more of a teasing touch and as he warms up, move to a firmer touch.

Once the penis begins to grow, move to the head. As you prepare to take it in, make sure your mouth is very wet. Play with him in a teasing manner as you go back and forth from his shaft to the head and back again, kissing, sucking, and even very lightly biting as you move up the shaft to the head of his penis.

Once he is very aroused, begin to take more control and be more aggressive. Stay on the head longer and with more regular strokes of your mouth. If you feel comfortable, use the technique called "deep throating" to take his penis deeper into your mouth. Be careful and go slowly—he'll like it better that way. Pay particular attention to the head and the edge where it meets the shaft. This area is very sensitive in most men, and he'll love the attention you give to it.

Many men like increased stimulation as they get further aroused. They tend to like a series of repetitive actions and strokes. Vary the intensity so that you have a sense of where your partner is in his arousal state. By beginning to create a kind of dance with softer, more sensual strokes to hotter, firmer suction, you'll be able to help train your man to last longer.

Turn Up the Heat

To take oral sex up another level, you can add in stimulation with your hands or breasts. Encourage your partner to receive more pleasure by stimulating other parts of his or her body as you're performing oral sex. Or you can ask your lover to touch you as you're doing it.

FACT

The smells that surround our genitals are made up in part of pheromones. These chemical messengers are highly erotic and draw us in closer to our lover's body. Breathe in their essence deeply. It will keep you turned on.

Caressing, teasing, rubbing, biting, blowing, pulling, cupping, even scratching lightly—all these things and more will add to the overall pleasure during oral sex. Try gently pulling the pubic hair around your lover's genitals. Comb your fingers through the pubic hair and use your hands to pleasure the breasts and nipples. Women, rub your breasts across his legs as you take his penis into your mouth.

Here are a few other fun suggestions:

- Try humming while engaged in oral sex. Gently vibrate the lips to add the sensation to both the vulva and the penis.

- See how it feels to give and receive oral sex while standing or kneeling. Men will often get harder when they are standing or kneeling.
- Relax into an overstuffed chair while engaging in oral sex. This works for either partner and keeps the neck of the giver from cramping.
- Many couples think the position 69 (with both partners giving each other oral sex at the same time) is the ultimate. It is sometimes difficult for women to receive a gentler touch because the man will often want a faster, firmer stroke. But both partners tend to melt into a similar speed and touch when in 69.
- Use ice cubes, warm liquids or liquors, or edible body butters for an added turn on. These may also be a great way to introduce a reluctant partner into trying oral sex.

ALERT!

Never coerce reluctant partners into doing anything that they feel isn't right for them. Do encourage them to talk about their feelings and attitudes about the subject, and do express your own feelings, but don't try to convince them to change.

Communication Is Key

As you explore oral sex, ask for your partner's feedback. If you're the giver, pay attention to what your partner is saying. If you're the receiver, don't just assume your partner knows your body or your mind. If you need help expressing yourself, use this simple communication technique:

1. Say something you like that is happening right then: "I love the speed that you are using."
2. Ask for a single change: "Would you try moving slightly to the left?"
3. Give some kind of a response: "Ah, thank you, that's great" or "Oh, that's not a good as I thought it would be."

This simple communication technique includes an acknowledgement, a single change, and a response. This can be used over and over to get the kind of touch that you love. It's training for your partner and for you to know exactly what it is that turns you on!

Anal Stimulation and Anal Sex

Anal sexual activity is a taboo subject for many people. Yet, just as oral sex was a few decades ago, anal sex and other forms of anal play are coming into more favor in recent years. Thirty percent of couples say they have at least tried some kind of anal stimulation.

Often it is the man who would like his partner to participate in anal sex. Men, if your partner is willing to try, great. But if she's not willing, you may suggest experimenting with other types of anal stimulation. The truth is that the anus and the area around it are full of nerve endings. There are a variety of things you and your partner can do to stimulate these areas besides anal intercourse. Men, don't miss out on receiving anal stimulation yourself. Pleasurable attention to the anus can lead both of you to much stronger orgasms and sexual ecstasy.

Women will like stimulation of the anus toward the area of the G-spot. The membrane between the anus and the vagina is very thin. Combining anal and G-spot stimulation adds to the sensual feeling for women.

Because the G-spot is analogous to the prostate gland, men will like this upper area also. Feel for the prostate gland. Hold pressure here when stimulating the man.

Finger Play

There's no reason to rush. Begin by talking about any beliefs or hesitations you might have with your partner. If you both agree to try some anal play, keep it simple, and communicate with each other while you are experimenting. Don't expect too much at first, and have the receiving partner be in complete control of the situation.

It's best if your first few experiences are limited to finger play. Before you begin, take a bath and be relaxed and clean. Open your partner up by massaging and being playful.

Introduce anal play by lubricating a finger and playing with the area immediately around the anus before moving toward the opening. Slowly and gently add a little stimulation without entering. Ask your partner if he or she is ready for you to enter. If you get permission, slowly and sensually insert one finger.

Latex gloves can be essential to have on hand for things like anal play. Keep gloves, finger cots, and condoms around for such occasions. They can add a sense of fantasy, play, and safety to your sexual exploring.

For both men and women, we suggest that you be turned on already before anal play starts. Men, try giving your partner oral sex first and then as she is close to orgasm, and after you have stimulated the outer area of her anus, ask her if you can enter her with one finger. For women, the same applies for your man. He should be turned on first—he will be much more accepting of penetration.

Anal Sex

Try experimenting with some anal toys before you have anal intercourse. Women may love having a small, soft anal plug inside them while having vaginal intercourse. Men, you'll love the tighter fit, too.

If you're ready for anal sex, be sure to use lots of water-based lubricant, because the anal cavity doesn't self-lubricate. And unless you are monogamous and both of you are HIV negative, use a condom during anal intercourse.

Before you begin, massage and warm your partner's anal area. Make sure she's relaxed and ready. The woman's anus will actually relax and open if you go slowly and let her set the pace. Place the head of your penis at the entrance and allow her to move toward you.

Good positions to start are with the woman on her back with her legs up and the man on his knees. Rear entry works well, but don't try this the first time you have anal sex, because the woman is less in control in rear-entry positions.

Remember, don't ever coerce or force your partner into anything he or she doesn't want to do. Learning to relax into anal stimulation is healthy. The anus and buttocks area holds a lot of tension and stress. It is to our advantage to learn to relax that region, both physically and emotionally.

Never put a finger, hand, penis, dildo, vibrator, or anything else into the vagina if it has just been in the rectum or anus. This can cause the woman to get a vaginal infection. Always wash very thoroughly anything that has been in the anus before inserting it into the vagina.

Fantasy and Role-Playing

Games, role-playing, and recreating some of your fantasies together can add new excitement and possibilities to maturing relationships. We make up fantasies because even the best of relationships needs new stimulus and input. The subject of fantasy is a whole book in itself. Everyone has fantasies. Even if you think you don't, you do have desires, and desires are a form of fantasy, too. We are creative and imaginative beings. When we feel cared for, safe, and trusting, we will often open up about our fantasy life.

ALERT!

Never coerce a reluctant partner into doing anything that he or she feels isn't right for them. Do encourage them to talk about their feelings and attitudes about the subject, and do express your own feelings, but don't try to convince them to change.

Fantasies are best when shared. Sharing fantasy can open up new realms for many couples. You may have had no idea that your partner wanted something that you wanted, too. Or, though it might not be something you had a fantasy about, it may sound good to you. Being willing to listen openly and sometimes try new things is a healthy sign. However, also be aware that some fantasies aren't necessarily for playing out. When you tell the truth about something that you've been keeping a secret, the fantasy tends to become less important or significant. We become less attached to having to play it out.

Be open to talking about your fantasies, starting out slowly and sensitively and then building up over time to some of the edgier ones. Keep a healthy perspective on what is doable and what is not. And don't assume that just because it's your heart's desire that your partner will feel like participating.

One important thing about fantasizing during lovemaking is that it is best to have it be up-front and in the open. That way when partners are making love, they can be 100 percent present with each other. There is nothing that will destroy a relationship faster than either partner being "somewhere else" or "with someone else" during lovemaking. Your lover will know that you are not in the moment and will feel disconnected and possibly abandoned.

There are plenty of sex catalogs out there that offer sexual aids, toys, and fantasy props that could be used during your lovemaking. If you and your partner are both interested, you could shop for these items together, an act that may serve you as foreplay.

Try Role-Playing

Role-playing is fantasizing together, and it's very important because we often get stuck in one or two ways of being that eventually limit us as individuals. For a man to explore his more feminine side by letting his partner take control for an evening can open up doors of understanding, food for thought, and conversation.

As a woman, you may easily identify with roles as mother, daughter, and wife, but how about senior executive, muse, virgin, hero, and priestess? Men, you may be a father, husband, and son, but how about shaman, traveling salesman, Don Juan, or the president? Have fun with some of the roles that may be out of the norm for you. It's only play, and when you realize this, you usually feel safe.

Swings, Velvet Handcuffs, and More

There are whole categories of extras that many couples enjoy to spice up their relationship. Make sure you both are in agreement before acting on your fantasies and desires. The most important thing is to have fun.

There are several varieties of love swings on the market. They are versatile, fun, and add variations to lovemaking positions. Love swings aid in G-spot stimulation and can be helpful for men interested in learning to last longer. They can be hung in a variety of places in the house and the yard as the imagination dictates.

If you are interested in playing with light bondage or S-M, there are books on the subject. It is suggested that you talk and do some research together before you agree to try this type of activity. Communication and trust are of the utmost importance, and you need to know how to approach the activities with care and knowledge. Couples may find new realms open to them through experiences such as these. E

Chapter 13

Aphrodisiacs and Sexual Aids

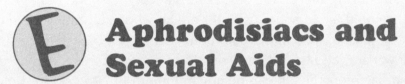

Throughout history, human beings have sought to enhance the sexual experience—through special foods, smoking, sexual toys, and by stimulating the imagination. As you will see from the description of the many kinds of sex aids in this chapter, almost anything can add to your pleasure if your mind associates it with sex.

The Power of Aphrodisiacs

An aphrodisiac is typically considered to be any substance that you either ingest or take part in to enhance pleasure or susceptibility to pleasure. The list of possible aphrodisiacs is probably endless, since every person alive has had different early life experiences associating certain foods, odors, or environments with sex. For instance, the sound of the toilet flushing could be an aphrodisiac for a man who used to flush the toilet when he masturbated in the bathroom as a boy.

Nowadays, events, clothing, sounds, and environments can have aphrodisiac properties. It can be fun and interesting to explore with your lover what your particular turn ons are.

FACT

Some of the well-publicized aphrodisiacs in ancient times were rhinoceros horn, elk antler, and powdered sea horse. There is little evidence that these substances actually work, however, and serious damage is being done to the environment today because of these ancient beliefs.

A good deal of evidence does exist that the following items do enhance sexual interest or arousal:

- Erotic art
- Flowers
- A sensual setting or room
- Watching a sexual video
- Reading to each other
- Compassion
- Vulnerability
- Looking at erotic books
- Deep breathing and relaxation
- Talking about sex
- Shared physical exercise
- Teasing and touch

- Words of love
- Certain smells and foods
- Many herbs and extracts

Pheromones—the Chemicals of Love

Pheromones are chemicals found in body secretions that attract the opposite sex. They don't have a smell or odor that is discernable, but humans have special detectors in their noses for pheromones. We respond physiologically to another person's pheromones, even if we cannot consciously smell them.

Pheromones are available for purchase; you can add them to your favorite perfume or dab them on separately. Appendix B lists Web sites and stores where you can purchase pheromones. The jury is out on their effectiveness, since there haven't been many studies done with manufactured pheromones, but they aren't too expensive, so try some out for yourself.

The word "pheromone" is derived from a Greek word meaning "to transfer excitement." Body temperature, skin conductance, heart rate, and blood pressure are just some of the functions that can be affected by our reactions to our partner's pheromones. (Women taking oral contraceptives seem to be less responsive to pheromones.) Pheromones have also been isolated as the cause for synchronized menstruation cycles among women who live in close proximity over a period of time.

Male and female pheromones are excreted from glands in the hair follicles, the underarms, and the groin area. Some men and women are greatly attracted to the smell of their partner's underarms and hair. Try burying your nose in your partner's hair the next time you want to become aroused.

Scents and Perfumes

Scents and perfumes have been used since time immemorial, possibly to mimic pheromones. One of the most popular is musk, which has a smell very close to the male hormone testosterone. The Romans used civet and ambergris as the carriers for lavish perfumes that were erotic in nature.

Vanilla, lavender, and flower essences have been used for thousands of years to add allure to our bodily scents. Many of the tropical forests in Hawaii were cut down in the eighteenth and nineteenth centuries for the delicate musky, earthy scent of sandalwood. The finest European fans for aristocratic women were made from sandalwood. This wood never loses its scent, so it served as a perfume when a woman seductively fanned herself.

When choosing a perfume, pick something that isn't too overbearing. It should complement the subtle scent of your own skin, hair, and pheromones. Try going without perfume sometimes, especially before a night of lovemaking. This goes for men, too. Don't always wear colognes. They can distract from natural erotic smells.

◀ Use scents and perfumes lightly.

The use of incense has a long history for enhancing the setting in which lovemaking takes place. Again, pick something that is appropriate and not overbearing. You might want to place it in an adjacent room like a bathroom so that the hint of it reaches you rather than having the full strength take over the room you are in. You can also "freshen" a room with incense and then put it out quickly, to give just a hint of the scent.

Lovemaking and Food

It's often been said that food is the way to a man's heart. Well, that can have a lot of different implications. Healthy eating is of course the optimum for all of us. But certain foods can have a positive effect on the libido.

Before we go on to examine what foods are compatible with the act of making love, a word of warning. Overeating before an evening of lovemaking can have a less-than-beneficial effect—both on the libido and on performance. Have you ever eaten a large meal and then had to go back to work and engage your brain for some critical thinking? The brain will often fail you in these times because the body has sent a lot of the blood supply to the stomach to aid in digestion. When we eat a meal, the blood flows away from the brain, away from the extremities, and away from the genitals.

QUESTION?

What other things turn you on?
Make a short list of items you know increase your desire and libido. Share this list with your lover and ask him or her to do the same. Notice the things that are the same and the ones that are different.

Time for Food, Time for Love

If you are planning an evening of lovemaking that includes food, make eating a part of the ritual or ceremony of loving. That way, you can include eating in the sensual evening without it stopping the action. Eating can be a fun addition. You can feed each other. Eat in courses so that eating takes a long time and is spread out between the "courses" of love.

Serving things like sushi, light pastas, small skewers of vegetables and fish, or a salad with many goodies in it would be perfect. Then dessert could come later. Maybe you present dessert on your inner thighs or you offer your partner the opportunity to become the platter. Find unique and fun ways to surprise yourself and your lover.

Suggestive Shapes

Try forming foods into shapes that are suggestive or downright sexual—you can use chocolates, little cakes, oysters, candies, breads, and main dishes. Your imagination can take you anywhere. Soak dried fruit in wine or liquors to enhance their flavor. Use fresh and dried fruit to dip into sauces that are sweetened and have a yogurt base. Dip fresh fruit into chocolate or butterscotch sauces. Raspberry sauce, whipped cream, and even ice cream can be used in erotic ways to enhance an evening of love.

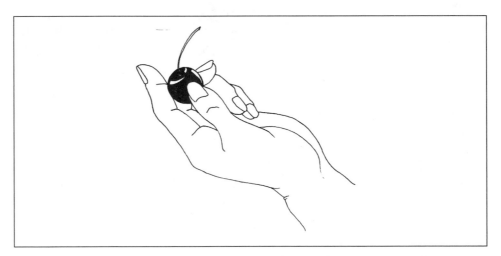

▲ Whip up a sexy dessert for your lover—and don't forget to put a cherry on top!

Spice Up Your Life

Some spices, seasonings, and foods with certain amino acids are good for getting the "heat" to rise. Adding a variety of spices to your food concoctions can have a wonderful effect of heightening arousal. Pumpkin pie spices, licorice, cinnamon, peppermint, curries, coriander, cardamom, lavender, chili peppers, sesame seeds, saffron, nutmeg, pepper—all these are believed to intensify sexual desire. They are generally also very good for your health and vitality.

Ginger, onions, and garlic are also considered aphrodisiacs by many cultures. Asparagus, figs, grapes, almonds, oysters, mussels, caviar, basil, bananas, mangos—the list goes on. Remember, anything can be erotic, and often what's erotic is unique to the individual, so create foods that appeal to you and your lover. It's fun creating and discovering new things together, and the time spent attending to the details will be rewarded. You are cocreating a ritual to honor your lovemaking.

Chocolate Temptation

One of the active ingredients in chocolate produces phenylethylamine, the chemical that the body manufactures when we fall in love. These chemical messengers speed up the flow of information that travels between our nerve endings. Phenylethylamine is similar in many ways to amphetamine, which dilates the blood vessels and creates energy and focus. It is not by chance that chocolate is so highly associated with love.

FACT

When the conquistadors invaded Mexico, Montezuma was reported to have drunk up to fifty cups a day of chocolate with chili and spices in it. He had to keep up his stamina to satisfy his many wives! Some women, as their hormonal balance shifts, crave chocolate as an unconscious remedy to lift spirits and provide energy.

In Drunken Bliss

Used in small amounts, alcohol can enhance the sensual/sexual experience. It can relax you and ease your inhibitions. In small amounts, it has been cited as an aid in helping men last longer so they don't ejaculate too fast. However, be aware that in larger amounts, it has the opposite effect.

Try using it in a ritual way by creating a ceremony when you drink it. Sip it during lovemaking. Share a kiss with a little liquor in your mouth and let it dribble down your cheeks.

Take some liquor into your mouth and then give your partner oral sex while you still have it in your mouth. Throw in the element of surprise. This can add new sensations to both your experiences. It can be licked and sucked off if any gets away from you!

Erotic Reading and Writing

Reading erotic materials to your partner can be exquisitely sensuous. As you read, you can place your own intention and inflection on the sentences you want to emphasize. You can even act out some of the parts and discuss or fantasize about what you are reading together.

Pillow books are books that have pictures, writing, and sometimes instructions—like position books. These provide a great resource for erotic adventure. Books like the Ananga-Ranga, the Kama sutra, and the Perfumed Garden are ancient erotic pillow books that not only brought pleasure, but also helped educate people over many generations. These books are available today in modern forms and are informative as well as evocative and titillating.

If you are inclined to write a love letter but feel intimidated, ask for help at the bookstore. Purchase a book of poetry by Rumi or another love poet and generously sprinkle some of their words in your letter. It'll turn your partner on in more than one way!

Writing poetry has long been a symbol of both romantic and erotic love. Even writers of little skill can successfully write poetry to their lover and have it be received as though it came from a master. The gift of writing from a lover is a gift of time, care, and love. Read and write poetry together. Try writing one poem together, and see what you come up with.

Even if poetry isn't something that turns you on, consider stretching yourself a little if it is something you think your lover would like. In addition, write little love notes that point to the anticipation of a particular erotic event that might be planned. Leading up to a date with notes and love letters is an outrageous way to create titillating tension. By the time you get together, you'll be all over each other!

▲ Write a love letter to your partner, hinting at an erotic encounter you plan to have with him or her.

Words of Love and Lust

For both men and women, words can be powerful erotic stimulators. In general, men will prefer lusty, teasing, more explicitly sexual language. Women tend to respond to more indirect language—hints, words of love and desire, compliments. Regardless of what you like, the idea is to start the erotic play before you get to the bedroom. The longer we are juiced up, the stronger our reactions will be when we get there.

Don't hesitate to use words liberally when making love. And make sounds to let your partner know how you are feeling. Here's an activity to try. It has several different variations. You may want to create new additional versions that are appropriate for times other than when you are making love. Sit facing each other when you do these, and take turns.

- Give each other the gift of one minute of compliments. Just say as many loving, complimentary words and phrases as come to your mind. Don't think too much—just let them flow.
- Each of you takes one minute to say as many erotic, hot, sexy words as you can come up with. Don't censor your words—just let them out.
- In one minute, say as many words of compassion, care, and sympathy as come to your mind. Use this one when one or both of you are experiencing hurt or vulnerability.
- Use words of gratitude and thanks for one minute each. This practice

helps us remember to speak about how precious our lives are. Use this one generously!

• Make up your own version with themes that fit your life.

Between the Sheets

There are a lot of toys, safe-sex products, lubricants, and creams that can be very handy and useful during sex. If you haven't tried some of these products, talk with your partner about purchasing the ones that intrigue the two of you. If you are single, you're sure to find something on this list that titillates you.

Vibrators

Vibrators are excellent for women who need help learning to orgasm. If a woman has been frustrated with her capacity to have orgasms, using a vibrator can open the door to that experience. Start with a small one designed for clitoral stimulation.

Some women like vibrators, while others prefer dildos, which are used inside the vagina. Or you can purchase a vibrating dildo. You may need to explore a few to discover what works for you. Each type has a specific purpose.

If you have a partner, talk to him about going to an adult store to look over the selection. Be sensitive to your lover's feelings about this. He may have feelings of inadequacy at not being the lover you want him to be. Reassure him that you only want to add to the repertoire of your adventures in bed.

Vibrators do have a downside—they can be addictive and desensitizing. Your lover may find that you are having a harder time reaching orgasm when he is giving you oral stimulation, if you have been using the vibrator a lot. Pay attention and modify its use if this seems to be a problem. Vibrators can be great to use during intercourse to stimulate the woman's clitoris. Either partner can hold it and add to the pleasure.

FACT

Vibrators were initially invented for people with disabilities. In the late nineteenth and early twentieth centuries, doctors used vibrators to cure women of "hysteria" or sexual frustration.

Men may have an interest in some of the sensations a vibrator has to offer. Try the small clitoral vibrators on the perineum during intercourse or while giving him oral sex. This is healthy stimulation and exercise for the prostate gland, too. It may stimulate more sexual excitement or may defocus the intensity, which helps to delay orgasm and ejaculation in men.

Dildos

Dildos come in all shapes, sizes, materials, and forms. There are combinations for stimulating the clitoris and for insertion into the vagina; there are ones just for the vagina; there are anal plugs for anal stimulation; and there are combinations for vagina and anus. Some will be battery-operated vibrators, and some will be without vibration. And in each of these categories there are literally hundreds of varieties.

There are so many options to choose from. Go to a well-equipped Web site or adult store when you make your first purchases. Web sites are great to browse and order from because they offer privacy and ease. There are some good suggestions in Appendix B.

Condoms and Gloves

Condoms, gloves, and other latex products can be fun to use, even for committed, monogamous couples who are free of sexually transmitted diseases. Even if you are in a long-term relationship and can safely have unprotected sex, try using a condom once in a while. They may fit into sexual fantasies for you or just be fun to try. The same goes for gloves. The use of latex gloves adds a fantasy dimension to lovemaking and they work very well for anal stimulation for both men and women. They can take the edge off trying these things if you are new to this kind of sexual exploring.

Lubrication

Some fun additions to a sex-positive bedroom are the slippery, wet, and creamy aids that help us get more comfortable physically. They will help you have a better time when you make love. They're fun to put on for yourself or for your lover. Lubricants, creams, and oils come in a variety of sizes, consistencies, and qualities. You'll need to try a few to see which ones you like and what works best for you. If you have a negative reaction to one, try another. Check the ingredients for things you know you might be allergic to, and compare desired effects.

ALERT!

Some lubricants have a petroleum base. Do not use these with anything made out of latex, like condoms and gloves used for safe sex. Petroleum breaks down latex and will compromise the protection that a condom gives.

Lubricants are available for any purpose you can come up with. Lubricants are generally used on the sensitive tissues of the genital region. They can go inside you. Some lubricants dry out rather quickly. Some are stickier than you might like.

Check if the lubricant you are selecting has nonoxynol-9 in it. This additive is a spermicide, meaning it kills sperm. If you do not need the protection for pregnancy prevention, it is recommended you don't use these products. It can be irritating or cause an allergic reaction.

Scents and Oils

Massage oils are fabulous for soothing or erotic massages. They should not go into the body, however—keep them on the outside. Choose a scent that you think you and your lover would like. The base should be made from good-quality natural oils. Anything with almond, wheat germ, olive, or coconut oil is great. You can even use cocoa butter, especially if you like the chocolate smell it has, though it's not edible.

Scents are best when they are natural, essential oils that are created to give the ultimate sensual experience. Popular essential oils used for erotic purposes are vanilla, musk, orange, ylang-ylang, rose, cedar wood, geranium, lavender, and lemongrass. Look for blends that turn you on. You may even want to try making your own—experimenting with different combinations of scents.

If you feel unsure at first about picking something out, go to a health food store or a natural product store and ask for help. Someone will be glad to assist you. If you decide to try your hand at mixing some of your own massage oils, you'll find that the leftover essential oils are a wonderful addition to the sensuous baths you and your lover will take. Simply add a few drops to the next bath for a heightened experience.

Heightening Creams

There are many new creams on the market that are designed with women in mind. Like Viagra, they are supposed to help with the physical aspects of sexual dysfunction that some women have in achieving orgasmic states.

FACT

In the first clinical trials that gave Viagra to women, fewer than 45 percent of the women had any positive response. A separate group determined that if the women were first screened for psychological problems and those subjects were removed, the remaining group of women who exhibited physical symptoms had a success rate of more than 90 percent.

The general function of these creams is to increase blood flow to the genitals. Blood flow causes the engorgement and arousal of the genital region. Many of these creams are based on the absorption of L-arginine into the blood supply in the immediate area of the genitals. L-arginine increases the nitric oxide available to the tissue, which in turn expands the blood vessels and allows more blood to flow to the region.

The creams that are currently on the market have varying degrees of success. This is a new area in the understanding of sexual response, and it is in its infancy. We can expect more of these products to be available in the coming years. It is exciting that the medical community is finally focusing some of its attention on women.

Sexual Response Remedies

Great sexual response and vitality is enhanced by sufficient sleep, low stress levels, exercise, good health, and limiting your consumption of alcohol and drugs. If these aren't enough, you may turn your attention to the many herbal remedies for sexual dysfunction that are currently available:

- **Ginkgo biloba and ginseng:** Both are recommended for blood flow to the brain and extremities. Ginkgo greatly increases the concentrations of dopamine and other neurotransmitters, the forerunners of increased pleasure, happiness, and alertness. Ginseng increases the production of sex hormones like testosterone and progesterone and helps keep up your stamina. It helps moderate stress, stimulates the immune system, and can decrease menopausal symptoms.

- **Avena sativa (wild oats):** This plant has long been known to have a direct effect on libido and health. It produces deep relaxation, increased sex drive, and stronger erections; it may also increase men's testosterone levels. Avena sativa is the active ingredient in Vigorex Forte for men and Vigorex Femme for women and other supplements found in health food stores.

- **Yohimbine:** This substance is derived from a tree native to Africa. It has a reputation for being a strong sexual stimulant, but it can be dangerous. Its powerful action blocks nerve activity, which constricts blood vessels, leading to problems in people who already take blood-thinning medications. When combined with some of the other herbal remedies that follow, but not used as the main ingredient in a formula, it can be a healthy addition as a sexual tonic.

- **Saw palmetto:** This herb is effective in stopping swollen prostate growth. While some claim that it can actually shrink a swollen prostate gland, most experts say that it is effective only in stopping additional swelling from occurring. This can help increase the flow of semen from the testicles, help with urinary problems in older men, and relieve the tension to the urinary tract caused by the enlarged gland. This tension often leads to an uncomfortable feeling during sex. Since men over age fifty are so susceptible to prostate enlargement, it is a good idea to take saw palmetto regularly, as a preventative measure.

- **Muira puama:** Also known as "potency wood," as it is called in its native Amazon, muira puama has been highly regarded as a potent sexual and nerve tonic. It heightens physical response and sensations to sexual stimulus. It increases libido and hardness in the penis during sexual stimulation. It contains the building block chemicals that are the precursors to other important hormones. Muira puama has no known harmful side effects and has been used in Europe for centuries, though it is only beginning to gain acceptance in the United States.

- **Black cohosh:** This herb is known for its balancing effect on female hormones. Both estrogen and progesterone levels are influenced by its properties. It is a great treatment for premenstrual symptoms and menopausal problems related to lubrication and sexual receptiveness.

- **Dong quai:** This remedy is a relaxant and pain reliever for female symptoms, including menopause and menstrual cramps. It contains many nutrients that support hormone production, balance estrogen production, and relax smooth muscles in the body. It has been shown to have a pain-relieving effect that is 1.7 times that of aspirin. All these attributes make it an ideal enhancer of sexual desire and blood flow to the genitals.

- **Ashwagandha:** This is a native plant of India that has been used in Ayurvedic medicine for thousands of years. Its aphrodisiac properties are attributed to a steroidlike effect, which produces precursors to testosterone and progesterone—hormones instrumental in activating sexual response and libido.

ALERT!

Smoking is recognized as one of the main causes of sexual dysfunction in men and women. It is implicated in the failure to have and maintain erections as men age. Smoking decreases blood flow, which is necessary for arousal in the genital regions.

In addition to these natural substances and herbal formulas, there are a few more supplements worthy of mention. Wild yam, L-arginine (taken orally), kava kava, Damiana, Pygeum, and stinging nettle are a few. You can find more information on these items and more through books, the Internet, and reliable health food stores. Not only are they healthful additives to your diet, they have the added distinction of whetting your sexual appetite. E

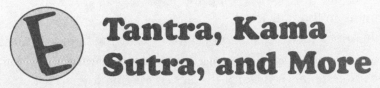

Chapter 14

Tantra, Kama Sutra, and More

Many people who experience deep, ecstatic sexual states liken these to transcendental spiritual experiences. They discover that the distinction between what is carnal and what is spiritual may not be so clear. They may even feel that they have come to know God, or ultimate reality, through sex. Tantra and the Kama sutra both view sexuality as vital aspects of the path to enlightenment.

Ancient and Modern Tantra

Tantra originates from India, where it has been practiced for thousands of years. Tantric practices were at their height between A.D. 500 and 1300. The spiritual, sexual, and personal transformative components of tantra include whole-body health and Ayurvedic medicine. Today, it remains a living system that is designed to promote rapid growth toward enlightenment in the individual.

In India, not everyone has the honor of studying tantra. In order to practice it, you must have a guru who deems you worthy of this art. In tantra, elaborate rituals transform the act of making love to a higher purpose. You need to be the type of person who is able to worship your partner as though he or she were a god or goddess.

What is most real (or experienced) is also most spiritual. In other words, when you allow yourself to be deeply moved by an experience—feeling it in your body, letting go of the ego's need to control things—you are having what mystics have called a spiritual experience.

Adopting Tantric Principles

Although most of you probably won't seek out a guru, practicing even the simplest of the tantric techniques can bring a sense of greater communion with your partner, your sexual nature, and, ultimately, with your soul. We become expansive because our spirit opens up when we engage in more trusting sexual practices that involve communication, the spirit of playfulness, and being open to discovery.

Most of us must teach ourselves the basics of love and sexuality through some form of trial-and-error process. Over time, and especially in long-term relationships, we tend to stop exploring and being inventive. When we can break out of those old patterns and learn new ways of being—physically, spiritually, and emotionally—we expand and open. In a sense, we transcend who we thought we were.

Today in the West, there has been a renewal of interest in tantric practices. Perhaps because our society is maturing, perhaps because of a widespread awakening of consciousness, we seem to be gravitating toward the lessons in conscious intimacy that tantra has to offer. Most of us know very little about our own bodies and our potential for pleasure. In this age of information, we are attracted to what tantra has to teach us about sex and love.

The spiritual seeking that many Westerners are involved in fits well with the practices that tantra offers. The modern seeker may find that many of the components of ancient tantric practices integrate well with our daily lives.

In fact, the experiences one has practicing tantra can be seen as a metaphor for other aspects of one's life and can give one "tools" for being more present and aware in general.

Tantric Sex

In essence, tantric sex is a spiritual practice—like meditation or yoga. It is not meant to be self-indulgent and pleasure is not its only goal. Tantra uses sexuality, with all of its rawness, social stigma, fear, vulnerability, and ignorance to crack open the ego so that we can be present with our lover, and, ultimately, with our self.

The approximate Sanskrit definition of *tantra* is "web," or that union of opposites that, when united, become one with everything in the universe. Tantric practice aims to unify the many and often apparently contradictory aspects of the self—masculine and feminine, spirit and matter, dark and light—into a harmonious whole.

Sexual Yoga

Tantra is actually a branch in the study of yoga, or practices that help to unify apparent opposites. The practice of hatha yoga, for example, tones the muscles, and massages and keeps healthy the vital internal organs in our bodies. It harmonizes the body and the mind by connecting conscious breathing with focusing the mind. When doing yoga, you are actually performing an active meditation. You are focusing your energy on certain internal as well as external points. You bring much more awareness to the body and mind with yoga.

Tantric Gods and Goddesses

Tantra is based on the gods and goddesses of the Hindu pantheon. One telling relationship in this pantheon is between Shiva and Shakti, representations of the male/female, yin/yang energies.

Shiva is the supreme god in Hindu tantra. He represents the male principle and the control and movement of time and all material things. His penis (*lingam* in Sanskrit) is upright, action oriented, and powerful. It commands a place of nerve and worldly power. Shiva's counterpart is Shakti—the female essence. It is Shakti's energy that literally runs the universe. Without Shakti, Shiva is nothing and would have no power in the world. She is the creator, the sustainer, and the destroyer all in one.

These two deities form a union that is necessary to keep the universe in perfect harmony, representing the life of every living human. According to tantric philosophy, life is a journey to become a balanced blend of both male and female, to become whole, or unified. Your sexual nature can lead you to this perfect balance of energies.

Your Guru

The role of the guru in classical tantra is that of guide—a guide who pushes the student to the edge. The guru knows the student and the limitations in that person's life. He or she sets a path for the student that will ultimately lead the individual to stretch and grow in ways that the student might not attempt on his or her own.

The beauty of tantra is that it is a partnered path of learning. In a sense, your partner is your guru. To trust another with your personal growth is the ultimate act of surrender, and that's where breakthroughs happen. If two people can do that for each other, taking conscious risks that gently stretch the limits of their comfort zones, they can realize great growth—both individually and as partners.

To risk the vulnerability of "doing it wrong," not looking good, being stuck emotionally, and facing your own shadows and life's challenges is to move closer to your own soul and to the power that resides in self-realization. If you discover, for example, a fear of intimacy and move toward it with courage and trust, not denying it or trying to hide from it, the benefits are great.

As you meet and face your fears and limiting beliefs, you will feel yourself becoming less fearful. How you face your sexual fears is a great metaphor for how you deal with fear in general. In sex, you cannot hide from the truth. If your body feels pleasure, it feels pleasure. If it feels numb, it feels numb, and you know it.

Harness the Energy of Your Chakras

In Eastern medicine, the chakras are seven energy centers situated along the spine in what is called the *subtle body*. Practitioners of Eastern medicine treat the subtle body as well as the gross physical body and see the chakras as very important to the overall health of the individual. Each of the chakras is associated with one of the basic core energies that we work with in life. The energy that flows through them and up the spine is called *kundalini energy*.

There are symbols, colors, sounds, elements, emotional "drives," and gestures associated with each chakra. As you extend your practices of tantra and other teachings relating to the body, you begin to see where you flow and where you get stuck in life. As you learn to sense the energies in your various chakras, through tantric practice, you can discover where your life energies are not flowing, where you are stuck, and where you need to put your attention in order to revitalize yourself.

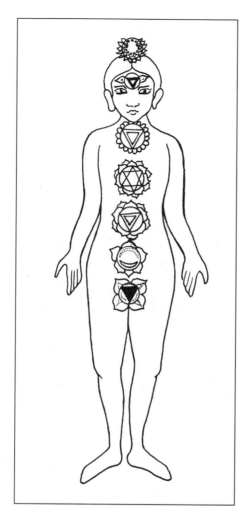

◀ The seven chakras

The First Chakra—Muladhara

The pelvis area at the perineum is where the first chakra resides. It represents being grounded and secure in the basic physical comforts of life: food, shelter, and the needs of our animal nature. Its element is Earth, and its color is red.

A secure first chakra enables us to feel confident in our abilities to care for ourselves. We can hold a job that brings us enough money to survive. We have a realistic concept of our physical body and its needs, and a sense of being grounded.

The Second Chakra—Svadhishthana

The genital area is the seat of the second chakra. It represents our sexual urges and fantasies, creativity, and procreation. Its element is water, and its color is orange. Sensations, pleasure, sexuality, and emotions are all associated with this chakra. When this chakra is "open" and healthy, we are likely to experience stable emotions, gracefulness, and self-acceptance.

The Third Chakra—Manapura

This chakra is situated at the solar plexus, or navel area, of our body. It represents our power, will, energy, authority, and longevity. Its element is fire, and its color is yellow, like the sun. Ego identity and self-esteem are the products of a healthy third chakra. Confidence, reliability, and autonomy without domination and manipulation produce the fire necessary to live a powerful yet compassionate life. When you have butterflies in your stomach, they may indicate a sign of excitement or fear. This is a temporary disturbance in the third chakra.

The Fourth Chakra—Anahata

The chest area and specifically the heart are the home of the fourth chakra. It represents our heart and all that is associated with it: sharing, love, service, compassion, and devotion. Its element is air, and its color is green. The heart is often considered the seat of the soul because, when it is open, it embodies the qualities just mentioned.

The increased incidence of breast cancer in women may be seen as a metaphor for what ails women. The breasts are the center of the fourth chakra. Finding a loving, wise, mature partner for many women is difficult. Being loved for who they are, regardless of how they fit the stereotype, often eludes them.

We can all recognize the times when our heart feels shut down. This tends to happen when we are mad, hurt, pitying ourselves, or when we don't feel loved. We actually can feel it as a stuck or tight area in the chest. Jealousy has been called the green-eyed monster, and in fact the heart chakra is represented by the color green. We say that our heart aches when we feel the emotions associated with this chakra.

The Fifth Chakra—Vishuddha

This is the throat area of the body and represents knowledge and speaking the truth of that knowledge. Its element is ether, or space, and its color is violet. The throat chakra builds upon the knowledge learned from the previous four chakras. It takes all that we know and have learned and dares to synthesize and help us speak what we know.

QUESTION?

When was the last time you had a lump in your throat? That is your fifth chakra telling you that you don't know all the facts, that you are afraid to speak up, or that you aren't being truthful in what you are saying. Stop, breathe deeply, notice what you are avoiding, and tell the truth.

The Sixth Chakra—Ajna

Located at the pineal gland, or "third eye," area of the forehead, the sixth chakra represents enlightenment and self-realization. It has no element as it is beyond the elements. Its color is bluish-white. Self-mastery, intuition, and insight are signs of an open sixth chakra. Symbolic and archetypal meaning is integrated into self-reflection. We can move to and through old, recurring patterns in our lives when our sixth chakra is healthy. Often this chakra opens up through a "spiritual" emergence or awakening.

The Seventh Chakra—Sahasrara

This chakra is at the top of the head located at the fontanel, that area where the soft spot is located on a baby's head. It is the open conduit to God and the guru within. Immortality is achieved at this level. It is the realm of saints and of holy men and women throughout the ages. Golden white light and a lotus flower with a thousand petals are the symbols of this uppermost chakra. A supremely conscious human being exhibits compassion, self-awareness, mindfulness, and awareness of the world. Such a person has a very evolved seventh chakra.

Achieve Tantric Balance

Tantra offers many easy-to-learn practices to help you and your partner evolve spiritually while enjoying great sex. Many of the practices and lessons in other chapters of this book come from or were inspired by tantric theory, like the repeated reminder to focus your mind on your heart and your partner's heart when you are making love.

Meditation

Meditation is being recognized, in many different circles today, for its value in bringing focus and quiet to the mind. Its simple techniques are easy to learn and are useful in a variety of ways. As little as twenty minutes a day can bring relaxation, concentration, and lower blood pressure.

FACT

When our bodies get this full-blown experience of love and when we practice enhancing it with different breath patterns, sounds, and "right-hand path" techniques, we have the potential to move into multiple orgasms and out-of-body sex.

Most people, at some time or another during sex, have found their mind wandering, or have found that they think about whether they are doing it right or about what they wish their partner would do. The highest honor and gift you can give a partner is focused attention. When you bring that quality to your loving, it doesn't matter what techniques you know—you simply *are* a great lover. Practicing meditation will enable you to focus your attention during lovemaking.

Let Your Heart In

Here is a simple practice you can try the next time you are making love. It's about connecting the heart chakra with the genital chakra. Both men and women need to learn to connect the genitals and the heart. Touching these two areas at the same time can bring immense healing, enabling you to experience this connection.

During foreplay or oral sex and while you are stimulating the genitals of your partner, place a hand on his or her heart chakra. Breathe love deeply into it. Think of the possibility of having a pure heart orgasm or extending the orgasmic release from the genitals up to the heart. You may even want to wave your hand over your lover's body with focus on the heart area. Remind the receiving partner that he can spread the orgasmic feelings all the way up to his heart.

Tantric Orgasm

Tantric philosophy talks about two seemingly different types of orgasm: the physical orgasm and the heart orgasm. At first appearance they may seem contrary to each other, but on closer inspection one supports the other perfectly.

As you go further into this practice, you are able to begin to have full-body orgasms, or energy orgasms, simply by breathing them, without any physical touch. This powerful energy is then much more available to you in your everyday life, sometimes simply by breathing!

Modern sexology recognizes that there are several forms of orgasm. In women there is the clitoral orgasm, which tends to be very localized to the genitals. There is the vaginal orgasm, which involves the G-spot and a few other areas of the vagina. There is the blended orgasm, involving the clitoris and the G-spot. Men's orgasms tend to be of one general kind. These are all forms of the physical orgasm. Through tantric practices the orgasmic plateau can be extended for long periods of time.

Moreover, tantra offers another kind of orgasm—the energy orgasm, or heart orgasm.

Orgasm from the Heart

Tantric practice encourages us to be in our hearts at all times. That blissful state can be equated to an orgasmic state of being in which "heart energy" is transferred to all that we experience and do during the day. In tantra this is sometimes referred to as the "right-hand path"; certain sects of practitioners achieve this optimum state of being through meditation, yoga, compassionate states of mind, mantra chanting, and celibacy.

In the "left-hand path," sexuality is the vehicle one rides to achieve this same blissful state. Sexuality is used as a form of yoga to go to the deepest spiritual levels one can attain. The orgasm is used as the gateway to recognize the bliss state. Once this state of being is recognized, you are able to use that recognition to develop the ability to attain higher states of consciousness that enable you to bring the bliss state to all aspects of life.

When the two paths are blended, the possibilities for personal growth expand exponentially, and the duality between the two types of orgasms vanishes. Just as breath is of the utmost importance in meditation, it is the consciousness of breathing that can be the tool to a transformational lovemaking experience.

The Kama Sutra

Best known to us for its variety of exotic sexual positions, the Kama sutra has as much to offer modern couples as it did their counterparts in ancient India. Perhaps the most well known of all love manuals, it was translated from Sanskrit in the mid-1800s by an Englishman named Sir Richard Burton. It shocked Victorian England, and upon Sir Richard's death, his wife burned many of the other books he had translated. Most of them have not been retranslated and indeed many may be lost to humanity forever.

It is believed that our version of the Kama sutra originated from oral traditions passed down in verse form, and that these verses were written down and compiled into one book by a man named Vatsyayana. The Kama sutra's descriptions of the positions are short and to the point. It's almost as if they were meant to be reminders to the couple, rather than detailed instructions. That fact supports the idea that the sutras were born of an oral tradition and were probably originally taught that way to couples.

The Richness of Detail

The variety and depth of information ranges from detailed kissing techniques to seduction and courting suggestions. It explores the idea of biting your lover to leave your mark on him or her. The instructions on scratching techniques are for the same reason and to heighten the sensual feel of the skin during lovemaking. Many different ways of thrusting are mentioned. The positions are named after animals, as this was a prime way of studying man's relationship to the natural world.

FACT

The Kama sutra exquisitely describes the "quivering" of the vagina that usually precedes orgasm and the "shuddering" that heralds it. It says that no two women make love alike and that one must be very sensitive to rhythms, sentiments, and moods of the individual woman.

Chapter 9 has some of the kissing and touching techniques from the Kama sutra that have been incorporated into a more modern interpretation. The book describes many different techniques to stimulate the clitoris like the ten types of "blows" that can be used to tap the clitoris with the penis for stimulation. It details the way in which a man might grasp his penis and churn it from side to side in the vagina of his lover. It outlines what areas in the vagina to stimulate and has special names for the sides, top, deeper areas, and the entrance area.

The Kama sutra also encourages lovers to learn as many of the Sixty-four Arts as they can, including music, singing, sciences, lovemaking, homemaking, poetry, dance, shooting of the bow and arrow, conversation, sewing, art, games, magic, chemistry, perfumery, and rituals. Refinement and accomplishment were important and were not gender specific.

QUESTION?

What does the term *Kama sutra* mean?
Kama is pleasure or sensual desire. It is the name of the Indian god that represents the sexual nature in man. *Sutra* is a short book or aphorism.

A Catalog of Aphrodisiacs

In ancient India, the use of aphrodisiacs and their preparation was common and well known to many. Items like datura, honey, ground black pepper, a corpse's winding-sheet, peacock bone, sulfur, pumpkin seed, bamboo shoots, cactus, monkey feces, and ram's testicle were used for enslaving, potency, and endurance.

Some of these ingredients, such as pumpkin seed and datura, are actually well known for their potency-enhancing qualities. However, it may be better for you to stick with some of the more easily procured supplements that are detailed in Chapter 13.

Other Ancient Sex Manuals

Ancient books like the Kama sutra are manuals on lovemaking that were written by people of various cultures for different purposes. For instance, many are guides for newlyweds on kissing, touching, positions in lovemaking, attitudes, moral obligations, and much more. Though Westerners know them to be about positions, these books have a lot more to teach us.

The Ananga-Ranga

The Ananga-Ranga was written in the sixteenth century in India. This manual includes morals, seduction techniques, sexual positions, hygiene, rituals and sexual spells, aphrodisiacs, and other erotic concepts. It pays particular attention to the woman learning to control her pelvic floor muscles to heighten the experience between her lover and herself.

The Perfumed Garden

The Perfumed Garden was written in Arabia in the sixteenth century. It has a treatise on the many different sizes and shapes of male and female sexual organs. Written primarily for men, the Perfumed Garden counsels them to find out from the woman what she likes and ask her for instruction on giving it to her. It speaks highly of God and the gift of pleasure that God has given to humans. It also contains teaching stories of various sorts and many intercourse positions.

The Ishimpo

The Ishimpo was a manual that originated in Japan as the erotic teaching manual for that culture. Similar to its counterparts in India and other parts of Asia, it depicts the sex act between man and woman as the essential force that controls the universe. It expresses the importance of making love as the force in nature that keeps Earth circling the Heavens.

FACT

Metaphors filled the erotic lives of ancient sexual explorers. In the Secrets of the Jade Bed Chamber, the penis is described as the Jade Stalk; the vagina is called the Jade Garden.

The Secrets of the Jade Bed Chamber

Exciting many Chinese couples, this treatise on sexuality and sensuality included recipes for potency remedies, exotic positions, and counseling on the ways of love. As with many societies that included eroticism in their cultural heritage, there is symbolism in the words selected for use in the books and by lovers.

Pillow Books

In addition to teaching manuals, China, Japan, and many other Eastern cultures also had pillow books, which were used by couples as erotic stimulants and as reminders of the vast sexual potential any couple could tap in to. Beautifully made pillow books were adorned with erotic pictures, poetry, writings, and suggestions that couples could partake of together to stir their passions.

In the past few decades, there has been a resurgence of erotic manuals, picture books, illustrated instruction books, and a wide variety of resources to educate and reconnect people with their sexual nature. As these materials become available, more people begin to speak openly about sexuality and sensuality. The result is an increasing awareness of our sexual nature and of the variety of touches and pleasurable sensations that turn each of us on.

Positions You Thought You'd Never Try

These ancient books have given us some positions we thought we'd never try. Trying some of them one evening may be just the thing you both need either to get you really involved in new ways to make love or to give you a great deal of laughter all evening long! With names like "donkeys in the third moon of spring," "crab position," and "tortoise position," don't you think you could have a little fun? Here are brief descriptions of a few positions:

- **The wheelbarrow:** The woman is standing on her hands and has her head on the floor or a pillow. The man is standing, holding the woman's legs. This position is very erotic to the man as he has a bird's-eye view of gorgeous buttocks and the pelvic freedom to thrust effortlessly. It's also known that inversion is quite good for your health, when done in moderation. A variation on this theme is to have the woman resting on a hassock or footstool so that she is a little higher up in relationship to her partner. Make sure the stool won't slip out from under the woman.

- **Suspended position:** The man stands against a wall or anything that will support his back, and the woman sits on his clasped hands as he holds her up. She is suspended by his arms and holds herself close to him with her own arms around his neck and her legs around his thighs. If she is very small, she can thrust by pushing her feet against the wall that is supporting the man.
- **Three legs position:** Both partners stand together. The woman places one foot between the man's two feet and lifts the other foot and leg so that her lover can hold her leg at the ankle at about the level of his waist.
- **Squatting position:** The man must have very strong, limber leg muscles for this one. He squats and his lover sits astride him, facing him. Her legs are left dangling in the air as he supports her. Subtle movements and rocking achieve the couple's ecstasy.
- **The swing:** What you need is any kind of swing that the two of you can fit on. If you have a love-swing, use that. A variety of positions can be played with, and best of all, one or both partners can be weightless.

Enjoy trying out these new positions, but be very careful, especially if you think any of these positions may be physically challenging. Endorphins, those chemicals your body produces when you're having fun, can cover up pain. (E)

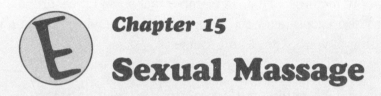

Chapter 15

Sexual Massage

Great sex should never be limited to sexual intercourse. One fun alternative is sexual massage. It's extremely pleasurable, and it's also about the safest of all safe-sex practices. Becoming an expert at massaging and erotically titillating your partner can be an exquisite addition to your sexual repertoire.

The Power of Pleasurable Touch

Learning many techniques to give and receive pleasure will benefit you and your partner throughout life. There will be times when intercourse isn't appropriate or when you want to give sustained pleasure to your partner so that he or she can simply focus on the pleasure without worrying about reciprocating it. Remember that sexual pleasure is a gift. Learning to give exquisite touch during sexual massage will deepen your understanding of your partner and yourself.

ALERT!

This chapter is written with two partners in mind, but the techniques described here are also very useful for masturbation. The strokes that will be described, when used in self-loving, can help you learn more about your own body. You can let your lover in on your discoveries when the time is right.

Massaging Your Man

During genital massage, find out if your man likes variety, change, and/or innovation. Be willing to ask for feedback and to try new things. Surprise him with some of the techniques in this chapter, then ask him how it feels. When you combine experimentation with focus and loving attention, you will be able to take him to new heights of pleasure. Some of the hand techniques in this chapter are useful for training a man to last longer, too.

Remember that when giving erotic touch, the giver's hands and heart should feel just as good—or even better—than the person receiving the massage. This may sound odd, but if you think about it, it makes perfect sense. We all know when someone is not present with us. We know when the heart is involved to its fullest. Be present with your partner. Focus your attention on how good it feels to give loving touch.

Men tend to like consistent strokes that are typically stronger and harder than women like when they are being touched sexually. They also like variety. Find out just how hard a touch he prefers and just how much variety he would like. Men tend to be very visual, so let your man see what it is that you are doing to him. Prop him up in a comfortable position and let him look.

When stroking his penis, you may have a "soft-on" or a "hard-on" to work with. Don't get the idea that one is better than the other. If he seems to be having a hard time relaxing, remind him to breathe deeply into his belly. Rub his belly to bring him into the present and remind him to just lie back and receive. Keep eye contact, when possible, and use lots of lubrication. He'll love the wet, shiny look; and the squishy sounds are erotic. Put the oil or lubricant on your hands first, to warm it up a bit.

Essentials for a sexual massage may include a candle, towels, good-quality oil, and water-soluble lubricant. Relaxing music is also a plus. And, of course, you'll need a warm, quiet area and some love and care to share.

Use your hands, feet, breasts, mouth, hair, fingernails, and anything else that might occur to you when stimulating him. Though we'll focus on hand strokes in this chapter, taking his penis and placing it between your breasts for a few strokes can be a real turn on!

Begin the Massage

Have your clean, relaxed partner lie down. Find a comfortable position that allows you to have both hands free. You may want to start with some light massage to his feet and chest and shoulders, as a warm-up. When you are ready to begin massaging his penis, put some lubrication or oil in your hands and gently rub your hands together to warm it.

With both hands, begin by gently stroking upward from his scrotum, up over his penis. Let your hands trail each other so that the motion feels continuous to him, one hand after the other. Move slowly at first and feel *your* hands enjoying the action.

For an extra-special treat, lovingly bathe your partner before a sexual massage. Use a warm towel to dry him and another to wrap him up as he lies down on the bed or another surface you've prepared.

Attention to the Head

Placing one hand firmly around the lower shaft of his penis, take your other hand and begin to gently pull upward with all your fingers on the corona, or the area where the shaft meets the head. This is a very sensitive area, and it loves attention. Pull, tug, and slide your fingertips around and under the head.

In a variation on this, while still holding the lower shaft with one hand, take the index finger and thumb of the other hand and make a ring around the corona. Now twist the two fingers around as far as you can go one way. Let go and make the stroke again and again. Don't move too fast. Ask your partner to coach you on the speed and pressure he likes.

Up and Down

This is the stroke that is the most commonly used by men to masturbate. It's also the one used the most by partners to stimulate the man. Using one hand, stroke the shaft of the penis evenly from the bottom to the head. Use a firm grip and a steady speed. Vary this stroke by putting more pressure on the thumb, either on the upstroke or the downstroke.

Another variation is to stroke just the head this way. You can add variety by doing a few strokes all the way up and down and then a few just over the head or tip of the penis. Then go deep again. You can also turn your hand over and lead downward with the thumb side of the hand, something a man would have trouble doing for himself.

Double-Handed Strokes

Using the basic up-and-down stroke, add the other hand to the base of the penis. Hold that hand in place, and use the other hand to do the stroking. The stationary hand can gently squeeze while the other hand is stroking.

Now, with the hand that is stroking, add a twist all the way down to meet the other hand. Twist up and then down. Get as much twist in as you can. Experiment with the pressure. And ask your partner for feedback.

Vary this by using both hands to do the stroking. Try them going the same direction, one after the other, and then try the hands going away from each other and then back together.

Exploring Down Under

Many men like their scrotum gently pulled. This can actually help keep him from ejaculating too quickly. In this move, gently cup his balls with one hand, making a ring around his scrotum with your index finger and your thumb. Pull down. With the other hand, stroke his penis in any way that feels good. You might try a long twist, all the way to the tip and back.

A full one-third of the penis is actually buried under the skin, behind the scrotum. With a liberal amount of lubricant, explore this area. Reach with your hand, under the balls, and gently feel for the root of the penis shaft. With enough lubrication, you can wrap your fingers around the whole shaft. Stroke up and down here while you are also stroking the exposed area of the penis. Men go wild over discovering this hidden area and its "virgin" nerve endings.

ALERT!

Time is a very precious commodity to most busy people. When you're receiving a sexual massage, be sure to show your appreciation with words, movements, and sounds. This will let your partner know how you feel and will assure her that she's giving you pleasure.

Another area that men often find very erotic is the area just to either side of the base of the penis. This is where the legs meet the body torso; many nerve bundles travel through this region. With lubrication, try stroking this area with an up-and-down motion.

You can also stroke and massage the perineum and anus areas while stroking the penis. Many men find this highly sensual and erotic. Some heterosexual men confess that they worry that they might be homosexual after discovering that they like to be touched in these ways. Anal eroticism is not unusual in heterosexual men. These areas have a high nerve count and are very erotic to the touch.

Taking It Higher

Invent some strokes of your own, combining a variety of moves. When you are ready to finish the massage, or if your partner has ejaculated, cup your hand over the penis and scrotum and just rest for a moment. Send your partner love and energy through your hands.

A massage like this can be the tool to learning and teaching ejaculation mastery. With the partner in control, having eye contact, using direct communication, and noticing things like breathing patterns, the two of you can be partners in training him to last for as long as he likes. This may eventually lead him to experience multiple orgasms without ejaculation.

Prostate, or P-Spot, Massage

The prostate gland and the urethral sponge, or G-spot, are very similar in composition. The prostate pumps the semen out the urethra during ejaculation. If a man is willing and wants to try prostate massage, it is highly recommended. Not only does it feel exquisite, it adds powerfully to the orgasmic sensations and helps keep the prostate gland healthy. While it doesn't take the place of seeing the doctor regularly, a man's partner can keep tabs on the health of his prostate, especially as he ages.

Prostate massage accesses the gland directly through the anus. While some may feel a little squeamish about this, it's not as unpleasant as you might think and the pleasure your partner may derive from it will make up for any initial discomfort you may feel. That said, prostate massage may not be for everyone, so don't push your partner to try it.

Step by Step

If you plan to give a prostate massage, make sure your man is very turned on. Perform oral sex, hand techniques, or any other form of foreplay to really turn your guy on. On a scale of one to ten, he should be at a seven or eight.

Have a latex glove, finger cot, or condom easily available. Use a high-quality lubricant and be generous in the amount you use. Don't use oil; use a water-based lubricant like Astroglide.

With the glove on, spread a liberal amount of lubricant over the area. Tease and play with him a little. Remind him to relax and just enjoy the sensations. Make sure you are continuing to stimulate his penis in whatever manner he likes.

When you feel he might be ready, ask permission to enter him. Use your longest finger. Go very slowly, reminding him to breathe deep into his belly and relax his anal muscles. Notice any changes in breathing, muscle tightness, and arousal. Heighten the stimulation to the penis. Be gentle when your finger is inside him. Move slowly.

Stimulating the Gland

Once inside, reach, with palm up, and feel for the gland. It will feel like a large, soft Life Saver. The center will have a slight, soft indentation, and the round structure should feel firm but somewhat pliable. It will be about the size of a walnut.

FACT

Medications cause about 25 percent of all cases of erectile dysfunction in men. Erectile dysfunction is twice as common in men who smoke as in men who don't smoke.

Gently explore the sides and center while keeping the stimulation going to the penis. Ask for feedback. As he becomes more turned on, try more pressure. Like the G-spot, the prostate generally can take quite a lot of pressure. Try tapping, rubbing, ringing around the edges, and just holding pressure on the middle indentation.

When you are both finished with this exploration or if he has had an orgasm with ejaculation, don't pull your finger out fast. Ask your partner to take a few deep breaths and as you remind him to relax, slowly bring your finger out. Thank each other for his vulnerability and for your willingness to try this technique.

The first time you try this, you may not get the full erotic feel of it. Keep exploring. After the second or third time, men, you'll really begin to enjoy this massage, but wait a few days before you try it again.

Massaging Your Woman

Women's sexual parts are for the most part hidden, but even so, there are many wonderful techniques that have been pioneered in the past by sexual explorers who have developed strokes and techniques in erotic genital massage for women.

Generally speaking, women like words. Loving words are like a massage to their inner being. Use them when you are giving attention to your woman. Women generally like a much softer touch than men do—especially when it comes to genital touching.

Some women need to learn that it is okay to have pleasure, period. You may find yourself playing an important role—being her guide in the realm of pleasure permission. If such is the case, be generous and compassionate with her.

A woman's vulva and genitals are comprised of mucous membranes that are tender and easily irritated. High-quality lubrication is required in liberal doses. A great guideline for touch is to pretend that there is a bubble of lubricant between the finger of the giver and the surface of her genitals. Then, you can let her know that she can ask for firmer touch when she's ready for it. Some women like consistent moves that continue for quite a while. Other women like to have the touch varied and for change to occur often. Find out what your woman likes.

Remember that, in general, it's less socially acceptable for women to touch themselves throughout their adolescence than it is for men. Your partner may never have explored herself and may need time to discover what works for her and what she likes.

Getting Started

After a relaxing bath, dry your lover with a towel and position her on the bed. She should be lying on a fairly flat surface and shouldn't use too many big pillows—they can keep the body from fully responding to orgasms by collapsing it and blocking the flow of energy. Remind her to breathe deeply into her belly and to relax.

Put some oil on your hands and rub them together briefly. Start with her breasts, and then move on to massaging her belly. Some men have a tendency to use firm touch, but your lover is more likely to respond if you use a light touch.

Apply some more oil and begin to gently brush your hands, one after the other, upward, over her pubic mound. Lightly brush the hair and move slowly. On about the fourth pass over her pubic mound, begin to let your two first fingers delve a little deeper, just over the labia majora, spreading the pubic hair as you do. Repeat these strokes for a while to really build up a charge.

Moving to the Inner Areas

Switch to a good-quality water-based lubricant now (massage oil and interior mucous membranes don't go together very well). Now with both of your hands, gently spread the lips of her vulva. Do this as if you are doing it for the first time—with wonder and awe. Look at her vulva for a moment and tell her how beautiful she is. Begin to lightly touch her inner labia. You can stroke with your fingertips and gently pull on the lips.

With your index and middle finger on either side, stroke from the bottom of her vulva, up, along both sides to the clitoris, and beyond. Repeat this stroke a few times. Now go in the opposite direction. Ask her how that feels. Does she need a firmer touch or a lighter touch? Would she like you to go faster or slower?

Attending the Clitoris

After you have explored this area thoroughly, move to the clitoral tip. Place your same two fingers above the clitoris and move the hood gently up and down. Now with one hand hold the hood back, away from the clitoris, and with your other hand apply some lubrication.

Begin to explore her clitoris slowly and gently. Move, in very small increments, around the whole outer edge. As you go around, ask your lover what she feels in that particular area. Notice if she reacts more in some areas than in others. Watch for signals her body gives like shifting or slight curling. These may be signs that she needs a lighter touch. Let her know what you are observing.

Once you have located her most sensitive spot, begin small movements in that location. Go in a clockwise direction first; then reverse. See which one she prefers. Now try moving up and down over this exact spot. How is that for her? Stick with the one she likes best for a while and make eye contact whenever you can.

ALERT!

The more we know about our bodies, the more we will know how to use them. It's like playing a fine musical instrument. The more practice, the more beautifully the instrument responds to the player.

The Clitoral Shaft

Move your two fingers up over the clitoris and place them on both sides. Run your fingers up and down slowly in this area and see if you can detect the clitoral shaft. Now that she is probably more turned on, you may be able to feel it under the skin. It will swell along with the tip of the clitoris.

Continue with this stroke. Bring your fingers close together so that the clitoris is actually slightly squeezed between the two fingers, as you go down over the top. This should be sending some exciting energy to your lover. You might try stroking one side and then the other. One of the sides may be more sensitive than the other because there are more nerve endings there.

If your partner is getting pretty turned on at this point, continue doing the strokes that she likes best. Listen to her responses, both audible and not. Remind her to breathe and relax as she moves deeper into higher levels of arousal. She may want to have an orgasm with just this stimulation or she may want to move on to G-spot massage.

Chapter 12 has detailed instructions for finding the G-spot and massaging it. Read this part of the book and refresh your memory if need be. If your lover is ready and desires to add G-spot stimulation, then proceed.

Massaging the G-Spot

Be sure you are positioned comfortably, so that your hands are free. Use one of your hands to continue stroking the clitoris and clitoral shaft. When you think she's ready, ask to enter her vagina with your finger. As you slowly do it, find her G-spot and hold your finger firmly on it for a few moments. Your lover should give you verbal or nonverbal indication that you're on the right area.

Begin to use some of the G-spot strokes you learned in Chapter 12. As you do, time your movements with the movements of your fingers over her clitoral shaft. As you do, be aware that you are stimulating both poles of the woman's sexual parts. As you may remember, the G-spot actually sits between the two legs, or crura, of the clitoris. As the clitoris and clitoral shaft swell with blood, so does the G-spot. These two hot spots are very close together, and as the woman begins to understand and recognize the feelings in this region, she experiences a much fuller sense of her sexual potential.

Continue with this massage for as long as your lover desires. Try the different modalities of strokes and change the pressure you apply to see what she likes. Watch her breathing. Her breath is the key to orgasm and multiple orgasm, so make sure she's breathing deep into her stomach.

Anal Massage

The anal area has many nerve endings and can be a wonderful addition to sexual massage. See if your partner is willing to explore some touch in that area. It doesn't have to mean that she'll be willing to have anal sex later. It just means she is willing to try having more pleasure.

Use a finger cot, a condom, or a latex glove if you'd like. Apply a liberal amount of lubrication. The walls of the anus and vagina are thin. Beyond the very sensitive entrance of the anus, she should be able to feel the G-spot through the wall of the anus. Try massaging her in that area and see. Gently explore around.

Continue to massage and stimulate her clitoris as you have been doing. Again, dance your fingers in time to each other. Be creative in your dance as a way of showing her that you love giving her attention.

Closing

When the two of you decide that you want to bring this session to a close, or if she has had an orgasm or two and wants to be finished, take a deep breath together and relax. Your hand should still be inside her. Now, let her know that you are going to remove your finger or fingers from her and ask her to "breathe" them out.

ALERT!

Never put a finger that has been in or around the anus into a woman's vagina—it may result in an infection. Play it safe by always washing with soap after any anal play.

When you are out, place your hands so that one is on her tummy and one is on her pubic mound. Eye gaze and breathe together. Hold her vulva close, as if protecting her, for a few minutes. The pressure on this area feels very good, supportive, and nurturing.

Thank your partner.

Chapter 16

Fun in the Bedroom

When it comes to lovemaking, there are a myriad of fun things you can do with your lover. As you get better at creating new things for you and your partner to experience, your communication and intimacy will increase. Deeper intimacy is a natural byproduct of shared fun.

Sexy Rituals and Traditions

The word "ritual" may sound daunting, but it need not be so. Anything you do to give an event special meaning or significance (like a birthday celebration) qualifies as a ritual. Rituals and traditions make ordinary occurrences more memorable.

A ritual or tradition can be anything you make it. It can be as simple as fixing a candlelit dinner with music and a sensual dessert or as elaborate as creating an entire evening that includes lighting incense, playing special music, toasting each other, erotic dancing or touching, and hours of intense lovemaking. A ritual is designed by you to fit your particular needs and taste.

The key to creating a ritual is to put your attention on it and your intention in it. You are creating a conscious event that is meant for a purpose. That purpose can be defined, acknowledged, and structured so that it enhances whatever state you want to embody or experience.

Putting It Together

For a sensual and sexual ceremony you will want to choose a theme and setting to enhance your intent. Consider the purpose of the ceremony. It may be that you have an anniversary coming up, a special day that was a first for you and your partner, or a birthday. Or perhaps you simply wish to celebrate your relationship.

Once you know what your intent is, you can put together your own ritual. Here are some ideas for what you may consider including:

- Create an invocation or intention for the occasion. This could be as simple as expressing your love for each other and your wish to honor that love by setting aside this special time.
- Light a candle together as a symbol of your union. A flame is eternal and can serve as a reminder of your everlasting love.
- Light incense to bring you to fuller awareness of all your senses. Our

sense of smell deeply affects our memory. It provides us with another anchor by which to associate an event. It can remind us of a deep religious or transcendental experience that we have had and this can extend to our memories of our beloved.

- Share how you feel about your partner, speaking from your heart. This creates emotional connection between you.
- Music has a powerful impact. Music sets a special tone that, when used wisely, will completely transform and guide an evening. Consider the tone you wish to set: soft and sensual to hot and spicy to holy and serene.
- Incorporate a new sex toy or sensual aid into your ceremony; you can try using a soft fur mitt, a feather, a soft paintbrush, a rose petal, velvet, silk, or sensual foods such as whipped cream.
- Movement and dance can be a powerful aid to building an erotic charge. Take turns following each other's movements, as a way of harmonizing and synching energy in the early stages of foreplay.
- Get silly, especially if this isn't normally the way you behave around your partner. What often makes a memorable experience is something out of the norm. Give yourself permission to try things outside the bounds of your usual expression.

When you create ceremonies for yourself and your lover, you are creating new stories of your relationship and staging a play in which you can be a hero, a siren, or even a villain! This ability to expand the limits of your lovemaking will soon extend into your everyday life, as well. It will give you permission to become more creative with other people and situations in your life.

Love Ceremony for Valentine's Day

Valentine's Day is the classic time to create a love ceremony. A special dinner, whether at home or out, sets the scene for giving gifts and flowers, spending the evening with your partner and loved one, and honoring the deep connection and special place you hold in your hearts for each other. The intention is clear and the event is universally recognized. Yet, within this one special day a year, there are many variations to be discovered and created. Here's a Valentine's Day ceremony you can adopt or use as inspiration to create one for yourself.

FACT

> Many pagan festivals were reincarnated later as Christian holidays. Valentine's Day originated in early Roman times as a festival of games of sexual license that foretold of the return of spring. It was later Christianized to a day of love and overseen by Saint Valentine, a Christian martyr.

Set aside two hours for the ritual and an additional hour to create the "set and setting" before the two of you get together. You may need to purchase candles, flowers, fruit (like mango, papaya, small juicy oranges, and kiwi), chocolates, and a sipping liqueur (if you drink alcohol). You may also wish to exchange gifts during the ritual.

Peel, slice, and arrange the food on a plate. This need not be a large amount as we are tempting the senses of smell and taste, not eating to be full. Pour a small single glass of the liqueur or whatever drink you desire. The two of you will share this glass.

Arrange the bedroom with clean sheets and pillows. Set the candles in several areas of the room that appeal to you. Place one or two candles in the bathroom. Pick soft, sensual music to play. If you've purchased flowers, place them on a table next to the fruit and drink, where you will be able to see them.

When you come together for your evening, tell your partner how excited you are to be having this special time together. Tell three specific things that you appreciate about him or her. At this time, you may also exchange gifts, or you can wait until later.

Take a sensual bath together. Dry each other slowly and accompany your partner to the bed. Harmonize your energy by lying in the "spoon" position. Place the top hand on the heart center and breathe slowly and deeply together for five minutes.

Exchange massages. Begin without using oils to give a light, fingertip-only massage and gradually explore the subtleties of touch on different areas of the body. Apply a little oil and use a firmer touch, making sure to keep it sensual. The hands giving the touch should be feeling just as exquisite as the body receiving it.

◀ To really connect, gaze into your partner's soul through the eyes.

Now face each other, eyes open, and gaze into each other's eyes. Spend a few minutes like this, breathing slowly and deeply into the belly. Gently begin your lovemaking.

There's no rush. Take it slowly and enjoy every moment. Remember to breathe into your belly—full, slow breaths. And remember not to get goal oriented by getting preoccupied about coming or not coming. Fill your senses with the sight, sound, and smell of your beloved.

Use the food and drink that you've prepared to excite the senses. Tease a little. Ask your partner to close his eyes and let him briefly smell what you are offering first. Lightly brush the morsel across his lips, allowing him to feel the fruit's texture.

Intimate weekends away are fun! As a surprise, bring a new sex game, some dress-up clothes, a sexy gift for your partner, sensual food, velvet handcuffs, or a pillow book with pictures of new positions. Spend lots of time in your hotel room together and feed each other the food provided by room service.

Weave and dance through your lovemaking. Speak to your beloved. Be vulnerable and open, even if it's not that easy for you to do. Remember that your lover wants to hear what you are feeling. Tell your partner how much you appreciate his love. Let him know how precious this time is to you.

Sensual Food Fun

Playing with your food takes on a whole new meaning in the sensual and sexual context. The possibilities are almost endless when you consider how many foods are considered either sensual in their texture and appearance or actually have aphrodisiac properties. Whipped cream and chocolate sauce in bed is just the beginning.

Create a sensual meal that is made up of finger foods. Include textures that are sensual to the mouth and lips. Place the food in a beautiful setting—why not recline over pillows strewn on the floor? Make a rule: Neither one of you can feed yourself, but you can feed each other!

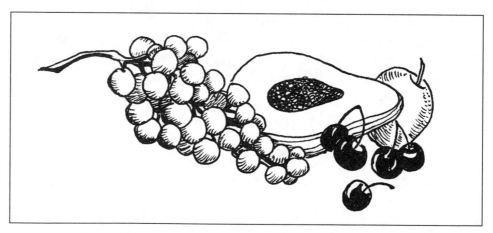

▲ Food can be a sensuous part of your foreplay.

There are good books available on this subject. Try Diana De Luca's *Botanica Erotica* for more fun ideas. She includes body butter recipes, erotic drinks, a guide to erotic herbs, and a variety of food ideas in addition to recipes for making your own tinctures.

Sugar is one of the worst things you can put into a vagina. Anything with even a slight amount of sugar in it can cause immediate reactions and can lead to a yeast infection in the woman, and possibly in the man. Be extra careful when playing with food applied to the body.

Intimate Games

Simple games can have a unique place in intimate relationships. They can be fun and they can be challenging. Some people will take to them a little easier than others. Know your partner and, if you are going to introduce the idea of games into your love-play, pick ones that will be fun for both of you.

Games can teach you new things about your partner. They can gently push boundaries and open new realms. And they can open up a Pandora's box full of dark secrets, perceived danger, and adventure. Mostly, though, they are fun and a good cause for humor and lightheartedness. They introduce a new approach to sexuality that we don't often come up with ourselves, and they can be cause for opening up the imagination for creation of your own fun and games.

It's important to remember to respect your partner at all times. If something isn't working for one of you, the game is over. Many love games involve surrender and receiving. It is difficult for some people to completely receive from the other. This is something that can be learned. Here are a few ideas to get the juices flowing.

Take Away One of Your Senses

Sight is a powerful sense—perhaps the strongest of all our senses. It is the first sense we draw on in everyday life. It is a powerful driver of experience. When we take it away, we give much more control to our other senses.

Play a lover's game that will help you heighten your senses and increase your awareness of touch and sensation. As part of an evening of experimental fun, you can create a game around the sense of touch without the sense of sight. Design an evening of exploratory fun that will also train the two of you to pay attention to your other senses.

Find a rose, a piece of very soft fur, a new art-style paintbrush, a feather, or anything that will produce a very sensual feel. You might even want to have a few ice cubes handy. Have a soft scent in a misting bottle and a gentle bell or chime handy. Gather at least four items. Set the scene by lighting candles, putting on soft erotic music, and having something to nibble (strawberries, a little chocolate, or some mango pieces will do!) and something to drink close by. Blindfold your lover. Now use your imagination.

Read erotic stories to each other. Find a "pillow book" like one of the ancient ones—the Kama sutra or The Perfumed Garden. Try some of the things that you read about.

Swimming in Oil

You can also create a fun game using warmed olive oil. To play, set the scene and the mood by lighting candles and making sure the room is warm. On the floor, throw some towels or an old rug that you don't mind staining. Also prepare extra towels and something to drink and nibble on, and 2 to 3 cups of olive oil, gently heated in a saucepan. You can add a few drops of a pure essential oil for fragrance, if you wish.

When you are ready to begin, both of you should shower. If you have long hair, you may want to pull it back. Put on your favorite erotic music. As you are sitting on the towels, begin to apply olive oil generously to each other's bodies. Go ahead and really get into it. You're going to get very oily!

As you oil each other, you'll notice an incredible freedom to slip and slide all over each other's bodies. Enjoy this sensual experience to the maximum. You'll feel as though you've never had so much of your body touched and stimulated at one time. Be playful. Fun is the name of the game here.

If you want to move on to making love, you need to clean off the oil first; salad oil may not be your lubricant of choice.

Talk to some of your friends about what fun and different things they've tried in their intimate relationships. Most people love to share this kind of information. You can exchange stories, and new ideas may pop up, too.

Pulp Fiction

Write your own "pulp fiction." Each of you can write an account of your ideal erotic fantasy, and read these aloud to each other. This is a great turn on! And it's a wonderful exercise in spontaneous self-expression. Get pens and paper, and just write. Don't think. Just write for ten minutes. Or pick another erotic subject that you have thought of ahead of time. Take turns coming up with the subject. Examples: "The best orgasm I ever had" or "The riskiest sex I ever had." Read these to each other.

Or you can use an intimate apparel catalog as a starting place for an intimate story. Have either the models in the catalog or you two be the subjects. Create an erotic adventure tale.

Use Your Imagination

There are hundreds of other games you can play with your lover. Here are a few more ideas:

- **The magic wand:** Give your partner a magic wand for an evening. You may actually want to decorate a wand and make it unique. Make a ceremony to present it to him or her. What will he or she wish for?
- **Servant and master:** Play a game of cards—any game will do. Have the loser be the slave or be in service to the winner for a half-hour. The winner should make sure to ask for exactly what she or he wants from the servant.

- **Strip tease:** Dress up in the sexiest clothes you have. Layer your undergarments so you have lots to take off—you can use a large filmy scarf, gloves, hats, and coats. Then, start stripping. When you're down to almost nothing, use the scarf or a sarong to do an erotic dance for your partner.
- **Toe zones:** Try a little toe sucking on your woman. As you begin, imagine that you're performing fellatio on her. Wet your lips and begin sucking really slowly, starting with the smallest toe—save the big toe for last. Try the moves you would like her to use when she's giving you oral sex.
- **Board games for lovers:** Purchase a board game or card game for lovers and present it to your partner as a gift. Get one that looks good to you and is not too silly. Try Erostrix from the Tantra.com catalog, at ✍ *www.tantra.com.*

Be Creative

As you move from games to lovemaking, be creative—don't just opt for the same few positions in bed. If you've got some privacy, explore the rest of your house. The kitchen table is often the perfect height for intercourse. Try the counter for oral sex. Have the woman bend over the arm of the overstuffed chair in the living room for rear entry. The women can also sit on the arm of the sofa and have her partner kneel on the cushions as he enters her. This is a good position in which to put one of your feet up on the back of the couch. Choose the side of the couch that will best allow you freedom of movement and maximum G-spot access.

ALERT!

The most important point here is that you should feel free to be creative and experiment. Take turns thinking up new places and ways to make love. You've nothing to lose and a whole lot of fun to gain!

Get yourselves a hassock—they are fantastic for a modified yab-yum position (see Chapter 10). The man sits on the hassock and his partner sits on top of him and closes her legs around him. He supports her back with his hands. This position is easy on the man's back. It gives both partners the freedom to rock, grind, and undulate to their hearts' content.

Another option is to forget furniture altogether and spread a lush carpet or blanket in front of the fireplace. Bring as many pillows out as you can find, to give you a variety of options for shaping your environment to suit the positions you might want to try.

Hanging Around

Consider the purchase of a love-swing. These are portable, fun, and versatile, and they work well for new position variations. Men find them a good tool for learning ejaculation control. They promote multiple orgasmic response in both men and women. Because they're so portable, you can hang them in strategic locations around your home and garden and enjoy them anywhere. Just put a few hooks up in the spots you like and hang it up when you're ready.

Take It Outside

The ancient Kama sutra texts talk about the physical health and psychological growth that can become available to you when you break away from your normal habits of lovemaking. When you move into nature, for example, you can mimic the birds and the bees, the lioness and her suitor, or two fishes swimming side by side. Being outdoors can add an element of mystery and erotic excitement to the sex act. You can become more aware of yourself and your partner when you remove yourselves from your usual surroundings.

It's often difficult, in modern living situations, to get to an outdoor place that feels safe for expressing sexual love. If you have a backyard that is private, you can create specially landscaped areas that may be conducive to lovemaking. Or try a gliding porch swing, a piece of lawn furniture, or a love-swing in different places around the yard or in the house. All these things will add titillating new variations to your lovemaking.

Animal Desire

You may be inspired by the wild sexuality displayed in mating rituals of different animals. Go to the zoo with your partner or look at nature videos. Check out how the animals do it. In many ancient societies, it was believed that animals can teach and inspire us in our own lovemaking.

Go out into nature and observe, and get inspiration for new positions. Swim like the fishes and try undulating together underwater. Use your nails to scratch lightly and your mouth to bite lightly. Use sound to add to the variety. Growl and howl, groan and whimper, moan and hum!

FACT

"An ingenious person should multiply the kinds of love-making after the example of the many different kinds of birds and beasts. For these different ways of loving, performed according to the traditions of different countries and the preference of individuals, generate love, friendship, and respect." —The Kama sutra

Share Your Fantasies

Everyone fantasizes at one time or another. Whatever your fantasies are, they're best shared with your partner. If you are fantasizing by yourself, you are not present with your lover. Your lover deserves your full attention, so bring him or her into your fantasy by sharing it.

When your lover receives all your attention, there won't be any room left for jealousy or feelings of being inadequate, and then you'll be free to share all your fantasies without the fear of offending your lover. Fantasies are part of the creative juice that fuels us. When you are creating a great meal or a love ritual, you are bringing a fantasy to life.

Tell each other your fantasies. Better yet, write them down for each other. That exercise alone will take off some of the edge for both of you. If you are both willing, pick one of your fantasies and plan to incorporate it into your lovemaking soon. Pick one you both like—one that takes some shared planning. That way you can both be completely involved and claim it for both of you.

Do you use fantasy in your lovemaking?
In an online survey of 2,400 people at Tantra.com, 9 percent answered "always," 26 percent answered "never," and 65 percent answered "sometimes." Of those who do use fantasies, 35 percent never let their partner know about the fantasy.

You'll get better at playing with fantasies if you keep your verbal communication going. Respect each other's boundaries, and make sure that what you are doing together is mutual. It's fun to risk a little of your ego and go for it sometimes, but remember that if any negative feelings come up, you should talk about them as soon as they occur. Discover new ways to make it a little safer next time or maybe even a bit more adventurous!

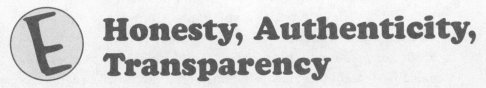

Chapter 17

Honesty, Authenticity, Transparency

Great sex depends on great communication. The only trouble is most of us grew up in families where communication was not so great. Too often, people avoid communicate in order to avoid trouble, but lack of communication makes it impossible for a couple to achieve deep intimacy. For intimacy and trust to flourish, you'll need to risk being completely honest.

Everyone Has Secrets

Do you remember what it was like as a child growing up? Was it safe to express yourself fully and spontaneously? If you are like most people, you learned early on that it's not always safe to tell the truth—especially if you have bad news to share.

So now that you have a lover or spouse, if you're bothered by something your partner does, you may be afraid to mention it for fear of offending your significant other. Or perhaps you have a secret sexual desire or preference that you don't want to let your partner know about because you think it might be considered odd or distasteful.

When doing active listening, it is very important that both people get a turn to be the talker and the listener—even if only one person appears to have a problem that needs to be discussed.

Just about everyone has secrets that they don't share with their partner. Secrets seem to be normal, given the fears of rejection and disapproval that most people live with. The only trouble with secrets is this: The more secrets you keep from your partner (that is, the more you withhold from him or her), the less intimate you are as a couple. Open, honest communication leads to intimacy, trust, and a feeling of closeness. Keeping secrets, avoiding certain topics, and playing it safe are all actions that lead to a less intimate relationship.

How Much Intimacy Do You Want?

It is your choice how intimate you want to be with someone. Take a moment to take stock of your past and current relationships. How honest are you? What do you tell yourself about how safe it is to be completely honest? Notice the choice you are making regarding how intimate to be. And notice if this is a pattern: Have you done things this way all you life?

Try not to view your choice as either good or bad. It is simply what you are comfortable with. Many people choose to have more comfort (i.e., playing it safe) and less intimacy (i.e., not risking showing who you really are). If this is true of you, you can at least admit that. You can at least be honest with yourself.

There are many reasons a person may choose to avoid being open with his or her partner; here are a few common explanations:

- My partner couldn't handle the truth.
- My partner would rather be lied to.
- It's not a good time.
- We don't know each other well enough yet.
- I don't want to make my partner uncomfortable.
- I don't want to hurt my partner.
- I'm afraid I won't be able to handle the reaction.
- I'm afraid my partner will reject me or leave me.
- I'm ashamed of what I did.
- I imagine I have to be perfect to be loved.

Risking Greater Intimacy

Let's say you have decided that you do want to create more intimacy in your life. So you decide you want to take more risks and be more open. You want to let your partner see your wants, likes, dislikes, jealousies, hurts, angers, fears, and vulnerabilities—even though you may also have some fears about revealing yourself to your partner.

Try to determine what risks you're actually taking by being honest and up-front with your partner. Is it foolish to fess up or to keep things hidden? What hurts you more, telling your partner what you think or keeping your thoughts a secret?

Let's take a look at what you imagine you might lose if you were more open, just so you'll know. Let's examine all the fears you have about speaking your truth. Here's an exercise to do right now:

1. Think of something you are afraid to tell your partner.
2. Make a list of all the "bad" things that you think could happen if you shared this.

3. Now, make a list of all the good things you imagine could happen if you shared it. Don't worry if they are likely or unlikely to happen. Just write what could happen.

4. Now, either write out or imagine how you would express your withheld communication to your partner. How do you feel now that you imagined saying this to your partner?

While you do not know exactly how this conversation would go in real life (you can't know that), the simple act of expressing your feelings, even on paper, helps you feel less fearful and more confident. You have been honest with yourself, and that is a big first step.

You may notice that you feel better after unburdening yourself like this. An act of honest self-expression often helps people feel lighter, freer, and more loving. Even the act of contemplating being more open—as you did in this exercise—can help.

Being Honest in Real Time

If you are committed to more real-life, up-close intimacy, which means communicating more openly with another person, the next step is to invite your partner to join you in this daring adventure. Intimacy is a game for two. It is one of the most fulfilling ways two people can be together. And when you add sex into the mix—WOW!!!

So if you want to invite your partner into your innermost being, start by painting a picture of how you envision this deeper intimacy enhancing your relationship. Here's how one woman described her vision to her partner: "Darling . . . I just read in this book about how sharing our deepest secrets, longings, wants, hurts, and everything makes people feel safer and closer and more trusting. I feel like I'm taking a risk in asking this, but I want that kind of a relationship with you—one where we don't keep secrets, where we can be open and vulnerable, even if it makes us uncomfortable and scared sometimes. What do you think?"

Then, she waited silently. Even though her partner took some time to respond, she just kept quiet. And when he did respond, she listened. She didn't interrupt when he expressed his reservations. Instead, she asked, "Tell me more about why you say that." And in the end, he had talked himself through all his fears and reservations and concluded, "Hey, let's try it. I'm not too good at this stuff, but I like the idea of feeling closer and more trusting. I like that a lot."

Sharing Your Wants and Longings

Once you and your partner have agreed that honesty is the best policy, the first step is to practice a very important honesty skill, which is "being transparent." Being transparent means you communicate what you are thinking, feeling, or wanting without any intent to change or control your partner. Your intent is simply to reveal yourself, to be transparent.

ALERT!

An important reminder: You can only be honest about yourself! Your judgments about someone else are *not* about yourself—unless they are shared as a self-disclosure with transparency as the goal.

Being Transparent in Lovemaking

Imagine that your partner is doing something to you in a way that feels irritating rather than pleasurable. Has this ever happened to you? If it has, you may have felt inhibited about speaking up about it. You may have told yourself that this would ruin the moment or hurt your partner's feelings or something along those lines. The only problem is, if you do not tell your partner what you are feeling, you are no longer present with him or her. Your mind is somewhere else. And how does this affect your partner? You might think, "What she doesn't know won't hurt her." But in something as sensitive as lovemaking, this is rarely the case. If you are not present, your partner will sense it.

What's a Lover to Do?

In attempting to be transparent in such a delicate situation, here are some things you could say; imagine yourself saying each of these things, and notice which ones might feel true for you:

- Sweetheart, I'm having difficulty being present. I'm thinking I'd love to have you do what you're doing a little softer (harder, faster, and so on).
- I'm distracted by some thoughts right now. Do you want to hear them?
- Honey, could you please do this (for example, stroke my breasts) now?
- What you're doing there is beginning to hurt. I'd like you to do that same thing, only over here.
- It would drive me wild if you would do that thing you did yesterday to me now.

If nothing on this list appeals to you, write your own list. And please don't worry about saying it just right. Even if you, or your partner, get uncomfortable, the important thing is that you express yourself in the interest of transparency. You'll get better and better with practice.

Dealing with Conflict and Differences

Once you make the choice to communicate honestly, you may begin to notice things about the relationship or your partner that you used to deny or be numb to. Giving yourself permission to speak the truth opens the way for more feelings to come up. This is a good thing. It means you're more alive, less shut down.

Given this heightened aliveness and openness, your differences are more likely to come up. You and your partner are going to need to practice another important honesty skill, "holding differences." Holding differences is the ability to listen to and empathize with another person's viewpoint without losing your own.

It does not matter if your differences are about sex or about some other area of your life. If you and your partner have unresolved disagreements, hurts, and resentments, it will affect your intimacy and ultimately your sex life.

There are a number of techniques that professional counselors use to help their clients learn to hold differences and resolve conflicts. Here are four very useful communication games that allow partners to vent their frustrations safely so they can get over them and get back into harmony: active listening, giving feedback, sharing withholds, and sharing resentments and appreciations. Each of these should be "played" or "conducted" at a certain agreed-upon time or in a certain agreed-upon "safe space."

Active Listening

This is a ritual that allows a couple to talk about something difficult. In this exercise, each person takes turns being the talker and the listener. When you are the talker, you make "I" statements about what you feel, think, and want, being careful to be honest about yourself and about your own experience (which is different from accusations or your judgments about the other person).

As the listener, you restate what you have heard, both so the talker knows you have been listening, and also so you practice describing a view that you may not agree with while still holding true to your own view. Once the talker feels heard, then the other person becomes the talker, and roles are reversed.

Giving Feedback

This exercise will help you learn a skill that is just as useful for preventing conflicts as it is for resolving them. It is a way of letting the other person know how his or her behavior has affected you.

Let's say you did not speak up last night when your partner was doing something that was irritating during lovemaking. Now it's the next day, and you get your partner's agreement that this is a good time to talk. Then you complete the following sentence: "When you [what was actually done, not the meaning you gave it], I felt [or I said to myself].

What I wanted [or what I would have preferred] was [this]." Then you might do a round or two of active listening.

Sharing Withholds

To perform this exercise, the couple holds this kind of a dialogue:

PERSON A: "There's something I've withheld from you. Would you like to hear it?"

PERSON B: "Yes."

PERSON A: "When you did or said [something that was actually done or said, not an interpretation], I felt [or I said to myself]."

PERSON B: "Thank you."

By talking in this manner, each person gets a turn to share his or her personal withholds.

Sharing Resentments and Appreciations

This is a practice that helps people clear the air on a regular basis, thus preventing little conflicts from turning into big conflicts. To begin, you'll need to decide together how often you will do the ritual: every day, every other day, weekly, and so on. Then assign one of you the responsibility of initiating the process (as in, "When is a good time to do our resentments and appreciations? Is now a good time?"). Take turns being the initiator, one week at a time.

Designate a safe, sacred space for the ritual by choosing a place in your home or yard where you will be uninterrupted and where you can sit facing each other. It's helpful to do the ritual in the same place every time you do it. That way when you walk into this room or area, you have the sense that you are entering a different mindset—a mindset in which you set aside any need to prove your point or bolster your position. Some people like to sanctify the space by doing something like lighting a candle, smudging, or burning incense.

Your aim is transparency—to know and be known. Revealing resentments is an act of making yourself vulnerable. We may fear that our resentments will appear selfish or petty or unenlightened and that it's a risk to reveal them.

Each person takes a turn sharing resentments. After that, each takes a turn sharing appreciations. It is best to start with resentments and end with appreciations, because if a person can clear their resentments first, their appreciations will be more sincere.

Use the words, "I resent/appreciate you for [this]," and be specific about what the other did, said, or did not do. If your partner is making an interpretation without giving you the data this is based on, ask, "Can you be more specific?" This is a signal for the partner to recognize that she or he is generalizing or making an interpretation. Asking for specifics also gives you the time to get centered so that you'll be less likely to overreact.

Some people like to decide on time limits for each person's turn. When it is the other person's turn, don't interrupt (except if you need to remind them to be more specific).

Then, share something that you appreciate about yourself. End the exercise by telling each other how much you appreciate being able to engage in this ritual for deepening your intimacy.

Going Out and Coming In Again

Another important honesty skill is the ability to "go out and come in again," to revisit a situation where things have gone badly between you and your partner. This is a nonthreatening way to take another try at resolving a situation that feels unfinished.

Think of a situation that you wish you had handled better. What specifically do you wish you had done, said, or not said? Now, imagine going to your partner and expressing this, sharing how you wish you had behaved. Do you notice any feeling of resistance to doing this?

Nobody's Perfect

One reason people deny themselves permission to go out and come in again is that they are busy criticizing themselves for not doing it right the first time. If this is true of you, do you really think that you can do everything right the first time? Everyone has the experience of thinking later what they wished they had done or said or not said. If you practice this honesty skill, you'll find that the gaps between when you had the opportunity to say something and when you actually do say it get smaller and smaller.

ALERT!

Don't try to be perfect in the way you communicate with your partner. As you get more practice going out and coming in again, you will become more self-forgiving and less of a perfectionist.

As you have probably already realized, intimacy does not require that you be perfectly honest. More often, it's about being *imperfectly* honest, that is, feeling and saying what you are aware of in the moment with the understanding that once you've expressed yourself, you'll realize that your true feelings are actually more or less than that. Or you may notice that your feelings have changed. That's why revising an earlier statement is such an important skill. You're never going to be "perfect, right, and done." You are always in process. Change is the name of the game of life.

Confront Your Fear

Usually when people allow themselves to imagine going out and coming in again, they become energized—a little scared, yes, but also excited. If you are contemplating trying this with a partner, and you're feeling fearful, tune in to the bodily sensations you normally associate with fear, and then notice whether it's excitement or fear that you are feeling.

Even if it's fear, you can probably still do it. Remember, in most cases fear is simply a sign that you're moving into unknown territory rather than a signal to turn back. Unknown territory is the domain of discovery and the breeding ground for self-trust. If, after you can feel and acknowledge your fear, it becomes less intense, then the risk is probably worth taking. You can probably handle it.

Making Amends

If you discover that your actions have harmed another person, going out and coming in again may not be sufficient. You may want to ask, "Is there some way I can make it up to you?" Asking this question is appropriate only if you sincerely wish to make amends. And while you're deciding if you sincerely want to, remember that achieving closure is as much for you as it is for the other person. It will help you feel complete, and you will not be distracted by unresolved issues.

Often just hearing that question from a partner helps to heal old wounds as well as the present one. People are often moved to completely let go of the hurt they were carrying: "No, I don't need anything from you. Just hearing that you're sorry means a lot."

FACT

Often when you take a risk and go out and come in again, your partner will follow suit and share how they, too, wish they'd done things differently. And that's what good communication is all about.

Practicing Making Amends: An Exercise

Think of a situation where you have done something that resulted in pain, harm, or loss to your partner. Recall exactly what you did or said, being as specific as possible. Notice any tendency you may have to make yourself feel guilty.

Guilt tripping can be a way of avoiding your true feelings. You focus more on how "wrong" you were (a judgment) than on what you actually did and how you feel (your experience). If you find yourself doing this, come back to the specifics of what you did and how you feel about what you did and about the consequences. Notice how you actually feel about the way your actions affected your partner. Feeling this, instead of focusing on what a bad person you were, is much more constructive.

Now make a list of things you might do for your partner to make up for whatever you did, to make amends. If you wish, contact him or her and make a time to meet in person so you can actually express what you feel and what you are willing to do about it. Let the other person look at your list and choose what he or she would like you to do to make amends.

Steps to Take When Revising

There are several steps you can take when dealing with any situation that needs revising:

1. First, let the other person know that you have had some second thoughts and make sure you have her or his attention. Invite your partner into conversation by stating that you'd like to revise what you said or did.
2. Don't make excuses. Take responsibility for what you said or did.
3. Report what has changed for you—what you are aware of now that you were not aware of at the time: "I had the realization that . . ." "I want to let you know what was really going on with me." "I want to make amends." In this step, use all the communication tools we have already identified in this book. Use "I" messages to help you stay in your own experience.
4. And, finally, listen to what the other person has to say, and aim to be more present this time. Leave space for the other to take a turn saying how she wishes she'd done things differently as well.

If you give yourself permission to revise and revisit whenever you need to, then you'll take each interaction more lightly. You don't have to try so hard to get things perfect the first time. Most things people do or say are not cast in stone. When your revision comes from an authentic place, usually the other person will sense the caring that it takes to make the effort to go out and come in again.

The Payoff

These communication practices teach you how to express and release emotions without getting stuck in them. You will discover that, after you express a feeling you have been holding back or suppressing, you feel more relaxed and whole. Your energy is flowing again, and with this renewed energy comes a sense of inner peace.

After doing one or more of these practices with a partner, you will soon find that topics that used to be off-limits are now easier to discuss. You will find it more natural to share your sexual desires, fears, fantasies, passions, and longings. As you grow closer in your communication, you will feel closer and safer with each other.

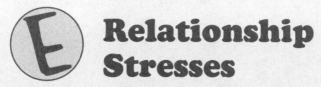

Chapter 18

Relationship Stresses

An intimate relationship is a container for sharing life's ups and downs with your partner. Over the course of your relationship, you will experience pleasure and pain, fulfillment and disappointment, harmony and power struggles—in fact, sex and money are the most frequent topics couples struggle with.

What You Can Expect

Power struggles are a fact of intimate life. If you've never been in an emotionally charged power struggle, you probably haven't been in a really intimate relationship! So what can you realistically expect? Certainly, it shouldn't be all work and no play! But neither is it all play and no work. When you're in a relationship, you can realistically expect the following:

- You will be disappointed.
- Your feelings will change.
- You won't meet each other's every need.
- You will learn how to forgive.

FACT

Research has shown that all couple relationships inevitably involve disappointed expectations. It's not the fact of being disappointed that affects trust; it's how couples communicate (or fail to communicate) about these issues.

You Will Be Disappointed

That's the bad news. The good news is that, with a little luck and a lot of work, you'll learn not to take these disappointments personally.

Intimate couples will inevitably encounter disappointment. When you know to expect this, when you know it does not mean "the beginning of the end," then you are more empowered to take disappointments in stride. You can communicate your hurt feelings to your partner and hear his or her response. You can discuss how you each experienced the incident in question. You can acknowledge that it was not your intent to hurt or disappoint, or that you wish you had not promised more than you could deliver. Then you can forgive and begin again—and again!

No Gunnysacking

In his classic *The Intimate Enemy*, famous "fair fighting" guru George Bach cautions couples to beware of saving up your disappointments and angers and then emptying the whole gunnysack onto your partner at once. When the sack finally gets so full it won't hold anymore and your partner does "one more thing" to set you off, you dump your collected grievances all over him or her:

- "You turned over and started snoring after we made love last New Year."
- "You cut me off in midsentence three times at your mother's birthday dinner."
- "How could you *not* know I was premenstrual when we took that workshop in New York back in 1999?"
- "You should never have walked out on me in front of the whole group!"

Imagine how you might feel receiving such a barrage of feelings. Would you feel defensive? Probably. Would you remember these incidents exactly as your partner did? Probably not! Would you wish you'd been told about these grievances sooner so you could clear up any misunderstandings? Perhaps. But just as likely, you might wish you could avoid such discussions entirely. You can, but if you do, the quality of your relationship (and consequently your sex life) will suffer.

ALERT!

Most people have unspoken expectations of their partner that they themselves may be unaware of. It's a good idea to have a conversation with your lover about both partners' secret expectations.

If You Really Loved Me

Saving up disappointments for later dumping is more likely to occur if you hold the belief that "if you really loved me, you would not do anything to hurt or disappoint me." Take a look right now at your own beliefs in this regard. Even if you have never uttered the words "if you really loved me," you may secretly harbor some ideas about what love means that your partner does not hold or that your partner does not realize that you hold.

To find out who expects what and which one of you will be disappointed by what, try this exercise with your partner. Each of you writes the sentence "If you really loved me . . ." at the top of a sheet of paper. Then, list all the things you can think of to complete this sentence:

. . . you would help around the house without my having to ask.
. . . you would buy me gifts when you go on business trips.
. . . you would hold my hand when we're walking down the street.
. . . you would touch me the way I've told you I like it without my having to repeat myself.
. . . you would tell me about the things I do right during lovemaking.
. . . you would tell me you love me at least once a day.
. . . you would tell me you're proud of me.

Of course, this list is just a sampling of the kinds of wants and longings partners keep secret from each other—until the gunnysack gets too full, and then everything comes tumbling out.

FACT

An expectation is a belief about how life should be. It is not necessarily how life is. This exercise is designed to help you get a healthy distance or detachment from your expectations. Maybe, after reading your list, you'll even be able to laugh at yourself a bit. That would be a good first step toward creating a relationship where disappointment (or disappointed expectations) is not taken personally.

Once you have both made your lists, read your partner's list, and discuss the differences, similarities, and surprises. Doing this exercise together can help you prevent needless disappointments. The statement

"If you really loved me, you would get home for dinner on time" can now be seen as nothing more than an expectation.

Your Feelings Will Change over Time

When you meet someone you find attractive, at first you will pay more attention to the positive, attractive aspects of that person. Even if you notice faults or foibles that you don't like, these will most likely take a backseat to the qualities you appreciate. This stage, which may be called the romantic stage, is just the first of five that most relationships go through as they mature. The other four are power struggle, stability, commitment, and cocreation.

It Begins with Romance

Romance is the stage in which we focus on our similarities and the things we like about each other. It is the stage in which we go out of our way to be pleasing. This allows a bond of trust to form, and we often feel that "here is a someone who will love me as I am. I can feel safe with this person."

Although this stage eventually passes, you can recall how it made you feel and bring some of those feelings back into the present. To help you reconnect with the essence of romance, recall what first attracted you to your partner. Take a few minutes to remember how you felt when you two were first falling in love. If you have never discussed this, or if you have not discussed it lately, make this a topic of conversation within a few days. It can help to rekindle some of those "young love" feelings.

As you reflect on that romantic getting-to-know-you period, you might also notice that some of the things that first attracted you have now changed. This fact could lead to disappointment, unless you can remember that change is to be expected. It's a necessary part of the journey. What most people do not realize is that once a strong trust bond is established in a relationship, partners tend to feel safe enough to reveal themselves and their negative aspects more fully.

If things have changed "for the worse," it's not because your partner was intentionally deceptive. It's more likely due to the fact that once a romantic bonding occurs, your partner feels safe and secure enough to be more open around you. This leads to the next stage, power struggle.

Intimacy doesn't just happen. It takes time, effort, and communication for a couple to become truly intimate with each other. While the romance stage is great, you won't achieve real intimacy until later stages in your relationship.

Power Struggle

During the romance stage, Curt and Vicki seemed to be perfectly matched sexually. They both had similar sexual appetites, and Vicki seemed to love everything Curt did. She would get turned on at his slightest touch. So why, after only a year, is their sex life almost nonexistent? Whenever Curt approaches her, she seems cold and unavailable. And when they do make love on occasion, why does she now complain that he's not present enough?

If anything like this has ever happened to you, remember that what you get to see of another person during the romance stage is like the tip of an iceberg. When you first meet someone, you cannot know this person all at once. You can't yet see what's hiding beneath the deep, dark waters—the other 85 percent of the iceberg that will get revealed over time.

The power struggle stage is the stage during which formerly hidden differences in wants, needs, and expectations rise to the surface. In Vicki's case, as she came to trust that Curt loved her, she was able to get more deeply in touch with dependency needs that had been with her since childhood—needs that she had not been conscious of herself.

Now, feeling the safety of her bond with Curt, she began to realize that her dad had never been there for her. This new awareness created in her a hypersensitivity to anything Curt might do that was similar to her dad. As a result, she became hypersensitive to Curt's "lack of presence" in lovemaking, and now he can't seem to do anything right.

Power struggles like this can be resolved if you and your partner are able to recognize that these struggles may originate in unfinished emotional business from your childhood. To get beyond such struggles, and heal any unresolved issues, you must enter the stability stage.

ALERT!

You know you're in the power struggle stage when you try to get your partner to change so that you can feel better. Stop and ask yourself why you feel you absolutely need those changes to occur. Can you love your partner for who he or she is?

A Time of Stability

As your relationship goes from the power struggle stage to the stability stage, you learn that the outer struggle mirrors the inner struggle—that is, if your partner's behavior triggers intense anger or hurt, this probably indicates an area where you have unresolved emotional issues within yourself—like Vicki's unresolved anger about her father's neglect.

Stability is the toughest stage to master. Having a partner, for most people, gives you a ready scapegoat. It's so easy to blame someone else for your pain—all he'd have to do is change one little thing and then you'd feel better! When you let go of blaming your partner, even secretly, and take responsibility for your own emotional triggers, then you are solidly in the stability stage.

From Stability to Commitment

If you succeed in mastering the lessons of the stability stage, the rewards are great. In the commitment stage, you can enjoy a genuine sense of safety—not the illusory safety of romance. Now you really feel your unity, your interdependence. You become a "we," where you naturally consider how your actions will affect your partner.

Such thoughtfulness comes, not from any sense of obligation, but from a deep knowing of and empathy for the other. But you need to go through the other three stages together before you can arrive at true commitment. Now your promises to each other are trustworthy. They were not before because you had not yet met and mastered the basic life task of taking responsibility for yourself (the task of the stability stage). Until you pass beyond stability, you are still secretly, or not so secretly, looking to be "taken care of," as in, "I want you to stop flirting with other women because it makes me feel insecure." (Translation: It triggers my insecurity.)

QUESTION?

Why is commitment stage four in a relationship? Doesn't it take commitment to get us started on the journey?
Yes, it does take a kind of commitment, but the ability to make agreements together that are really trustworthy comes only after your relationship has weathered a number of power struggles and uncovered each person's hidden sides. Only then do you know yourselves and the relationship well enough to make really trustworthy commitments.

Cocreation

Once two people are aligned in their oneness and secure about their ability to make and keep agreements without any sense of obligation, they can create things together with a real sense of partnership. They might create simple things like nice dinner parties for their friends. They might coauthor articles or teach classes together. Or they might use their bond to support each partner's individual self-expression in the world.

Cocreation is where you reap the rewards of the work you have done in the other four stages, and where you give back to the world from what life has taught you. The couple's journey from romance to cocreation helps both partners learn to be comfortable with change. It can help you avoid needless disappointment over the fact that "you're not the person I first fell in love with."

You Won't Meet Your Partner's Every Need

Even when you're first falling in love, you are probably aware, in theory, of the fact that you will not meet your partner's every need. Theory is one thing, but hearing your partner say they want to go somewhere with a special friend instead of with you—well, that might not be so easy to accept. Has this happened to you? If it has not, be prepared, for it probably will.

And if it never happens, your relationship is not very mature. You're probably still "babying" each other or the relationship, treating it as too fragile to handle such conflicts. In any relationship, there will be things one partner wants to do that do not include the other person. If you try to avoid mentioning such things, so as not to cause discomfort, then you will not progress very far in the couple's journey.

Sure, it can hurt to hear your partner say that he or she would rather be with someone else, or alone, than with you. It hurts, but it's good for you, in the sense that by facing the truth that you do not meet each other's every need, you also grow in your ability to handle life as it is.

ALERT!

Life is full of things that are not in your control. Accepting this makes you stronger. If you insist on having things your way all the time, you will stay immature, and so will your relationship.

Learning to Accept Differences

Here is an exercise to try with your partner:

1. First, each of you should make your own list of all the things you love to do.
2. In the left-hand column next to each item, write *A* (for things you prefer to do alone), *Y* (for things you prefer to do with your partner), and *O* (for things you like to do best with someone other than your partner).
3. Now share your lists and talk about your feelings. As you share feelings, be sure and start with the words "I feel." Using these statements will prevent you from attacking, blaming, or judging your partner.

After doing this exercise, give yourselves credit for taking on the challenge of being honest about difficult things. Being honest about your needs for separate space will bring you to a deeper level of intimacy and trust—trust that is no longer seen in terms of "I trust you to never hurt me" (which is unrealistic), but rather in the following way: "I trust myself to be able to handle whatever feelings come up between us. I trust that if you do something that hurts me, I will talk with you about it. And I trust that you and I together can listen to each other's feelings nondefensively so we can get to forgiveness." This is a real grown-up relationship.

You Will Learn to Forgive

Forgiveness is an essential survival skill in any relationship. No matter how mature and responsible two people become, at times they will do dumb or hurtful things. Forgiveness can occur in an instant. But more often it is a process that takes place over time.

Usually there are several elements or stages in the forgiveness process:

1. Figuring out what happened.
2. Investigating what you feel.
3. Expressing what you feel to your partner.
4. Listening to your partner.
5. Expressing other feelings.
6. Forgiving each other.

Beware of premature forgiveness. Many people cannot stand the discomfort of anger or resentment, so they say "I forgive you" before they have even found out what happened or fully felt their feelings about it. To get to true and lasting forgiveness, you need to be willing to go through all the stages until you feel within yourself a change of heart regarding the troubling event.

What Happened?

The first step in any forgiveness process is to identify what the other did that you felt hurt about. You need to think clearly here, because people are often hurt by something they imagine or by their interpretation of their partner's actions.

Ask yourself, "What really happened? What did my partner actually do or say?" Then ask, "What happened after that? What was my reaction? What did I actually feel? What did I say or do about those feelings?"

What Do You Feel?

After identifying what you felt after it happened, notice what you feel right now. Are you still upset? Are you feeling pain or hurt feelings? Notice the actual feelings and bodily sensations, and do not be confused by your labels and judgments: "I feel betrayed" is actually not a feeling. It is an interpretation about the other's actions—you think that someone has betrayed you.

If you are thinking, "I do feel betrayed," see if you can pinpoint the exact feelings in your body that you associate with betrayal. Often some old feelings get triggered—feelings that happened long ago but were never fully admitted or expressed and so were never released. So now, when a similar feeling occurs, it gets mistaken for that same old wound. You overreact in the present to an experience that appears similar to some unresolved hurt in your past.

By noticing the quality of your present feelings in detail, you will be better able to communicate to your partner in a genuine, grounded way. You will be more authentic and more believable (not acting hysterical or sounding dramatic).

Expressing What You Feel

For most people, this step is the hardest of all. You may fear that your partner will be defensive or maybe that you'll create a mess. Well, it's true that these things might happen. But if you take that risk now, you won't have to carry the burden of your unexpressed hurt and anger all by yourself. And you probably will get over it once you talk about it with your partner. Remember—the purpose of expressing your feelings is to get over them, to get to forgiveness. (Chapter 17 offers some communication tools to assist you in expressing yourself in difficult situations such as this.)

Listening to Your Partner

After your partner has heard you out, listen to him expressing his own feelings and perceptions. Ask clarifying questions to help your partner be more specific, but don't put him on the witness stand. Questions that begin with "Isn't it true that you . . ." are forbidden. If you can save these for the courtroom, you'll be less apt to wind up in a courtroom-type battle.

As you listen to your partner, it's a good idea to use "active listening" (described in Chapter 17). Repeating what your partner has just said keeps you grounded and present and prevents you from reacting impulsively. It also helps your partner feel that you are present and open, thus increasing the likelihood of resolution.

Expressing More Feelings

Now check in and see if you need to express anything more. Sometimes simply stating your resentments clearly, specifically, and directly leads to a sense of forgiveness: "I'm over it now. . . . I can forgive you. . . . I just needed to express myself and be heard."

Other times, you may still feel almost as upset as you did when you began, so you will need to repeat yourself. Simply restate what you said before; if you become aware of some new feelings, express them as well. After each expression, check in with yourself to see if you feel "clear" yet. Do you have a sense of resolution or closure?

Keep expressing yourself, even if you think it sounds repetitive, until you feel complete. Sometimes, the process of expressing strong anger will result in a surfacing of fear or pain. Sometimes after expressing hurt or painful feelings, anger will surface. Do not be alarmed if you discover something hidden underneath your initial feelings.

Sometimes, to get to a feeling of completion, you may need to repeat these steps together a few more times. If a present hurt is similar to one that you suffered in childhood, the wound may not heal all at once. Be patient. Accept that emotional wounds, just like physical ones, can take time to heal.

The human psyche is like an onion with many layers. Once you express yourself fully about a particular incident, feelings about another event might come into your awareness. Sometimes, you will be reminded by the current situation of something that happened to you long ago, maybe when you were a child. If this happens, then be sure to tell your partner that old buried feelings are now coming up. This allows your partner to be a compassionate listener and not get triggered. Then ask your partner to bear with you, and just keep expressing yourself.

Forgiving Your Partner

Once you feel complete in your expression, you are probably ready to forgive. It helps if you can take responsibility for the fact that you were triggered by your partner's actions. Your partner is not to blame for that. Your partner is responsible for his or her actions, but no one is to blame for what you experienced.

You need to remember that blame is not real. It is a defensive reaction that people use to feel more in control about something that happened. It is more mature to admit that you do not have control over things done by another person. The blaming habit supports an unrealistic view of reality—a view that says, "If I hurt, it's someone else's fault." Pain happens. The best way to deal with life's painful moments is to feel the pain, talk about it, forgive, and continue living.

Affairs Happen—How to Cope

The discovery of a secret sexual affair can be one of the most painful things a couple ever experiences. If this happens, it is important to attend carefully to each of the six stages of forgiveness. Find out what really happened, asking any questions you have. Do not protect your partner by suppressing questions you fear may be uncomfortable. But don't punish your partner or rub it in. Remember, your goal is to get to forgiveness by increasing your understanding of your partner and your partner's understanding of you.

You're in Shock—Now What?

When you find out your partner has been keeping such a secret from you, you may feel so out of control that your natural inclination is to try and get back in control by immediately taking decisive action—such as leaving or threatening to leave. Usually this is a bad idea.

Do not leave any relationship until you have at least expressed all your feelings about the matter and heard all that your partner has to say. If you leave a situation at the height of emotion, you will most certainly carry with you a lot of unresolved issues. Such emotional baggage will follow you into your next relationship, or prevent you from engaging in future relationships at all.

FACT

In a study conducted for the book *The Day America Told the Truth*, by James Patterson and Peter Kim, 37 percent of married people admitted to having had secret sexual affairs.

A Checklist of Questions

When you're in shock, you may be so numb or so angry that you can't think straight, and yet this is a critical time and you have a lot to consider. Here is a list of questions you need to ask:

- What actually happened? (If your partner will not tell you, find out why. Your partner shouldn't be afraid of being honest with you.)
- What is going on presently between your partner and this other person?

- What are your partner's wants and intentions?
- What does your partner want you to do or want from you?

Often, an affair is a wake-up call for a marriage—a signal that one or both partner's needs are not being met. Now that this information is out in the open, you can do something to remedy that situation.

Forgiveness

Each person is unique in what it takes to fully forgive. Yet the six stages give you a general outline of what is needed for most people. Sometimes, forgiveness is only the beginning, however. After this, the two of you may need to come up with a new vision of what you each want in your relationship and a plan of action for how to make your vision a reality. The forgiving person may request that the partner make some sort of amends.

If you get stuck in communicating about any of this, please seek professional help. Nowadays most mature couples realize that we all need third-party help at times. View this as a commitment to yourselves and to your relationship, not as a sign of weakness. And remember—love between two people can be stronger in the broken places. Ⓔ

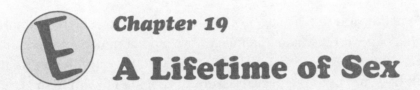

Chapter 19

A Lifetime of Sex

Life is full of change. It's a given that you can't escape, yet it holds wonder and mystery. Our sexuality is no different. From first learning about sex and your first sexual experience through your sex life, there's a lot of information that could help you along the way. It's never too late to learn more about sex and your sexuality.

The Very First Time

We have "firsts" for everything we do in life—first job, first time driving, first kiss, and first love. When you feel secure, empowered, and self-confident, most things you do for the first time will go well. Having information, knowledge, and resources helps you have even better life experiences for the first time.

Whether you're a teenager or older, you need to remember that sex can happen with or without intimacy, love, and commitment. Sex may be a part of a young person's explorations of who they are. It can be the result of giving in to the peer pressure of keeping up with friends. It can be a way of testing both how lovemaking might feel and how or who one is in relationship to gender and sex.

Don't Rush In

Generally, parents, clergy, and educators all feel that teenagers and young adults should put off sexual activity. Young people who feel like adults and are out to test their boundaries and experience life don't often follow that advice.

ALERT!

If you are a parent of a teenager who is interested in sex, sometimes all you can do is to trust that you have done a good job of educating your children and that they will make wise decisions because of that.

If you think that you're ready for your first sexual experience, and you would like it to be healthy and fulfilling the first time, there are several things you may want to consider. Make sure you have spoken with your potential partner and that you both agree that you're ready to be together; ideally, you will also be able to speak with a parent or another trusted adult in your life, especially if you have any fears or frustrations. It's also important that you have a safe, comfortable place to be with your partner.

Many young people don't know much about sexuality. Have a conversation with your potential lover that is vulnerable and open.

Chances are, this is a first for him or her as well, and you may discover that both of you share some of the same fears.

Your first sexual experience is something you'll remember for the rest of your life. Try to make it the best possible. It will get you started on the right foot on the road of sexual growth that will take you through the rest of your life.

FACT

Here's what *Boston Globe* columnist Ellen Goodman noted in her column of June 23, 2002: Statistics show that though most parents favor abstinence, 82 percent want sex education in schools to cover contraception as well as abstinence.

Talking to Kids about Sex

It is necessary to have safe, open conversations with your children about many things in their lives. You won't be able to talk about sex easily with your child unless you like it yourself and have already had other conversations with them about important things in their lives. Start talking to them now so that you can do it later when it's really important. Here is what you need to keep in mind as you begin:

- Don't leave the sex talk up to the school. It will be a rich experience if you can talk to your teen about sex. Today, over two-thirds of eighteen-year-olds have already had sexual intercourse. Most health professionals believe that the current abstinence-only sex education offered in schools doesn't delay intercourse or prevent pregnancy. The programs can't talk about contraceptives, except to mention their failure rates.
- Studies show that parents make a difference. Teach your child to think wisely. This starts early in life, with parents giving choices to their children that are easy and age-appropriate. As the child matures, the choices become more challenging but still within the reach and scope of the child. In this way parents can teach the skills that the child needs to say "no."

- Always be on the lookout for "teachable moments." Don't lecture—ask your child what he or she thinks about something presented on TV or in a magazine. Construct your questions to be nonjudgmental, so that your child feels permission to speak up. The conversation will last longer that way.

- Teach equality and self-esteem to your child. The current thinking among teens is that oral sex isn't sex. It's a very popular activity, and it allows girls to claim they are still virgins. Most of the oral sex is performed on the male, not on the female. This sets up a girl-pleasing-boy scenario and an early imbalance in sexuality and intimacy. It perpetuates the cultural permissiveness of sexuality for boys and the double standard of "innocence of body" for girls.

- Engage your children in all sorts of topics. Although it's known that extracurricular activities like sports, clubs, and church can delay the advent of sex, having a good relationship with your children is best. Let them know that you are interested in having them come to you with questions, no matter how hard that might be for you. Encourage them to go to friends and mentors, too.

QUESTION?

When did you lose your virginity?
Recall the experience and think about as many of the details as you can remember. Share what you recall and how you felt about it with your lover or a close friend. Ask them to answer the same question.

Protect Your Children

One of the unfortunate outcomes of our modern society is the increasing incidence of child abuse and rape. Estimates are that one in four girls and one in six boys will be sexually abused before age eighteen. The most shocking part is that often the perpetrator is someone they know and trust.

Small children need advocates. It is often impossible for them to be able to judge what is appropriate and what is inappropriate behavior from a trusted adult. You can educate them in nonfearful ways. You can be watchful over the children in your life. It is very appropriate for any adult who suspects a child may be being abused to talk about it with other adults. Don't just watch from the sidelines—if you suspect abuse, do something about it.

FACT

Of studies done of women over the age of eighteen who have been forced to have sex against their will, only 4 percent were forced or raped by a stranger. The number one prevention for abuse and rape is a good sense of self-worth. If a child, woman, our man feels worthy, has good self-esteem, and knows how to stand up to the perpetrator, he or she is more likely to be able to prevent the abuse from occurring.

Sexual abuse victims tend to feel inferior all of their lives. Not only will they have a difficult time having a good sex life as adults, they will likely feel inadequate in many other areas of their lives as well. Their trust in people is shattered and they tend to withdraw from intimacy and close personal relationships.

If you have been sexually assaulted or abused, don't be afraid of reaching out for help. Tell your story to someone you trust, for it is in that way that the healing begins. Keeping an experience of sexual abuse a secret is unhealthy. But if you seek help, you can break the cycle of fear. There are rape crisis hotlines across the country. Check Appendix B for additional resources.

Making Love with a New Partner

Chances are, you have had a few sexual partners in your life. Some of these relationships may have been more casual than others. The more special your partner was to you, the more shyness, fear, or even guilt you may have felt the first time you had a sexual experience with this person.

When you are just starting out a new relationship, you may feel pressured to impress your new partner sexually, and you may want to "do it better" than in the past. You ask yourself if you really did learn anything from your mistakes and struggles from your previous experiences.

You can use the communication, intimacy, and touch techniques covered in this book to get to know your partner intimately in a fun, relaxed manner, before you decide to take the next step toward sex.

ALERT!

> For both young and old, being naked in front of your partner for the first time may be very frightening or it may be erotically charged—or both! If you anticipate having a new lover, take it slowly and express that you are feeling vulnerable. It may help to undress each other.

Each of you has the opportunity to begin again in a new loving relationship that feeds your souls. You have the chance to create the highest possible communion with the divine in both yourself and your lover. Never doubt that there is someone for you to love and be loved by. If you find yourself in this place, remember to have a beginner's mind.

The "Highs" of a New Relationship

Many people are addicted to the "rush" they get from a new relationship. Often when you begin a new relationship, the endorphins take over and cloud your vision for a while. You feel on top of the world and the relationship feels indestructible.

Eventually, though, you'll come back down to Earth. It's then, as the relationship continues for the long term, that you will need the tools to help you stay clear and loving. If you take things slowly and build your intimacy skills and connection in the new relationship, it will go well. You will both be able to sustain those "highs" that attracted you to each other in the first place.

A Beginner's Mind

Even if you are in a long-term relationship, you may find it helpful to have a beginner's mind—being open, vulnerable, and trusting in your sexuality. A beginner's mind isn't full of judgments or complaints about how you want things to be. It accepts things as they are and works to transform both the interior struggles and the behaviors that bring the problems.

FACT

A study of 10,000 high school students, concluded in 2002, found that 54 percent were virgins. This statistic had increased from 46 percent a decade before. Birth rates among adolescents have been declining as well.

In meditation practices, we are reminded that when our mind wanders, we need to come back to paying attention to our breath. The breath is the best reminder of being in the moment. A person with a beginner's mind stays in the moment during sexual experience, and this state helps the two lovers to communicate and make improvements. The techniques in this book can be helpful in fostering the beginner's mindset.

Sexually Transmitted Diseases

Sexually transmitted diseases (STDs) are very prevalent today, as they have been throughout history. Though we have good prevention methods and effective treatments, STDs remain a growing concern among doctors, young adults, parents, and sexually active adults.

What Are STDs?

Sexually transmitted diseases are contracted through the following forms of sexual contact:

- Genitals (including the anus) to genitals
- Mouth to genitals
- Genitals to hands to genitals
- Mouth to mouth (this is only true for some of the STDs)

STDs may be caused by bacteria or a virus. The bacterial forms are generally treated with strong antibiotics. The viral forms cannot be cured, although their symptoms can be treated with antiviral drugs.

QUESTION?

Where did you first have sex?
Myth has it that first sex often happens in the backseat of cars or outdoors. In a 2002 report, it was reported that most teen sex occurs at home. In the report, 70 percent of teens said they were at home in their own rooms and that only 50 percent of parents were aware that their teen had had sex.

Common Sexually Transmitted Diseases

Except for HIV, the viral infection that causes AIDs, all common STDs have been plaguing humans for thousands of years. The symptoms are more noticeable in men, so women are more likely to have STDs that go undiagnosed and are therefore carriers of the disease. However, because men are more likely to engage in promiscuous behavior, they are more likely to infect more partners.

Here are descriptions of common sexually transmitted diseases that you should be aware of. Chlamydia, syphilis, and gonorrhea are bacterial infections; the rest are viral.

- **Chlamydia:** This STD is very common and hard to detect. Three-quarters of women have no symptoms. Symptoms can include discharge, burning, and pain during intercourse.
- **Syphilis:** This chronic disease is acquired from someone with an active infection. The first signs are painless sores that go away easily; long-term effects include damage to the heart, brain, eyes, bones, nervous system, and joints.
- **Gonorrhea:** There are often no symptoms associated with gonorrhea. When symptoms do appear, they may be mild but can include discharge from the penis, vagina, or rectum, and burning and itching during urination. There is an alarming increase in gonorrhea of the throat in teens who perform fellatio on their partners.

- **Human papilloma virus (HPV):** Genital or venereal warts is the most common STD in the United States. It is very contagious and is becoming associated with cancers of the genital regions. The warts are fleshy growths in the genital regions; they do not cause pain.
- **Genital herpes:** The symptoms of this virus include itching, burning, and blisters in the genital area or buttocks. The open sores are painful and the lymph nodes can become swollen in the groin area.
- **Hepatitis B:** This virus is acquired by piercing the skin with needles and through exposure to semen, blood, saliva, and urine from an infected person. Most infections clear up, but if it doesn't, it affects the liver and can be deadly.
- **HIV/AIDS:** The human immunodeficiency virus develops into AIDS after the virus has been in the infected person for a while, destroying the immune system and leaving the person vulnerable to infections. To date, there is no cure.

The AIDS Epidemic

With the advent of the AIDS epidemic sweeping the world, greater knowledge and preparation is needed by every human being. In an age when pleasure can quite literally kill, education, open discussion of sexuality, and resource availability must become the norm. Following is a list of the main ways HIV is transmitted:

- Anal or vaginal intercourse with an infected person.
- Oral–genital sexual activity with an infected person.
- Contact with semen or vaginal fluids of an infected person.
- Organ transplants or blood transfusion from an infected person.
- Contact with infected blood through the use of contaminated needles from drug users or tattooing, ear piercing, or steroid injections.
- Transfer from mother to child during gestation, birth, or soon after birth (breastfeeding is risky for an HIV-positive mother).

The most typical fluids through which HIV is transmitted are blood, semen, and vaginal secretions. It has been documented to be present in urine, saliva, tears, and feces, but there is no evidence of anyone contracting the disease through any of those avenues.

If You're Infected, Seek Help

Often people are embarrassed to seek help if they think they might be infected with an STD. Pelvic inflammatory disease can develop in women who have not been treated for STDs. This can cause infertility and other serious symptoms. Seek treatment before any serious damage has occurred. Once you are sexually active, it's important to get regular pap smears once a year. These detect any abnormal cells in the vagina and on the cervix.

ALERT!

It is possible to get some sexually transmitted diseases through oral sex and even kissing. Generally, though, anything that involves touching with the hands is safe. This is especially true if you wear latex gloves while caressing and touching your lover's genitals.

Practice Safe Sex

The frequency of infection goes hand in hand with multiple sex partners and starting sexual activity at a young age. If you are going to be sexually active, make sure that you're protected! Don't be afraid to ask your potential new lover about his or her sexual history, and be willing to talk about your sexual history as well. Your lives may depend on it.

See your doctor frequently. If you have any question in your mind, get tested. If you don't want to go to your regular doctor, you can go to a number of sex clinics where you can be tested anonymously. Check your local phone book for HIV clinics or check the references in Appendix B.

Being a Conscientious Lover

Having good self-esteem and a conscientious attitude when discussing personal sexual histories with a new partner is very important. The accepted method of clearing yourself and a new partner for unprotected sexual activity is to be tested at the time you decide to take your relationship to a deeper level. During the waiting time for your test results, you can begin to share intimate experiences that do not involve intercourse or other risky behaviors.

Knowing a lot about sensual and sexual touching techniques can help when being with a new partner. The previous chapters have many techniques to choose from. You can begin to get to know each other's bodies until the time you decide to take the next step to intercourse. Of course, you have the option of using condoms, too.

FACT

A study of 10,000 high school students found that 58 percent of the sexually active kids used condoms in 2002 compared to 46 percent a decade earlier. The study noted an increase in oral sex activity due to fear of pregnancy and contracting AIDS.

Latex, Condoms, and Finger Cots

Condoms made of latex are the safest method, outside of abstinence, for staying disease-free. They can prevent pregnancy, though they are not failsafe, by keeping the male ejaculate from entering the vagina. And by preventing direct contact between the penis and the female sexual organs, condoms protect both the man and the woman from contracting sexually transmitted diseases.

There are also female condoms available, though some women say they can bump the cervix and are slightly uncomfortable. That may change as new products are introduced to the marketplace in the next few years. Dental dams are square pieces of latex that can be used to cover the female's genitals for oral sex. Plastic wrap can be used, too. Finger cots, or condoms for a single finger, are good for anal stimulation and erotic touch over the genital areas.

All of these items provide a good barrier to the transmission of sexually exchanged diseases. Don't hesitate to use them. They can even add fun to the experience. If you are having sex in a situation that warrants protection, make it fun and worry-free for both of you.

Responsibility

Many women say that they feel it is ultimately up to them to make sure they are having safe sex. They say it is important to be prepared and to not be talked out of using male or female condoms if they feel it is warranted. This can be difficult if you have self-esteem issues that might keep you from defending your boundaries.

Both men and women need to be tolerant and agreeable when faced with discussing safe sex with their lover. You certainly wouldn't want to be responsible for another person getting an STD and you wouldn't want to be in that person's position, either. Take responsibility. Your lives may depend on it.

Practice Virtual Sex

Cybersex and phone sex can be seen as safer sex because there is no physical contact between lovers. Both of these ways of having sex are about self-pleasuring in an erotic situation with another person, though this person is not physically near you. If you are in a close relationship but are physically apart, sometimes phone sex can be a great way to connect intimately. These are also great ways for playing out fantasies with your partner.

However, if you are not in a relationship and you are frequently paying for phone sex or using the Internet for sexual relations, you may want to talk to a psychologist. The possible emotional and physical costs in terms of avoiding relationship with a real person are great. If you feel as though you might have intimacy problems, see a specialist. The rewards of true connection and deep intimacy are great. Everyone needs real touch and caring.

Sex During Pregnancy

Most doctors agree that unless there are medical complications during a pregnancy, there is no reason a couple cannot have normal sexual relations. Your doctor may not broach the subject with you, but you can bring it up if you have questions. Your own intuition should serve as a good guideline for sexual activity.

Typically, by the third trimester a woman may have difficulty with some sexual activities because her uterus becomes distended. During intercourse, her cervix may get bumped, causing slight pain. She may also not be as interested in sex, as her hormone levels will be changing.

Most couples find other ways of enjoying each other. Use some of the suggestions in the chapters of this book to invent new ways the two of you can pleasure each other during pregnancy. It's a great time to get good at oral sex and other forms of sexual activity.

Finally, and especially if you're pregnant with your first child, this will be the last time for a while that the two of you are just "two." Find ways of being sexual, sensual, and intimate now, even if you have to modify what you do. After the baby is born, it's typical for the woman not to engage in sexual activity for at least two to four weeks, and some women have a much longer period of not wanting to engage in sexual activity. Your doctor will tell you not to have intercourse until you have stopped bleeding completely. Sleep, time, and energy will be harder to come by. Most sexual activity is fully resumed after six to twelve months.

Sexuality and Aging

Adapting to changing hormones and body agility and accepting the changes that our bodies go through as we age is challenging. Today, we have many options for staying perpetually young in looks, health, and spirit, so middle age isn't so daunting on the surface. When it comes to sexual vitality, though, things do change as your body ages.

Health Issues

The good news is, we're living longer and you'll want to have sex longer as well. The bad news is that as a culture we are more overweight, on prescription drugs much more than our parents' generation, and have higher incidences of cancer. These cancers are prevalent in the areas of the body that have to do with sex. Breast cancer, testicular cancer, prostate cancer, and uterine cancer are all on the rise.

Maintaining a healthful lifestyle is very important for great sex. Eat well, stay fit, and see your doctor regularly. Educate yourself on matters concerning health and sexuality so that you will be well informed when aging issues come up.

FACT

In the last few years, we as a society have begun to see a synthesis between sexuality and spirituality. As the median age of the U.S. population increases, there is a growing trend toward a more sacred association with sex.

Maintaining Sexual Desire

Desire can be elusive throughout your life. Many people experience ups and downs in their level of desire. Depression, stress, and anxiety all contribute to lowered levels of the brain chemicals that keep us optimistic, healthy, and full of desire.

Lowered hormone levels during pregnancy, illnesses, personal crisis, and work and family problems can cause the loss of sexual desire. Midlife menopause in both men and women can cause confusion about desire and desirability. Many modern medications and drugs used for depression and stress-related illnesses can cause a complete lack of libido.

One woman put it like this: "I've been married for thirty-two years. I was once very open to sex. I don't want sex anymore. I work hard, am very attractive, and I don't smoke. My children are grown and out of our home. What is going on?"

Very often, after women have had their children, they go back to work with a vengeance. They put in long hours and come home to more hours of creating and maintaining a sanctuary in their home. They may be absolutely enjoying themselves, but it does make for a long, exhausting day.

At the same time, they are gently aging. Their testosterone and estrogen levels are dropping. Estrogens regulate the monthly cycle and help stabilize the emotions, side effects, and physical sensations of menopause. Testosterone gives women energy and sexual vitality the same way it does for men, although women need a much smaller amount of the hormone than men do.

Men's testosterone levels drop as they age, too. Their desire may begin to wane, though it may be more attributed to performance anxiety and fears associated with declining libido and perceived "sexiness." Men seem to be much less willing to address the issues. The sales of motorcycles and sports cars to middle-age men have increased tremendously as baby-boomers age!

Training Your Mind

Desire has a lot to do with how you've trained your mind to think about sex and sexual attraction. If you have been sex-positive for most of your life, it's likely you'll be more sexually active as you age. If you find that you encounter problems, you will be more likely to seek out remedies and solutions for them.

Our brain is our biggest sexual organ. We can enable ourselves to feel sexy, stimulated, and desirable by training our brains. It's never too late to start. Sex and desire are healthy, normal functions of any human being. If you or your partner is concerned about the lack of desire and libido, consult your doctor and ask for a referral to a sexologist.

Dealing with Impotency

Impotency problems may have psychological roots or a physical basis. Today, we are blessed to know much about the human body and its functions. It's known that poor blood circulation can cause erectile problems in men and arousal problems in women. As men age, the one-way valves that allow blood into the penis become fatigued and allow leakage of blood back out sooner than is desired. Good diet, lots of exercise, keeping cholesterol counts low, and a enjoying a happy, active sex life all lead to prolonging a great sex life.

Impotency problems may also be the result of stress, chronic smoking, diabetes, or taking prescription medicines.

ALERT!

Viagra is a short-term solution for some men. Take it ONLY under your doctor's care. In coming years, new solutions will become available that will have fewer side effects and may even be available over the counter.

Psychological problems can be short-term or long-term, depending on the situation. Consult your doctor or urologist first and if you determine that you need the help of a sexologist or psychiatrist, you can get a good referral. Often just opening up and having a frank conversation with your partner will help deal with psychological impotency.

Dealing with Menopause

As women age, they experience different problems. One common complaint is vaginal dryness. Many women wonder if it is the result of menopause or a psychological effect of decreased desire.

If you are a woman who has questions about the onset of menopause, see your doctor. Hormone levels, both of testosterone and estrogens, affect our libido. Have the basic blood tests that will tell you if your hormone levels are getting low. Once the test results come back, you'll have some decisions to make.

Large government studies on hormone replacement therapies for women have recently been halted. Sighting serious side effects, the FDA will conduct public forums and try to set guidelines for future research. It has left women wondering what to do. Although you may decide that hormone replacement is right for you, there are alternative avenues to choose from as well. Luckily, there's a lot more you can do to alleviate your experience of menopause. Here are a few suggestions:

- Physical activity is key to leading a healthy lifestyle; find an exercise program that you enjoy, and make it a part of your everyday schedule.
- Avoid stress; take more personal time for yourself and cut back your work hours.
- Create sensual (but not necessarily sexual) time with your lover. Be playful and innocent—it doesn't have to go anywhere as long as you

enjoy touch, massage, and cuddling.

- Practice your PC muscle exercises. Being proficient at these will bring more blood flow to your pelvic floor area, keep you toned, and will actually help to build your sexual energy and sexual desire.
- Try estrogen and testosterone topical creams.
- Attend a sexuality or tantra workshop with your partner. Workshops can put a tremendous amount of new sensual energy into relationships.
- Consider taking up yoga and meditation. These activities teach you to focus your attention and keep your body supple. Focusing techniques can help you respond better to the sexual stimulus that you get.
- Don't be afraid to use lubrication, if needed. It can be erotic and fun to apply. There are many products on the market already, and new lines are appearing that are organic and natural.
- Keep a sense of play and innocence when introducing new experiences. And most important, have fun!

Don't be too hard on yourself. Many women experience a lack of libido as they age. This becomes an excellent time to reflect on what is truly important in your life and to act on it.

Get yourself a good book on menopause; one good option is *The Everything® Menopause Book*. There are a few available that will give you all the information you need to understand what is happening to your body, mind, and soul. There are new products coming on the market designed for women. Speak to your doctor if this is an avenue that appeals to you.

Chapter 20

E A Do-It-Yourself Sex Workshop

Now it's time to put together everything you've read about in this book so that you and your partner can enjoy a lifetime of great sex together. This final chapter will present six specific sexual self-help programs: four are for couples; one for partners who are just beginning a sexual relationship; and one for people who wish to prepare themselves for great sex with a new partner.

Adding New Spices to an Old Recipe

If you are fortunate enough to have been together with your partner for many years, it may be time to spice up your sexual and romantic life. Perhaps you have gotten into a routine that is comfortable but lacks excitement. Perhaps you have begun to avoid sex entirely due to a backlog of incomplete communications. Perhaps there are still things, after all these years, that are frustrating or difficult. Perhaps you feel the need for variety, but don't want to go outside the relationship for it. If any of these issues speak to you, read on!

Breaking the Routine

It takes conscious effort to get out of your rut, but the effort is well worth the time it takes. If both of you have read this book, it's now time to have a conversation with your partner about which ideas for adding spice and variety appeal to each of you.

In Chapter 16, you learned about many ways to make the place where you make love more sensual and beautiful by using colors, flowers, and fragrances, and by bathing each other, feeding each other sensual foods, and dressing erotically. Some of these ideas may bring up fear or embarrassment, but you need to go beyond these initial feelings—all of these suggestions may be just the thing for spicing up your sex life.

ALERT!

Your partner can be your greatest ally and healer! Don't give up too easily. A recent study found that married people had far less depression than those who are not married. Choose to do the intimacy work that will make both of you overflow with happiness.

If you do something that feels a little scary, it means you are taking a risk on behalf of the relationship. You are stretching your comfort zone, and your relationship is growing. You may have heard the saying "grow or die." This means that if you're not stretching in a relationship, your relationship is dying. Don't let your sex life die an untimely death. Keep it alive and fresh by consciously changing things every so often.

Getting Back in Touch

No matter how long you have been together, you never outgrow your need for touch. Being touched in sensual, sexual, and nurturing ways helps people feel relaxed, loving, and loveable. Chapter 9 presents a wide range of touch exercises to revive your senses and renew your capacity for whole-body pleasure.

If you two have been together a long time, you probably have not had a "how I like it served" conversation recently—what feels good to you during foreplay and beyond—which is something that couples need to address often. Just because "things are working fine," doesn't mean that you should fall into being complacent.

Sometimes people's needs change over time. Sometimes, as you get more comfortable with yourself or your body, you learn new things about yourself. Don't let yourselves get out of touch with each other; keep communicating and trying new things.

If you are in a long-term relationship, ask yourself what transformations you'd like to see in the relationship. List three things that you would like to change in yourself and three things you'd like to see change overall. Write them down and be specific.

Still Wishing and Hoping

Even after years of marriage, many couples have secrets they have not told their partner. One of the main areas of secrecy is sex. Take a moment now to think about your own situation. Are there things that you wish your partner would do for you that you have not spoken about lately? Why is that? What are you trying to avoid? Chapter 17 offers many communication games and tools that you can use to 'fess up about your secret needs, wants, and longings. Remember—you are most loveable when you are most transparent and vulnerable.

If Variety Is the Missing Spice

There are many ways to add variety to an already satisfying relationship. Try a new position. Do it outdoors or on the kitchen floor. Try one-way sex in order to give each person the chance to simply receive pleasure. Try having sex without orgasm for a month.

QUESTION?

I need a shift from the routine. What can I do?
Imagine a weekend away at a luxury hotel, a camping trip, a cabin in the mountains, or a seaside resort. Pick a place were there isn't much to do except stay in your wonderful hideout. Take along a Kama sutra kit, massage oil, scarves, a love game, lingerie, champagne, or anything else your creativity conjures up!

If you have not explored the G-spot or the anal area, see what that holds for you. Dress up as someone different and act out the part (maybe you still have that old cheerleader outfit stored away somewhere). Have a fight about something you've both been avoiding. All these things can renew your feelings of love and lust. Try any of them that appeal to you, or better yet, try them all.

Connecting with Her Sexual Essence

It has been said that if sex works for the woman, it works for the man. Many of the tantric and other ancient practices described in this book offer ways that allow the woman's response to guide the way for both partners.

Foreplay Revisited: Don't Rush It

If the woman is not enjoying sex as much as you both would like, the first place to look to remedy that situation is foreplay. Often, the same old foreplay routine can feel boring for the man. But if that's what she likes, it will behoove you to learn to "tune in" to her needs rather than viewing it as simply "servicing" her.

When two people feel connected, when they are tuned in to each other, boredom disappears. A woman can help her man tune in to her by giving him verbal and nonverbal feedback about how he's doing. Most men report that they'd like a lot more feedback from their partner about what feels good.

Moaning and making other sounds are one good way to do this. Chapter 11 recommends using breath and sound—both as a way to help your partner know where you are and as a way to enhance your own responsiveness.

Open up and talk to friends about your sexual and intimate life. Be vulnerable with trustworthy friends in your life and you will create long-lasting connections. You may discover that your problems are universal and that you are not alone. Solutions, answers, and new possibilities will arise spontaneously.

Communicating Wants

Many women are shy about asking for what they want. If this is true in your partnership, it's good to talk about this outside the bedroom. First talk about her fears—what she's afraid will happen if she were more expressive. Then talk about what she wants. It's the old "feel the fear, and do it anyway" principle. Fear is a fact of life. Let's not let it limit us too much.

If the man wishes to help the woman express herself more freely, he can use some of the communication practices from Chapters 4 and 17. One of the techniques that helps a lot is to give her a multiple-choice question to answer, such as, "Would you rather have me do this with more pressure or less?" With this type of question, a woman who is afraid of hurting the man's ego, or even one who doesn't know what she wants, can be helped to accept and reveal her preferences.

Trying New Positions

Often the position that works best for the man is not the woman's favorite position, and vice versa, so please don't allow yourselves to gravitate to the man's favorite if he happens to be the one who is clearer about his wants.

This may cause the woman to yield in ways that are not in the best interests of great mutual sex. So, even if you have gotten into a pretty good routine together, don't assume that things could not get even better. Keep experimenting with new positions.

ALERT!

Make sure you don't use the tools and techniques you are learning in this book as weapons. There's nothing that kills sensual and sexual energy like an accusation of not following the rules or of not doing something "right."

Sexual Yoga

Many couples whose sex life brings up frustration, fear, awkwardness, or pain find it useful to refrain from having intercourse for a while and instead practice this "sexual yoga" exercise.

For at least twenty minutes per yoga session, lie down facing each other in a comfortable cuddling position. Breathe slowly and deeply as you feel the sensations of your partner's body next to yours. Just lie still, breathing together and feeling your sensations.

This exercise helps to balance and harmonize your sexual energies. Often one person is paced more slowly and the other's energy has a quicker pace to it. Lying together and quietly breathing together gets your two bodies feeling safe and "at home" together. Do this practice at least three times a week for a few months. It is good preparation for starting your sexual relationship over from a new place.

Enhancing His Pleasure

Sometimes it is the man who needs more help enjoying sex. Because of the fact that a man's self-esteem is often closely tied to his sexual performance, he may be reluctant to admit that things could be better for him. Yes—men fake sexual interest just like women do—they just do it differently.

To reduce the likelihood of pretending, withholding, or faking, partners need to help each other feel safe admitting when things aren't feeling quite right. Give your partner permission to tell the truth about what he wants.

Don't take his self-disclosures as criticism of you. If he tends to use a blaming tone, ask him to reread the section in Chapter 17 about how to ask for what you want.

Men Need Warming Up, Too

Somewhere in high school many men got programmed to believe that they should be "always ready"—just in case the opportunity ever comes along! As they mature, however, and as sex gets to be more available and less of an "opportunity," this attitude becomes inappropriate. A man should not expect himself to be always ready whenever the woman wants it.

This being the case, a woman needs to learn to feel comfortable with a limp penis. Do not wait for your man to be hard before you touch him or put your mouth on him. And pleasure his whole body, not just his sexual parts. This book offers a wealth of ideas for getting him, and yourself, in the mood.

FACT

Letting his lover be active in lovemaking is healing for the man. It helps him outgrow his conditioning to be always active and in charge. It helps him learn to let go of needing to run the show and discover that he is loveable even when he is not doing anything to earn love.

Passive and Active

Most women are conditioned to be passive. Don't deprive your man of the pleasure of feeling your hunger for him. Just because you were conditioned to act a certain way, doesn't mean you have to stay that way. If you think you'd like to learn to be more active in sex, a good way to start is by giving your man a full-body massage that culminates in an erotic massage, as described in Chapter 15.

Don't Be Afraid to Ask

A man has to learn to ask for what he likes. If your man does not ask, show, or tell you what he likes, it's your job to ask. You can use the multiple-choice technique or any other ideas from Chapters 4 and 17 that appeal to you.

If you are a man who is shy about asking, try using sounds to indicate what works and what doesn't. And remember, it's okay to move your lover's hands or mouth or body so things fit better for you. Even if you have no trouble communicating during sex, it's usually good for partners to have regular talks outside the sexual context to discuss what they like, including what worked and didn't work for each person the last few times they made love.

Sex after Sixty (and Well Beyond)

Sixty is not so old anymore. People are taking better care of themselves and living longer. Many men and women older than age sixty have sex that is just as satisfying as when they were younger. They usually do it less frequently, however.

Letting Go of What Used to Be

Some people feel sad when they notice their sex drive growing less intense. Others celebrate this fact! If you are in the former category, the secret to making this transition successfully is to allow yourself to experience your feelings of sadness and loss fully.

It's also important to be honest and transparent with your partner about such feelings. She's not as hot for you as she used to be. He has a hard time climaxing. How do these changes feel? If you can remember to express feelings, instead of focusing on your interpretations of what they mean, you'll grow more intimate from sharing your feelings.

Let's say, for example, that your partner doesn't reach orgasm as easily as before. How do you feel about this? Do you feel afraid? If so, what meaning are you giving to this fact that creates the fear? Or maybe you feel angry. Again, what are you telling yourself about what this change means?

If you imagine that it means something significant, be willing to check out your assumption. Ask, "I notice you didn't come the last few times we've made love. I'm afraid that means you're no longer interested in sex. Is that true?"

ALERT!

It is not change that interferes with intimacy, but rather the unwillingness to openly express our feelings about the change. Expressing feelings together almost always leads to a deeper sense of connection—even if those feelings are painful.

So, it's true that she has more wrinkles now, and her skin doesn't feel like it once did to your touch. And he has a belly, which makes him less physically attractive, and perhaps he is less agile than he once was. The changes associated with aging can bring about shame or compassion. Your ability to speak with your partner about these things will help you choose compassion over shame.

Shame is healed by feeling and expressing vulnerability and having it openly received. For inspiration in this regard, reread the children's storybook, *The Velveteen Rabbit*. Here, the well-loved, well-worn toy rabbit reminds his owner that how you "get real" is by being loved so long that most of your hair is gone, maybe one of your eyes is hanging by a thread, and at least one of your limbs is ready to fall off. Being real comes from letting yourself be seen and loved, imperfections and all.

Less Busyness Equals More Bliss

Sex after sixty can be better than in earlier years because you may now have more time to enjoy it without as many distractions. If you are no longer working at a regular job, and no longer responsible for kids, you have a lot of time freed up to explore the subtler aspects of sexuality.

Throughout this book, we have emphasized the importance of simply being present in each moment. When your lifestyle is less pressured, you may have more chances to fully experience the moment-to-moment nuances of sexual sensations, including how your sensations are influenced by your breathing and by where you put your attention.

Feelings of love, conscious breathing, and paying attention to your bodily sensations are still the best aphrodisiacs there are. These things can continue to develop over an entire lifetime. They are not limited by age.

No Erection Necessary

Tantric sex teachers encourage men and women to become as comfortable with a soft-on as they are with a hard-on. Lots of pleasure can be achieved by rubbing your two bodies and pelvic areas together. Many people find this a wonderful alternative to penetration—especially if the woman's vaginal tissue has become thin or sensitive.

A soft-on can also be inserted into the lubricated vagina. From there, experiment with various movements to see how they feel. Often, if this feels good to the woman, and she lets him know it, it will start feeling good to the man as well. If you are willing to accept what is and work with what you have, rather than focusing on what you don't have or can't do, you will continue to discover new realms of pleasure well into your later years.

FACT

Oral sex is fabulous when your man has a soft-on. There's less urgency, softer tissue, and more time to play. You may have the experience of having him "grow" in your mouth, and then again, you may not. Simply enjoy the experience without any expectation.

Positions That Are Restful

If you have never made love lying on your side, try it. This can be done face-to-face or in "the twinning branches" position, mentioned in Chapter 10. Spooning is another relaxing position—a favorite for before or after intercourse. As you age, you may need to take breaks during more vigorous lovemaking sessions, using one of these more restful postures.

Staying Fit with Great Sex

Research has shown that sexual pleasure is related to overall health. Let's review some of the key things you can do to stay in tip-top sexual condition:

- Have regular sex.
- Eat a diet rich in whole grains, high-quality proteins, fresh fruits, and vegetables.
- Do your Kegels (they are beneficial for both men and women).
- Do regular aerobic exercise.
- Manage your stress—balance play and work.
- Be moderate in your eating and your alcohol consumption.

You're Never Too Old for Erotic Touch

Even if you have little or no desire for intercourse, you still need to be touched in a loving way. If sexual intercourse does come to a halt or a hiatus, don't stop teasing, touching, kneading, and stroking each other's whole body, including the genitals. You never outgrow your need for touch.

ALERT!

If you're taking Viagra or another sexual enhancer, don't keep the fact of your use a secret from your lover. Secrets kill intimacy. If you have a secret, you'll be distracted from being fully present by your fear of being found out.

Beginning Things Right

If you are in a new sexual relationship, it may be fresh and exciting; but that's no reason to get complacent. Now is the very best time to explore conscious lovemaking and expand your capacity to experience pleasure.

Communicating Expectations

Talk to your new lover about what having sex means for your relationship. What are your expectations of each other? Does having sex carry hidden expectations or hidden fears?

If you have secret questions or fears about this topic, or secret expectations that you aren't aware of, this conversation will help clear the air so you can be more present to each other during lovemaking. If you leave these sorts of things unaddressed, you'll be thinking about them when you'd rather be enjoying your newly found love.

Sex Lessons

The second conversation that needs to occur should examine what each one of you likes. What turns you on? What secret longings do you harbor? What fetishes and fantasies do you have but are reluctant to disclose?

A good way to have this conversation is to do part of it as a show and tell. While in a relaxed, tender mood, allow your partner to see what you do to turn yourself on. Let him or her move your hand to the spots that give you most pleasure. Let your partner play with you as you give feedback on what feels good, better, and best. It's often fun to give your preferences numbers, like, "That's a ten . . . that's a seven . . . that's only about a two," and so on.

Read this book together, perhaps taking turns reading chapters to each other. Then discuss anything you think you might want to try. Talk about any feelings or shyness that comes up. And have fun.

Creating a Romantic Mood and Setting

Make your first sexual experiences special by creating a romantic setting for lovemaking. Delegate one of you to set the stage, preparing a special atmosphere that honors both partners.

Simply sitting together very closely and gazing into each other's eyes for five or ten minutes is an experience of bonding, trusting, presence, and relaxation. It's a great thing to do on one of your first dates with a potential new partner. You'll both learn a lot from the unspoken.

Leave lots of time for sensual exploration and foreplay. Do not rush it. If your lives are too busy, plan some time away from your normal routine. And definitely turn off your phones and avoid other distractions. It's important that your early sexual experiences leave time for lots of trial-and-error learning. That way you will not fall into habits that need to be corrected later.

Time to Bond

The early stage of a relationship is a time for sexual bonding. Busy people often do not take the time to bond properly. This takes more time than you might think.

Bonding occurs when two people share unstructured tender time together, both inside and outside the bedroom. So if your love is new, spend a day in bed together now and then, talking, cuddling, resting in each other's arms, and, of course, pleasuring each other and getting to know each other's bodies.

Getting Yourself Ready for Love

If you do not have a sexual partner, reading this book and doing the exercises will help you get ready to have one. People say that chance favors the prepared mind. You have a better chance of attracting a great sexual relationship if you have prepared yourself with the necessary knowledge and skill.

◀ Love is like a rose—soft and thorny at the same time.

Love is one of the great mysteries of life. As such, it cannot be controlled. But you can get yourself ready for it—so you'll be ready when it hits you, so your fears stemming from past hurts won't scare it away, and so you'll be able to receive it.

Are You Ready?

Is anyone ever fully ready to love and be loved without reservation, without fear? Probably not. So if you don't feel completely ready, don't make too big a deal out of this. The truth is, practice makes perfect.

There is someone out there for you right now—someone who could love you just as you are. There could be many possible reasons you have not connected with this person, and some of these are beyond your control. However, one thing is in your control, and that is your degree of preparation. You can, for example, keep sexually fit even if you do not have a partner. You can use every social situation as an opportunity to hone your communication skills. You can do whatever you can to heal your unresolved issues from the past. And you can get clear about what you truly want in a sexual relationship.

How's Your Sexual Fitness?

It's important to stay healthy and fit, whether you're in a relationship or not. Do not neglect this aspect of life just because you don't have a partner at the moment. If you let this go, you will be less attractive to potential partners. Health and sexual vitality are a turn on. You will feel more attractive and alive when you have a positive relationship with your own body.

ALERT!

If you are really out of shape sexually, get involved with a practice such as hatha yoga, tantra, tai chi, or chi gung. Or join a gym or an aerobics class. These practices bring more oxygen into your cells, leading to an overall sense of well-being and confidence.

Healing from Past Wounds

Perhaps you do not feel ready to begin a new relationship due to unresolved conflicts from your past. Maybe you have felt betrayed or have simply been disappointed too often. If this is the case, it's good to recognize that your next relationship may not be the love of your life. You are probably not ready for that. You may need to have a "learning relationship" or a "healing relationship" first.

In seeking such a relationship, start by being honest with yourself that you want someone with whom you can be yourself and who will not expect you to be other than who you are. This means he or she will not demand a commitment from you. You may find someone with similar needs. You can admit that you're not ready for a full-on commitment, and look for someone to share what you do have to offer.

Becoming a Good Communicator

Some people have trouble getting started. They may be shy, or they may feel uncomfortable in social situations. Once again, chance favors the prepared mind. If you can see each social event you go to as an opportunity to practice being a better communicator and risk-taker, then you'll be better and better prepared when you do meet a potential partner.

When you learn to generate your own orgasms and take full responsibility for your own pleasure, you will feel a deep sense of personal empowerment. You will experience what it's like to be self-ignited.

Poor communicators often have no trouble attracting a partner, but they may have trouble sustaining a relationship. If this is your situation, please reread and study the material in Chapter 17. Additional resources on becoming a skillful communicator can be found at ✍ *www.thegettingrealgame.com* and ✍ *www.susancampbell.com*. Especially recommended are two books by Dr. Susan Campbell, *Getting*

Real: 10 Truth Skills You Need to Live an Authentic Life, and *Truth in Dating: Finding Love by Getting Real.*

Being Clear about What You Want

To figure out what you want, try to boil it down to a few specific terms that you can write down. Don't use generalizations or abstractions. Paint a specific picture with your words that you can see and feel. And put yourself and the other person in that picture. For instance: "I want someone who will pick me a bouquet of flowers from his garden, and kiss me every time he goes out and comes back home." Or, "I want us to make a fire in the fireplace and build a nest of pillows and blankets and just lie together cuddling, fondling each other, and listening to Madonna or Peter Gabriel on the stereo."

Being specific like this is a creative way to visualize having what you want. It brings your body and mind into a unified picture instead of just having abstract thoughts that do not include the whole body. This prepares you to receive what you want, and when you finally meet that person, you'll know you found exactly who you were looking for. Ⓔ

Appendices

Appendix A

Glossary

Appendix B

Additional Resources

Appendix A
Glossary

ABSTINENCE: Refraining from having sex.

ANAL INTERCOURSE: A sexual behavior in which a man's **penis** is inserted into another person's **anus.**

ANUS: The opening of the rectum.

APHRODISIAC: A substance that is supposed to increase sexual desire.

CLITORIS: A small, highly sensitive sexual organ in the female, located above and in front of the vaginal entrance.

COITUS: Sexual **intercourse.**

CONDOM: A latex or lambskin sheath that is placed over the erect **penis** as protection against pregnancy and sexually transmitted diseases **(STDs).**

CRURA: The internal branches of the clitoral or penile shaft.

CUNNILINGUS: Oral stimulation of the female **genitals** for sexual purposes.

EJACULATION: The expulsion of seminal fluid from the **penis,** usually during **orgasm.**

ERECTILE DYSFUNCTION: A **sexual dysfunction** characterized by the inability to have or maintain an **erection** despite adequate stimulation and interest; commonly known as **impotence.**

ERECTION: The enlargement and hardening of the **penis** due to vasocongestion that occurs during sexual arousal.

EROGENOUS ZONE: Any area of the body that is especially sensitive to sexual stimulation.

EROS: The god of love in Greek mythology.

ESTROGEN: The principal female **hormone,** secreted from the ovaries or testes, and also from the placenta.

FELLATIO: Oral stimulation of the male **genitals.**

FOREPLAY: A term used to refer to sexual activities other than **intercourse.** The term comes from the view that all activities of a sexual nature are designed to lead up to intercourse.

FORESKIN: The sheath of skin covering the tip of the **penis;** it is removed during circumcision.

FRENULUM: A highly sensitive area of skin on the underside of the **penis,** where the glans meets the penis shaft.

G-SPOT OR GRAFENBERG SPOT: A sexually sensitive area on the upper wall of the **vagina** approximately two inches from the opening.

GENITALS: The reproductive and sexual organs of males and females. Also sometimes known as genitalia.

HETEROSEXUAL: A person who is sexually attracted to members of the other gender.

HOMOSEXUAL: A person who is sexually attracted to members of her or his own gender.

HORMONES: The chemical messengers of the body, secreted by the endocrine glands, which regulate several functions including sexual development.

IMPOTENCE: Another term for **erectile dysfunction.**

INHIBITED ORGASM: Persistent difficulty in having **orgasm** or inability to have orgasm; in males, also called ejaculatory incompetence or retarded ejaculation.

INTERCOURSE: Sexual activity in which the **penis** is inserted into an orifice such as the **vagina** or **anus;** the term is often modified accordingly (e.g., anal intercourse).

INTIMACY: The experience of deep connection, closeness, and vulnerability.

KEGEL EXERCISES: A set of exercises designed to strengthen and give voluntary control over the muscles surrounding the **genitals** (known as the **pubococcygeus,** or PC, **muscles**) and thereby increase sexual pleasure and awareness.

LIBIDO: Term used by Freud to refer to sexual energy; Freud believed the libido to be the driving force in humans.

LINGAM: The ancient Sanskrit word that means **"penis"** or "phallus."

LUBRICANT: The slippery fluid secreted from the walls of the **vagina** during sexual arousal; synthetic lubricants are also available to supplement or replace the natural version. The synthetic version is also used for other activities that require lubrication, such as hand jobs or **anal intercourse.**

MASTURBATION: Self-stimulation of the **genitals** for sexual pleasure.

MENARCHE: The onset of **menstruation;** the first menstrual period.

MENOPAUSE: The cessation of **menstruation** at the end of a woman's reproductive capacity; menopause usually occurs during late middle age.

MENSTRUATION: The more-or-less monthly sloughing of the uterine lining, which results in a bloody discharge from the vaginal opening.

MONOGAMY: A relationship in which both partners have committed to dating, being married to, or having sexual activity only with each other.

MULTIPLE ORGASMS: Having several **orgasms** in a short period with no refractory period in between.

ORGASM: An intense sensation that occurs at the climax of sexual excitement; it is accompanied by rhythmic muscle contractions and intense pleasure, followed by release of sexual tensions. In men, orgasm is usually accompanied by **ejaculation.**

PENIS: The primary male sexual and reproductive organ through which both urine and **semen** pass.

PERINEUM: A strip of sensitive tissue that runs between the **genitals** and the **anus.**

PHEROMONE: A sexually arousing chemical substance that is secreted by many kinds of animals, including, possibly, humans.

POMPOIR: The act of using uterine muscles to squeeze or "milk" the penis during intercourse.

PREMATURE EJACULATION: A **sexual dysfunction** characterized by the inability to control or delay **ejaculation** as long as desired.

PROSTATE GLAND: A muscular gland encircling the urethra that produces much of the seminal fluid.

PUBOCOCCYGEUS (PC) MUSCLES: A set of muscles that form a muscular sling stretching from the pubic bone in front to the tailbone in back; PC muscles control urine flow and contract during **orgasm.** Also see **Kegel exercises.**

SCROTUM: Sack that contains the man's testicles.

SEMEN: The alkaline fluid expelled from the **penis** during **ejaculation,** containing fluids combined from several glands as well as sperm.

SEXUAL AROUSAL DISORDER: Failure to obtain or maintain **erection** or vaginal **lubrication,** despite adequate interest and stimulation.

SEXUAL DYSFUNCTION: A difficulty with sexual response that causes a person subjective distress (for example, anorgasmia).

SEXUAL ENHANCEMENT: Improvement or enrichment of sexual relationships among otherwise healthy, well-functioning individuals.

SEXUAL RESPONSE PATTERN: The pattern of response that both men and women go through during a sexual encounter that leads to **orgasm.**

SPECTATORING: The process in which a person begins to observe and evaluate his or her sexual activities, rather than merely enjoying them, thereby often causing **sexual dysfunctions** or disorders.

SQUEEZE TECHNIQUE: A technique used by sex therapists for the treatment of **premature ejaculation** in which the man or his partner squeezes the erect **penis** below the glans when he feels the likelihood of ejaculating, thereby reducing the urge.

START-STOP: A sex therapy technique in which a man learns to control **ejaculation** by repeatedly ceasing stimulation prior to **orgasm.**

STD: Acronym for "sexually transmitted disease."

TESTOSTERONE: The major natural androgen **hormone,** it is secreted by the testes and serves to maintain secondary sex characteristics, sperm production, and sex drive. This hormone is also found in smaller amounts in women.

TUMESCENCE: Sexual excitement and swelling of sexual tissues, such as the erection of the penis.

VAGINA: The tube-shaped muscular organ in the female into which the **penis** is inserted during **intercourse** and through which a baby passes during birth.

VULVA: Female sexual parts that make up the entrance or opening to the **vagina.**

YONI: The ancient Sanskrit word meaning "**vulva.**"

Additional Resources

Internet Resources

✐*www.tantra.com,* ✐*www.tantra.org*—The portal for tantra, the Kama sutra, and sacred sexuality that offers articles, discussion forums, interviews, Q&As, workshops, personals, instructional materials, and an online catalog with 200 unique items.

✐*www.susancampbell.com*—Visit the Relationship Coach Web site for tools and support for using authentic communication as a spiritual awareness practice. Susan has created three educational games to teach people how to have more transparency and intimacy with others and is the author of seven books.

✐*www.altsex.org*—This Web site is dedicated to the exploration of the miracle of human sexuality, in all its wonder and diversity.

✐*www.sexuality.org*—An educational organization that promotes understanding of adult intimate relationships and sexual expression.

✐*www.siecus.org*—The Sexuality Information and Education Council of the U.S. (SIECUS) is a national nonprofit organization that supports healthy sexuality.

✐*www.plannedparenthood.org*—Planned Parenthood offers information on professional training, patient education, and community education programs on human sexuality; it also lists community resources for reproductive control and health checks.

✐*www.positive.org*—This Web site is a good resource for teens, offering information they need to help them take care of themselves in areas like sex education, sexuality, reproductive control, and condom availability.

Hotlines

National STD Hotline: ☎ 1-800-227-8922

National AIDS Hotline: ☎ 1-800-342-2437

Further Reading

Anand, Margot. *The Art of Sexual Ecstasy*. (Los Angeles: Jeremy P. Tarcher, 1989).

Berman, Jennifer, M.D., and Laura Berman, Ph.D. *For Women Only: A Revolutionary Guide to Overcoming Sexual Dysfunction and Reclaiming Your Sex Life*. (New York: Henry Holt & Company, 2001).

Campbell, Susan M. *The Couple's Journey: Intimacy as a Path to Wholeness*. (San Luis Obispo, CA: Impact Publishers, 1980).

Camphausen, Rufus C. *The Encyclopedia of Sacred Sexuality*. (Rochester, VT: Inner Traditions, 1999).

Chia, Mantak and Maneewan Chia, *Healing Love Through the Tao: Cultivating Female Sexual Energy,* (Huntington, NY: Healing Tao Books, 1986; reissued, 1991).

Chia, Mantak and Douglas Abrams. *The Multi-Orgasmic Man*. (San Francisco: HarperCollins, 1997).

Douglas, Nik and Penny Slinger. *Sexual Secrets: The Alchemy of Ecstasy*. (Rochester, VT: Inner Traditions, 1979; reprint, 1999).

Meletis, Chris D. *Better Sex Naturally: Herbs and Other Supplements That Can Jump Start Your Sex Life*. (New York: Chrysalis Books, 2000).

Muir, Charles and Caroline Muir. *Tantra: The Art of Conscious Loving*. (San Francisco: Mercury House, Inc., 1989).

Ramsdale, David and Ellen Ramsdale. *Sexual Energy Ecstasy: A Practical Guide to Lovemaking Secrets of the East and West*. (Playa Del Rey, CA: Peak Skill Publishing, 1991; reprint, New York: Bantam Doubleday, 1993).

Stubbs, Kenneth Ray, Ph.D. *The Essential Tantra: A Modern Guide to Sacred Sexuality*. (New York: Jeremy P. Tarcher, 2000).

Zilbergeld, Bernie, Ph.D. *The New Male Sexuality*. (New York: Bantam Books, 1999).

Index

for men, 283
not rushing, 280–81
See also Games; Massage; Oral sex
Foreskin, 68, 73, 294
Forgiveness
for affairs, 257
steps, 252–55
Fourth marriages, 15
Fragrances. *See* Pheromones; Scents (aromas)
Free association, 39
Frenulum, 68, 73, 294
Fun games, 221–24

G
Games, intimate, 221–24
Genital herpes, 267
Genitals
defined, 294
heart and, 80, 196
stimulation exercise, 30–31
See also specific body parts
Ginkgo biloba, 184
Ginseng, 184
Giving, pleasure from, 29–30, 114, 204
Gloves (latex), 167, 181, 209, 268, 269
Goddess spot. *See* G-spot
Gonorrhea, 266
Grafenberg spot. *See* G-spot
Great sex (overview), 1–10
as bonding experience, 4
book assumptions, 7–9
as communication, 4
controlling and, 6
Divine oneness from, 4
as life metaphor, 4–5
life purpose and, 7
maintenance sex vs., 2–3
presence as basis, 3–4, 9, 233–34, 265
relating and, 6
required elements, 4
social mores complicating, 2
trusting yourself, 10
G-spot, 156–59
anal stimulation and, 166
defined, 156, 294
exploring, 59, 156–59, 213
location, 54, 59, 156
massaging, 213
orgasms, 83, 86–87, 125, 146
penis stimulating, 71

prostate gland vs., 69
stimulating, positions, 121, 124, 126, 127, 129–36, 139, 149–51, 159
thrusting patterns and, 150–51
urethra/urethral sponge and, 54
Guilt, 22, 88

H
Hair
pubic, 50–51, 57, 67, 112
pulling, 50, 57, 67, 112
Healing relationships, 291
Heart
genitals and, 80, 196
giving, receiving and, 29–30, 114, 204
orgasms from, 197
Heart hold, 46–47
Hepatitis B, 267
Herbs, 184–86
Herpes, 267
Hirsch, Alan R., 98
History, of sex/love, 11–20
current situation, 14–15
early humans, 12
Kama sutra. *See* Kama sutra
Middle Ages, 13
mythological figures, 12, 18–19
procreation and, 12, 13
sexual liberation, 14
symbols, 15–16
Twentieth century, 14
Victorian Age, 13
HIV / AIDS, 266, 267–68, 297
Holding differences. *See* Differences
Honesty
affairs and, 255–57
expressing desires and, 233–34, 279, 281, 284
eyes revealing, 16–17
faking interest and, 282–83
fear and. *See* Fear
forgiveness and, 252–55, 257
as intimacy prerequisite, 7–8
perfection and, 238
revisiting situations, 237–40
secrets and, 230, 232–33, 279, 287
throat chakra and, 194
transparent expression, 233–37
Hormones
defined, 294–95
sexual response remedies, 184–86

Hotlines, 297
HPV (Human papilloma virus), 266
Human papilloma virus (HPV), 266
Hymen, 54

I, J
Impotence, 209, 273–74, 295. *See also* Sexual dysfunction
Incense, 174–75
Inhibition. *See* Fear; Vulnerability
Intercourse
as dance, 150
defined, 295
thrusting patterns, 150–51
See also Ejaculation; Orgasms (female); Orgasms (male); Positions; Sexual response
Internet
resources, 297
virtual sex, 270
Intimacy, 33–47
arousal from, 81
clearing negative energy, 46–47
comfort levels, 230–32
communication and. *See* Communication
conquering fear, 34–35, 37, 191, 238–39
controlling vs. relating and, 6
creating safe, sacred space, 38
defined, 33, 295
desires and, 233–34, 279, 281, 284, 292
enhancing, 38–39
eye gazing for, 16–18, 45–46, 144, 288
fear of, 20, 34–35, 231–32
free association and, 39
games for, 221–24
honesty and. *See* Honesty
meditation and, 39, 144, 195
openness and, 36–37, 67, 121–22, 139–40, 231–32, 233–34
overcoming differences. *See* Differences
prerequisite, 7–8
rekindling romance, 92–93
rituals for. *See* Rituals
secrets and, 230, 232–33, 279, 287
sexual addiction and, 20
sexual healing and, 5
silence and, 38
today, 14–15

Prostate gland *(continued)*
  reducing swelling, 184–85
  saw palmetto for, 184–85
  vibrators and, 181
Psyche, 12, 18–19
Pubic bone, 51, 67
Pubic mound, 67, 73
Pubis, 50–51
Pubococcygeus (PC) muscles
  experiencing, 60
  function, 56, 296
  location, 56, 60
  See also Kegel exercises

R

Raqs sharqi, 27
Readiness, sexual. *See* Sexual response
Reading erotic materials, 178
Rear-entry positions, 132–36, 159
Receiving, giving and, 29–30, 114, 204
Relating, controlling vs., 6
Relationship(s)
  affairs and, 255–57
  beginner mind for, 264–65
  bonding in, 289
  cocreation in, 250
  commitments, 249–50
  communication and. *See*
    Communication
  desires and, 233–34, 279, 281, 284, 292
  disappointments, 244–47
  dumping grievances, 245–46
  enduring, 20
  expectations in, 244, 246–47, 287–88
  feelings stages, 247–50
  forgiveness in, 252–55, 257
  healing, 291
  lifestyle options, 15
  mutual benefit in, 7
  new, 263–65, 287–89
  power struggles, 248–49
  preparation, 289–92
  presence in, 3–4, 9, 233–34, 265
  romance stage, 247–48
  stability stage, 249
  unmet needs, 250–52
  variety in, 278–80
  See also Differences; Honesty; Intimacy
Reproductive organs. *See specific organs*
Resentment
  overcoming, 39–43

sharing, 236–37
  See also Differences
Resources
  books, 298
  Hotlines, 297
  Web sites, 297
Responsibility
  for own experiences, 8–9
  for pleasure, 8–9, 142, 291
  for safe sex, 268–69, 270
Right-hand path, 195, 197
Risk-taking, 8. *See also* Fear;
  Vulnerability
Rituals, 216–20
  composing, 216–17
  sharing resentments/appreciations,
    236–37
  Valentine's Day ceremony, 217–20
Roll-playing, 169
Romance, rekindling, 92–93. *See also*
  Intimacy; Mood setting;
  Relationship(s)
Routine, breaking, 278–80

S

Sacred rituals, 10
Safe sex, 268–70
  condoms for, 17, 167, 181, 182, 209,
    269, 294
  female condoms, 269
  finger cots for, 167, 209, 269
  responsibility for, 268–69, 270
  STDs and, 265–68
  virtual sex, 270
Sandalwood, 174
Saw palmetto, 184–85
Scents (aromas), 97–99
  emotions and, 97–98
  experimenting with, 98
  of food. *See* Food
  incense, 174–75
  natural oils, 98–99, 174, 182–83
  perfumes, 174
  sandalwood, 174
  stimulating genital blood flow, 98
  See also Pheromones
Scrotum, 67
  defined, 296
  exploring, 73–74
  massaging, 205, 207
Second marriages, 15

Secrets, 230, 232–33, 279, 287
Secrets of the Jade bed Chamber, 200
Self-confidence
  dancing and, 27–28
  pleasure capacity and, 26
  from risk-taking, 8
  self-doubt and, 22
  through intimacy, 5
Self-expression, 10, 231–32, 233–34. *See*
  also Desires; Honesty
Sensory deprivation game, 221–22
Servant/master games, 223
Sex education, 261–62
Sexology exams
  for men, 72–75
  for women, 56–60
Sexual abuse, 262–63
Sexual addiction, 20
Sexual aids, 180–85
  condoms, 17, 167, 181, 182, 209, 269,
    294
  dildos, 181
  gloves, 181
  heightening creams, 183–84
  herbs, 184–86
  lubricants, 182
  sexual response remedies, 184–86
  Viagra, 183, 274, 287
  vibrators, 180–81
  Web sites, 297
  See also Aphrodisiacs; Food;
    Pheromones; Scents (aromas)
Sexual arousal disorder, 296. *See also*
  Impotence; Sexual dysfunction
Sexual dysfunction
  defined, 296
  heightening creams for, 183–84
  impotency, 209, 273–74, 295
  in men, 88–89, 209, 273–74
  research, 82
  sexual response remedies, 184–86
  smoking and, 88, 186, 209
  in women, 89–90, 145
Sexual healing, 5
Sexual liberation, 14
Sexually transmitted diseases (STDs),
  265–68, 296, 297
Sexual massage. *See* Massage
Sexual response, 77–90
  aging and, 272–75
  arousal time, 80–81

curve (patterns), 78–82, 296
ejaculation. *See* Ejaculation
excitement phase, 79, 81, 83
heart, genitals and, 80, 196
in men, 79–80
menopause and, 274–75
multiple orgasms, 82–84, 85, 149, 195, 295
orgasm phase, 79, 80, 81–82, 83
plateau phase, 79–80, 81, 83
readiness and, 78
remedies, 184–86
resolution, refractory phase, 79, 80, 82, 83
visual stimulation, 79
in women, 80–82
See also Orgasms (female); Orgasms (male); Sexual dysfunction
Shakti, 12, 190
Shiva, 190
S-M, 170
Smoking, 88, 186, 209
Social mores, 2
Soft-ons, 71–72, 205, 283, 286
Soul. *See* Psyche
Sounds, making, 149, 281
Special events. *See* Rituals
Sperm, 69
Spices, 176–77
Spirituality, 272. *See also* Kama sutra; Tantric sex
Splitting bamboo position, 126–27
Spooning, 46–47, 139–40, 218
Squatting position, 202
STDs (Sexually transmitted diseases), 265–68, 296, 297
Strip tease games, 224
Subtle body, 191
Suppression, of sexuality, 2, 5, 22
Suspended position, 202
Swings, 169–70, 202, 225
Symbols, of sex/regeneration
eyes as, 16–18
of females, 16
history of, 15–16, 68
of males, 16, 68
Syphilis, 266

T, U

Tantric sex, 187, 188–97
balance in, 195–98
chakras and, 191–95
defined, 189
gods/goddesses, 190
gurus, 190–91
history, 188
meditation and, 195
orgasms, 196–97
principles, 196–97
sexual yoga, 189–90, 282
Teenagers. *See* Kids
Testes
cancer, 193
exploring, 73
function, 69
size variation, 73
Third eye, 194
Third marriages, 15
Three legs position, 202
Thrusting patterns, 150–51
Toes, sucking, 224
Touch
aging and, 287
erotic exercise, 30–31
erotic foreplay, 111–12
giving, receiving and, 29–30, 114, 204
great, technique, 29–30
key to, 29–30
knowing your pleasures, 153–54
pleasure of, 30–31
See also Massage
Toys. *See* Sexual aids
Transparency, of expression, 233–37
Trust
honesty and. *See* Honesty
for intimacy, 36–37
vulnerability and, 4, 36–37, 231–32
Two peas in pod position, 133–34
Union of balance position, 138
Urethra, 54, 58, 68
Urethral sponge. *See* G-spot
Uterus, 55

V, W, Y

Vagina
anatomy, 53–55
categories, 58
cervix and, 54–55
defined, 53, 296
exploring, 58–59
hymen, 54
as Jade Garden, 200
Kama sutra on, 58, 198
orgasms, 83, 86–87, 125, 146
os and, 54–55
proper fit, 121–22
quivering, 198
scent of, 53
scents stimulating, 98
sensitive areas, 59–60
sugar caution, 221
tightening. *See* Kegel exercises
vestibule, 53
vulva vs., 51
See also G-spot
Valentine's Day ceremony, 217–20
Variety, adding, 278–80
Vestibule, 53
Viagra, 183, 274, 287
Vibrators, 180–81
Virtual sex, 270
Vulnerability, 4, 36–37, 231–32. *See also* Fear
Vulva, 50–53
defined, 50, 51, 296
exploring, 57–58
as "Jade Garden", 56
labia, 51–52
massaging, 211
pubis, 50–51
vagina vs., 51
varying characteristics, 52
Web sites, 297
Wheelbarrow position, 201
Woman on top positions, 128–32, 159
Word fasting, 38
Worrying, 2
Writing erotic material, 178–80, 223
Yab-yum positions, 136–38
Yates, Gayle, 93
Yawning position, 125–26
Yin/yang, 120
Yoga, sexual, 189–90, 282
Yohimbine, 184

THE EVERYTHING ROMANCE BOOK

By Donald and Pamela Baack

Trade paperback
$12.95 ($19.95 CAN)
1-58062-566-5, 304 pages

Enhance the intimacy, passion, and energy in your relationship now! *The Everything® Romance Book* is filled with suggestions that will help you charm and delight your partner—from simple displays of affection to elaborate celebrations for holiday or relationship milestones. From the first date to a fiftieth wedding anniversary, you'll learn there is no wrong time for romance. *The Everything® Romance Book* is packed with recommendations for exciting seasonal treats and adventures, tips on creating just the right ambience, ideas for romantic weekend getaways, and more!

OTHER *EVERYTHING®* BOOKS BY ADAMS MEDIA

BUSINESS

Everything® **Business Planning Book**
Everything® **Coaching and Mentoring Book**
Everything® **Fundraising Book**
Everything® **Home-Based Business Book**
Everything® **Leadership Book**
Everything® **Managing People Book**
Everything® **Network Marketing Book**
Everything® **Online Business Book**
Everything® **Project Management Book**
Everything® **Selling Book**
Everything® **Start Your Own Business Book**
Everything® **Time Management Book**

COMPUTERS

Everything® **Build Your Own Home Page Book**

Everything® **Computer Book**
Everything® **Internet Book**
Everything® **Microsoft® Word 2000 Book**

COOKBOOKS

Everything® **Barbecue Cookbook**
Everything® **Bartender's Book, $9.95**
Everything® **Chinese Cookbook**
Everything® **Chocolate Cookbook**
Everything® **Cookbook**
Everything® **Dessert Cookbook**
Everything® **Diabetes Cookbook**
Everything® **Low-Carb Cookbook**
Everything® **Low-Fat High-Flavor Cookbook**
Everything® **Mediterranean Cookbook**
Everything® **Mexican Cookbook**
Everything® **One-Pot Cookbook**
Everything® **Pasta Book**

Everything® **Quick Meals Cookbook**
Everything® **Slow Cooker Cookbook**
Everything® **Soup Cookbook**
Everything® **Thai Cookbook**
Everything® **Vegetarian Cookbook**
Everything® **Wine Book**

HEALTH

Everything® **Anti-Aging Book**
Everything® **Diabetes Book**
Everything® **Dieting Book**
Everything® **Herbal Remedies Book**
Everything® **Hypnosis Book**
Everything® **Menopause Book**
Everything® **Nutrition Book**
Everything® **Reflexology Book**
Everything® **Stress Management Book**
Everything®**Vitamins, Minerals, and Nutritional Supplements Book**

All Everything® books are priced at $12.95 or $14.95, unless otherwise stated. Prices subject to change without notice.
Canadian prices range from $11.95–$31.95, and are subject to change without notice.

Everything® **Investing Book**
Everything® **Money Book**
Everything® **Mutual Funds Book**
Everything® **Online Investing Book**
Everything® **Personal Finance Book**
Everything® **Personal Finance in Your
  20s & 30s Book**
Everything® **Wills & Estate Planning
  Book**

PETS

Everything® **Cat Book**
Everything® **Dog Book**
Everything® **Dog Training and Tricks
  Book**
Everything® **Horse Book**
Everything® **Puppy Book**
Everything® **Tropical Fish Book**

REFERENCE

Everything® **Astronomy Book**
Everything® **Car Care Book**
Everything® **Christmas Book, $15.00**
  ($21.95 CAN)
Everything® **Classical Mythology Book**
Everything® **Einstein Book**
Everything® **Etiquette Book**
Everything® **Great Thinkers Book**
Everything® **Philosophy Book**
Everything® **Shakespeare Book**
Everything® **Tall Tales, Legends, &
  Other Outrageous
  Lies Book**
Everything® **Toasts Book**
Everything® **Trivia Book**
Everything® **Weather Book**

RELIGION

Everything® **Angels Book**
Everything® **Buddhism Book**
Everything® **Catholicism Book**
Everything® **Jewish History &
  Heritage Book**
Everything® **Judaism Book**

Everything® **Prayer Book**
Everything® **Saints Book**
Everything® **Understanding Islam Book**
Everything® **World's Religions Book**
Everything® **Zen Book**

SCHOOL & CAREERS

Everything® **After College Book**
Everything® **College Survival Book**
Everything® **Cover Letter Book**
Everything® **Get-a-Job Book**
Everything® **Hot Careers Book**
Everything® **Job Interview Book**
Everything® **Online Job Search Book**
Everything® **Resume Book, 2nd Ed.**
Everything® **Study Book**

SELF-HELP

Everything® **Dating Book**
Everything® **Divorce Book**
Everything® **Great Marriage Book**
Everything® **Great Sex Book**
Everything® **Romance Book**
Everything® **Self-Esteem Book**
Everything® **Success Book**

SPORTS & FITNESS

Everything® **Bicycle Book**
Everything® **Body Shaping Book**
Everything® **Fishing Book**
Everything® **Fly-Fishing Book**
Everything® **Golf Book**
Everything® **Golf Instruction Book**
Everything® **Pilates Book**
Everything® **Running Book**
Everything® **Sailing Book, 2nd Ed.**
Everything® **T'ai Chi and QiGong Book**
Everything® **Total Fitness Book**
Everything® **Weight Training Book**
Everything® **Yoga Book**

TRAVEL

Everything® **Guide to Las Vegas**

Everything® **Guide to New England**
Everything® **Guide to New York City**
Everything® **Guide to Washington D.C.**
Everything® **Travel Guide to The
  Disneyland Resort®,
  California Adventure®,
  Universal Studios®, and
  the Anaheim Area**
Everything® **Travel Guide to the Walt
  Disney World Resort®,
  Universal Studios®, and
  Greater Orlando, 3rd Ed.**

WEDDINGS

Everything® **Bachelorette Party Book**
Everything® **Bridesmaid Book**
Everything® **Creative Wedding Ideas
  Book**
Everything® **Jewish Wedding Book**
Everything® **Wedding Book, 2nd Ed.**
Everything® **Wedding Checklist,
  $7.95 ($11.95 CAN)**
Everything® **Wedding Etiquette Book,
  $7.95 ($11.95 CAN)**
Everything® **Wedding Organizer, $15.00
  ($22.95 CAN)**
Everything® **Wedding Shower Book,
  $7.95 ($12.95 CAN)**
Everything® **Wedding Vows Book,
  $7.95 ($11.95 CAN)**
Everything® **Weddings on a Budget
  Book, $9.95 ($15.95 CAN)**

WRITING

Everything® **Creative Writing Book**
Everything® **Get Published Book**
Everything® **Grammar and Style Book**
Everything® **Grant Writing Book**
Everything® **Guide to Writing
  Children's Books**
Everything® **Screenwriting Book**
Everything® **Writing Well Book**

Available wherever books are sold!
To order, call 800-872-5627, or visit us at everything.com

HISTORY

Everything® **American History Book**
Everything® **Civil War Book**
Everything® **Irish History & Heritage Book**
Everything® **Mafia Book**
Everything® **World War II Book**

HOBBIES & GAMES

Everything® **Bridge Book**
Everything® **Candlemaking Book**
Everything® **Casino Gambling Book**
Everything® **Chess Basics Book**
Everything® **Collectibles Book**
Everything® **Crossword and Puzzle Book**
Everything® **Digital Photography Book**
Everything® **Family Tree Book**
Everything® **Games Book**
Everything® **Knitting Book**
Everything® **Magic Book**
Everything® **Motorcycle Book**
Everything® **Online Genealogy Book**
Everything® **Photography Book**
Everything® **Pool & Billiards Book**
Everything® **Quilting Book**
Everything® **Scrapbooking Book**
Everything® **Soapmaking Book**

HOME IMPROVEMENT

Everything® **Feng Shui Book**
Everything® **Gardening Book**
Everything® **Home Decorating Book**
Everything® **Landscaping Book**
Everything® **Lawn Care Book**
Everything® **Organize Your Home Book**

KIDS' STORY BOOKS

Everything® **Bedtime Story Book**
Everything® **Bible Stories Book**
Everything® **Fairy Tales Book**
Everything® **Mother Goose Book**

EVERYTHING® KIDS' BOOKS

All titles are $6.95
Everything® **Kids' Baseball Book, 2nd Ed.** ($10.95 CAN)
Everything® **Kids' Bugs Book** ($10.95 CAN)
Everything® **Kids' Christmas Puzzle & Activity Book** ($10.95 CAN)
Everything® **Kids' Cookbook** ($10.95 CAN)
Everything® **Kids' Halloween Puzzle & Activity Book** ($10.95 CAN)
Everything® **Kids' Joke Book** ($10.95 CAN)
Everything® **Kids' Math Puzzles Book** ($10.95 CAN)
Everything® **Kids' Mazes Book** ($10.95 CAN)
Everything® **Kids' Money Book** ($11.95 CAN)
Everything® **Kids' Monsters Book** ($10.95 CAN)
Everything® **Kids' Nature Book** ($11.95 CAN)
Everything® **Kids' Puzzle Book** ($10.95 CAN)
Everything® **Kids' Science Experiments Book** ($10.95 CAN)
Everything® **Kids' Soccer Book** ($10.95 CAN)
Everything® **Kids' Travel Activity Book** ($10.95 CAN)

LANGUAGE

Everything® **Learning French Book**
Everything® **Learning German Book**
Everything® **Learning Italian Book**
Everything® **Learning Latin Book**
Everything® **Learning Spanish Book**
Everything® **Sign Language Book**

MUSIC

Everything® **Drums Book (with CD)**, $19.95 ($31.95 CAN)
Everything® **Guitar Book**
Everything® **Playing Piano and Keyboards Book**

Everything® **Rock & Blues Guitar Book (with CD)**, $19.95 ($31.95 CAN)
Everything® **Songwriting Book**

NEW AGE

Everything® **Astrology Book**
Everything® **Divining the Future Book**
Everything® **Dreams Book**
Everything® **Ghost Book**
Everything® **Meditation Book**
Everything® **Numerology Book**
Everything® **Palmistry Book**
Everything® **Psychic Book**
Everything® **Spells & Charms Book**
Everything® **Tarot Book**
Everything® **Wicca and Witchcraft Book**

PARENTING

Everything® **Baby Names Book**
Everything® **Baby Shower Book**
Everything® **Baby's First Food Book**
Everything® **Baby's First Year Book**
Everything® **Breastfeeding Book**
Everything® **Father-to-Be Book**
Everything® **Get Ready for Baby Book**
Everything® **Homeschooling Book**
Everything® **Parent's Guide to Positive Discipline**
Everything® **Potty Training Book**, $9.95 ($15.95 CAN)
Everything® **Pregnancy Book, 2nd Ed.**
Everything® **Pregnancy Fitness Book**
Everything® **Pregnancy Organizer**, $15.00 ($22.95 CAN)
Everything® **Toddler Book**
Everything® **Tween Book**

PERSONAL FINANCE

Everything® **Budgeting Book**
Everything® **Get Out of Debt Book**
Everything® **Get Rich Book**
Everything® **Homebuying Book, 2nd Ed.**
Everything® **Homeselling Book**

All Everything® books are priced at $12.95 or $14.95, unless otherwise stated. Prices subject to change without notice.
Canadian prices range from $11.95–$31.95, and are subject to change without notice.